The Sovereign Remedy?

The Sovereign Remedy?

Trade Agreements in a Globalizing World

A. Estevadeordal and K. Suominen

OXFORD
UNIVERSITY PRESS

OXFORD
UNIVERSITY PRESS

Great Clarendon Street,
Oxford ox2 6DP

Oxford University Press is a department of the University of Oxford.
It furthers the University's objective of excellence in research, scholarship,
and education by publishing worldwide in

Oxford New York

Auckland Cape Town Dar es Salaam Hong Kong Karachi
Kuala Lumpur Madrid Melbourne Mexico City Nairobi
New Delhi Shanghai Taipei Toronto

With offices in

Argentina Austria Brazil Chile Czech Republic France Greece
Guatemala Hungary Italy Japan Poland Portugal Singapore
South Korea Switzerland Thailand Turkey Ukraine Vietnam

Oxford is a registered trade mark of Oxford University Press
in the UK and in certain other countries

Published in the United States
by Oxford University Press Inc., New York

© A. Estevadeordal and K. Suominen 2009

The moral rights of the authors have been asserted
Database right Oxford University Press (maker)

First published 2009

British Library Cataloguing in Publication Data

Data available

Library of Congress Cataloging in Publication Data

Data available

Typeset by SPI Publisher Services, Pondicherry, India
Printed by the MPG Books Group
in the UK

ISBN 978-0-19-955015-9

10 9 8 7 6 5 4 3 2 1

To Jordi Nadal and Jeffrey Williamson
AE

To Margaret E. Scranton
KS

Acknowledgements

This book is the result of the work of great many individuals. We wish to thank our cadre of diligent and patient research assistants who have worked on this book over the past four years—Akiko Oncken, Mari Nishie, Masahiro Matsumoto, Raul Cabrera, Yusuke Kuwayama, Kevin McCown, Margaret Mitchell, Cristina Dengel, Naoko Uchiyama, Pedro Martínez Alanís, Carlos Velasco, Carlos M. Gutierrez Jr., Santiago Florez Gomez, and Sara Marzal Yetano. Two IDB colleagues, Matthew Shearer and Jeremy Harris, have made extensive contributions to various papers and articles that form part of the basis of this volume; our thanks to their many insights, comments, and sheer hard work.

We are grateful to the numerous colleagues around the world—too many to mention here—who have critically shaped our thinking over the years. Our humble thanks also to the countless committed trade policy officials in Asia, Americas, and Europe, who have provided a reality check for our work, and taught us more than we could ever teach them.

We also wish to thank the anonymous referees for insightful and useful comments. Particular thanks to the referee of the complete manuscript, whose comments improved this volume significantly. Our very special thanks to the hugely professional team at Oxford University Press—Sarah Caro, Harriet Ayles, Emma Lambert, Virginia Williams, and Jennifer Wilkinson. All interpretations and errors remain ours alone.

We dedicate this book to our professors Jordi Nadal and Jeffrey Williamson, who over the years taught Antoni the importance of an interdisciplinary approach to economic thinking, and to Margaret "Peggy" Scranton, a tireless mentor who first sparked Kati's love for the study of international politics.

Summary Contents

Contents

Contents

Abbreviations

ABF	Asian Bond Fund
ACP	African, Caribbean, and Pacific
AFTA	ASEAN Free Trade Agreement
ANZCERTA	Australia–New Zealand Closer Economic Relations Trade Agreement
APEC	Asia-Pacific Economic Cooperation
ARO	Agreement on Rules of Origin
ASCM	Agreement on Subsidies and Countervailing Measures
ASEAN	Association of Southeast Asian Nations
ASEAN+3	ASEAN, China, Korea, and Japan
BIS	Bank of International Settlements
BIT	bilateral investment treaty
CACM	Central American Common Market
CAFTA	Central American Free Trade Agreement
CARICOM	Caribbean Community
CBI	Caribbean Basin Initiative
CEFTA	Central European Free Trade Agreement
CEPR	Centre for Economic Policy Research
CET	common external tariff
COMESA	Common Market for Eastern and Southern Africa
CRO	Committee on Rules of Origin
CU	customs union
DOTS	Direction of Trade Statistics
DR–CAFTA	US–Central America–Dominican Republic Free Trade Agreement
EAC	East Asian Community
EAVG	East Asia Vision Group
ECOWAS	Economic Community of West African States

Abbreviations

EEA	European Economic Area
EEC	European Economic Community
EFTA	European Free Trade Agreement
EMEAP	Executives' Meeting of East Asia Pacific Central Banks
EPA	Economic Partnership Agreement
EU	European Union
FDI	foreign direct investment
FTA	free trade agreement
FTAA	Free Trade Area of the Americas
FTAAP	Free Trade Area of the Asia-Pacific
GATS	General Agreement on Trade in Services
GATT	General Agreement on Tariffs and Trade
GDP	gross domestic product
GSP	Generalized System of Preferences
GSTP	Global System of Trade Preferences
HS	harmonized system
IADB	Inter-American Development Bank
IIE	Institute for International Economics
IMF	International Monetary Fund
INTAL-ITD	Institute for the Integration of Latin America and the Caribbean–Integration and Trade Division
ITO	International Trade Organization
LAIA	Latin American Integration Association
MEFTA	US-Middle East Free Trade Agreement
MERCOSUR	Southern Common Market
MFN	most favored nation
NAFTA	North American Free Trade Agreement
NBER	National Bureau of Economic Research
OCT	Overseas Countries and Territories
OECD	Organization for Economic Cooperation and Development
OP	outward processing
PECS	Pan-European Cumulation System
PTA	preferential trading arrangement
QIZ	qualifying industrial zones
RoO	rules of origin

ROW	rest of the world
RPG	regional public good
RTAA	Reciprocal Trade Agreements Act
SACU	South African Customs Union
SADC	South African Development Community
SAFTA	South Asia Free Trade Agreement
SAT	substantially all trade
SEP	Strategic Economic Partnership Agreement
SPARTECA	South Pacific Regional Trade and Economic Cooperation Agreement
SMEs	small and medium-sized enterprises
TA	Trade Agreement
TCRO	Technical Committee on Rules of Origin
TRAINS	Trade Analysis and Information System
TRIMs	Agreement on Trade-Related Investment Measures
TRIPs	Agreement on Trade-Related Aspects of Intellectual Property Rights
TRQ	tariff rate quotas
UN	United Nations
UNCTAD	UN Conference on Trade and Development
WCO	World Customs Organization
WTO	World Trade Organization

The Sovereign Remedy?

Yet all the while there is a remedy which, if it were generally and spontaneously adopted by the great majority of people in many lands, would as if by a miracle transform the whole scene, and would in a few years make all Europe, or the greater part of it, as free and as happy as Switzerland is to-day. What is this sovereign remedy? It is to re-create the European Family, or as much of it as we can, and to provide it with a structure under which it can dwell in peace, in safety and in freedom. We must build a kind of United States of Europe. In this way only will hundreds of millions of toilers be able to regain the simple joys and hopes which make life worth living. The process is simple. All that is needed is the resolve of hundreds of millions of men and women to do right instead of wrong and to gain as their reward blessing instead of cursing.

(Winston Churchill's speech to the academic Youth, Zurich, 19 September 1946)

Unhampered trade dovetail[s] with peace; high tariffs, trade barriers, and unfair economic competition, with war ... if we could get freer flow of trade ... so that one country would not be deadly jealous of another and the living standards of all countries might rise, thereby eliminating the economic dissatisfaction that breeds war, we might have a reasonable chance of lasting peace.

(Cordell Hull (1948), *The Memoirs of Cordell Hull*. New York: Macmillan)

1

Introduction

I. The Proliferation of Trade Agreements: New Policy Questions

War, energy, immigration, financial bubbles, food crises, and poverty are among the most contentious issues dominating our news daily. So is trade. Hardly a week goes by without articles in global newspapers about the fortunes of the Doha Round, agricultural subsidies, US trade balance, Chinese export competition, or the political maneuvering surrounding the negotiation of new free trade agreements.

Trade debates are intricately and explicitly connected to the other headline-makers. Indeed, trade and the rapidly proliferating preferential trading arrangements (PTAs) have not only aroused passions for decades; they have in the popular parlance long been linked to major trends in the global economy and politics.[1] While some blame PTAs for exporting jobs, sowing poverty, furthering illegal migration, robbing national sovereignty, and balkanizing the world trading system, others praise them as lynchpins of growth, pillars of peace, guarantors of security, and engines of globalization. Still others view them as useful instruments for fostering trade and investment, yet ones that are only a second-best option to global trade liberalization and effective only when accompanied by "open regionalism"—simultaneous liberalization toward non-members—sound macroeconomic policies, rule of law, and first-rate infrastructures.

One point on which all pundits agree is that these conjectures are valid hypotheses. Trade agreements have become one of the most important

---

[1] Trade agreements here encompass our entire set of more than four thousand trade agreements for 1875–2005. They can be bilateral, plurilateral, and multilateral. PTAs, the main focus of this volume, form a subset of (nearly four hundred) trade agreements, and are inherently signed in the post-war period. They are also inherently bilateral or plurilateral in membership, rather than multilateral.

and potentially highly consequential phenomena in today's global economy since the formation of what we consider the first PTA, the European Communities, in 1958. The number of PTAs notified to the World Trade Organization (WTO) surged to 200 by the end of 2007; the figure is far higher when the dozens of deals that are not notified to the WTO are considered. The wave of PTAs is only just starting to swell: according to the WTO, the number of PTAs will soar to 400 by 2010.

The wave of enthusiasm for PTAs has swept through the world. Today, only one country—Mongolia—remains outside the web of PTAs, and many countries belong to multiple agreements. Among the most prolific integrators are the United States and Singapore with 14 signed agreements, Mexico with 12, and Chile with ten. If the world is indeed flattening, countries are pushing to get an edge and to get ahead.

PTAs have transformed the global economic landscape. Some one-half of global trade is carried on among partners to a trade agreement; for countries such as Chile, Mexico, or Turkey that have formed PTAs with the main trading powers, the bulk of foreign trade flows are with their trade agreement partners.

Not only has the number of integration schemes grown, their content has become more complex and encompassing. Most agreements have advanced beyond market access for goods to so-called "behind-the-border" issues, such as investment, intellectual property rights, competition policy, and government procurement. Sub-regional pacts have taken collaboration even further to issues ranging from macroeconomic co-operation and labor mobility to coordination of positions in multilateral trade negotiations.

Do PTAs merit the blame heaped on them, or do they live up to the hopes pinned on them? Why do countries keep forming PTAs? What are the most constructive ways to harness the good and pre-empt the bad aspects of the rapidly growing trade agreement network? Can PTAs be the "Sovereign Remedy" that will fuel economic exchanges and perpetuate peace, as Winston Churchill surmised at the dawn of the post-war era?

The purpose of this book is to open avenues to answering these questions. We purport to examine PTAs in a historical context, map out their key contents, analyze their effects, and propose ways to make more of them for the benefit of global free trade and welfare.

Rather than focusing on any one agreement, or analyzing the effects of PTAs on any particular country, this book is more about the systemic issues surrounding PTAs—the contours, characteristics, and implications of the now global web, or "spaghetti bowl", of PTAs. We start from the premise that this system can have distinct and unintended effects separate from those of its parts, and that its effects are beyond the control of any one country. We focus on five main sets of questions.

- How has the system of PTAs evolved in history? How is it related to the rise of different types of trade agreements in the past 200 years? What are its unique properties, and why did it emerge when it did? What kinds of constellations are arising, who is linked to whom, and which countries are the leaders and which the laggards in pursuing agreements? Is the global architecture of agreements marked by hub-and-spoke patterns that could yield welfare-decreasing trade diversion, or is it more multipolar? Do PTAs risk metamorphosing into a handful of continental blocs that could silo global commerce, or proliferating into a mosaic bilateral agreements that could balkanize the world trading system?

- What does the rise of PTAs imply for other forms of cooperation? What are its effects on international institutions beyond trade—international agreements and organizations formed in such areas as monetary policy, transportation, and international security—that have mushroomed since the founding of the United Nations and the Bretton Woods system? Do PTAs—and trade opening—make countries more vulnerable and suspicious of one another, hindering cooperation, or do they tie countries' fortunes together, inducing them to cooperate further? Do PTAs sow global conflict or cooperation? Conversely, does international cooperation facilitate trade integration?

- How much built-in liberalization does the PTA architecture contain? How are PTAs structured, and how much trade do they free up and when? Do they liberalize trade on all products and do so quickly, or is liberalization less comprehensive and prolonged? What issue areas do they cover, and how? Why are some agreements more liberalizing and comprehensive than others? Who are the laggards and who the leaders in liberalization? How compatible are PTAs with one another? Are there families of certain types of PTAs, and if so, where and why?

- What do PTAs mean to the multilateral trading system? What are the implications for the non-discriminatory most-favored-nation treatment provided at the multilateral level? How do PTAs relate to the body of multilateral trade rules that the 152 current WTO member countries have diligently crafted over the past six decades? Do PTAs bypass the General Agreement on Tariffs and Trade (GATT) and the

WTO Agreements, or do they complement the multilateral trade rules? Do PTAs entrench protectionist forces around the world, or do they galvanize liberalizing lobbies to push harder for freer global trade? How can complementarities between PTAs and the global trading system be advanced?

- What are the key policies for making PTAs work for trade and growth? How should the web of PTAs be shaped so as to guarantee the effective operation of international trade, investment, and production? How can PTAs add greater value to their end-users—traders and investors—who navigate the layers of global trade rules on a daily basis? What issues should governments be most aware of and why—what are the potential good and bad aspects of the current PTA framework? What measures should be pursued at the multilateral level to shape the future of the PTA spaghetti bowl? How might regional neighbors address the spread of PTAs? How can countries best leverage PTAs for trade, growth, and productivity?

While the policy debate on these questions is intensifying, analysts have yet to devise conclusive answers. One reason is that despite the fact that PTAs come in many different shapes and sizes and thus could have different effects, most studies have failed to differentiate between these arrangements. This methodological choice undercuts the credibility and usefulness of the arguments of those who view PTAs as discriminatory instruments that obstruct global trade liberalization and dent welfare, and those who regard PTAs as conducive to multilateral opening and as engines of economic growth.

Further, most analysts of economic integration have focused on capturing PTAs' trade effects. Less attention has been paid to exploring PTAs' meaning for the sweeping trends in international economy and politics. And yet, should PTAs have any of their presumed effects on the multilateral trading system, global production patterns, and international cooperation, their relevance will surely extend well beyond their immediate trade effects.

II. Organization and Main Findings

That is where this book comes in. We employ new extensive and detailed data on PTAs to understand the features of the current trade agreement wave, examine the broader implications of PTAs for the future of global trade and politics, and put forth proposals to make PTAs a more constructive phenomenon in the globalizing world.

The various components of this volume are to an extent tested and tried. They derive from and build upon some of our prior research, articles, papers, and presentations over the past half dozen years, on which we have received commentary and further insights from several colleagues from around the world—in fact, too many to thank here.

This book is divided into two parts. The first part—Chapters 2, 3, and 4—takes a broad historical look at the "ecology" of PTAs and other types of trade agreements through history, and subsequently focuses on the "anatomy" of PTAs, detailing and dissecting the intricacies of these arrangements.

Chapter 2 endeavors to place PTAs in the historical context of the rise and fall of different types of trade agreements around the world over the past two centuries. It takes a *tour d'horizon* of the waves of trade agreements around the world over the past 130 years, examines the economic and political environment in which they have taken place, and discusses the various political economy interpretations accounting for the rise and spread of different kinds of trade agreements and of PTAs, in particular. There are five main findings.

First, the on-going proliferation of PTAs is but one of four main trade agreement waves over the past century and a half. Indeed, PTAs are but a subset of the vast body of international trade agreements forged over the years. The first and largely Euro-centric wave surged in the mid-1800s and receded at the beginning of World War I. The second wave took place in the inter-war era and was propelled by defensive bilateral agreements and trade blocs spearheaded by various European powers. The third wave started after World War II, swelled forcefully in the 1970s upon various developing countries' entry into the system of trade cooperation, and ebbed in the face of the economic downturn of the early 1980s.

Today's wave gained momentum in the early 1990s. It stands out in many ways from the waves of the past: driven by PTAs, it is the most liberalizing of the waves, containing manifold agreements that free up trade on the bulk of goods and do so quickly. Its agreements also are highly complex and comprehensive across trade and economic policy spaces, covering such issues as services, investment, and competition policy rules. It has also a transcontinental quality, with agreements increasingly being formed among countries across oceans. And it is taking place against the backdrop of an unprecedentedly liberal and globalized multilateral trading order.

Second, the geographical fault lines of PTAs have transformed over the past century. The most significant recent development is the move away from multi-member regional integration schemes among geographically proximate partners for bilateral, transcontinental agreements. In the meantime, coherent megablocs outside Europe, such as the Free Trade Area of the Asia-Pacific (FTAAP) or the Free Trade Area of the Americas (FTAA), have yet to materialize. More importantly, even if regional megablocs were to emerge, they would be inherently linked to the other world regions by virtue of the regional states' transcontinental connections.

Third, the trade agreement waves differ dramatically from each other in terms of their relationship with the multilateral trading system. For one thing, the first two waves surged prior to the creation of a multilateral trade institution—GATT and, subsequently, the WTO. Moreover, the backdrop for them was creeping multilateral protectionism in the late 19th century and outright closure of global trade in the inter-war era. In contrast, the post-war wave and certainly today's wave of PTAs have ridden on the back of multilateral trade opening. Should the historical record be a guide, it seems that PTAs have in the past substituted for multilateral liberalization, today they have properties conducive to complementing multilateralism.

Fourth, the importance of PTAs in global commerce has grown in the past two decades. The share of world trade among the partners to the most liberalizing of these agreements—free trade agreements and customs unions—has grown to about one-half of global trade flows. This has implications for the members—rules embedded in PTAs are increasingly important in their trade policy portfolios—as well as for non-members, given the preferential treatment that they forgo in the member states' markets. The growing importance of regional rules as referees of global commerce also has implications for the multilateral trading system as the nucleus of rulemaking in world trade.

Fifth, these patterns entail some serious risks. Granted, the global trading system today has multiple insurances against the type of protection that has engulfed the world in the past—an encompassing multilateral system with a credible dispute settlement mechanism, well-organized export lobbies, and the large stake that most states have in the fortunes of both the global trading system and their trading partners. However, trade cooperation at any level is fragile: our analysis of earlier eras of integration shows that isolationist sentiments and economic hard landings can decelerate liberalization or result in outright global protectionism, particularly if gripping the leading trade powers. A further challenge is posed by potential frictions between PTA rules and rules of the multilateral trading system. And still another set of challenges stems from the geography of trade integration: the spread of PTAs risks a balkanization of the global trading panorama into multiple, overlapping agreements that can create disincentives for the most efficient supply chains and production patterns in the global economy.

Chapter 3 takes a step further back to chart the backdrop to trade agreement waves, the evolution of international cooperation. A vast body of political science literature has shown that cooperation in one issue area can encourage states to expand their cooperation into other areas. The hypotheses turn on the idea that any cooperation requires a focal point, such as an international institution, which enables states to overcome Prisoner's Dilemmas inherent in international relations. PTAs can be a particularly potent focal point by spurring positive externalities (such as greater trust and contacts forged during the negotiation process) or negative ones (such as increased traffic congestion) that induce economic actors to demand further cooperation (so as to facilitate trade and create new transport corridors).

However, the empirical understanding of the linkages between trade and other forms of international cooperation is nascent. Employing data on international agreements over the past century, we strive to start filling this gap. Our historical narrative shows that trade and other types of cooperation agreements have ebbed and flowed together over the past 130 years: surges of PTAs are closely related to surges in cooperation agreements. We also find that PTAs may have spillover effects: countries that cooperate most extensively with each other in the area of trade tend to be each other's most favored partners also in other areas of cooperation.

What does this mean for the current wave of agreements? Should PTAs be building blocks for further cooperation, their ongoing spread could translate into a wave of cooperation agreements. Conversely, should cooperation agreements help propel trade and PTAs, cooperative international relations could be thought of as necessary, if not sufficient, for advancing trade integration. The policy implications are straightforward: if PTAs and cooperation agreements are mutually reinforcing and complementary, honing one can further the other, potentially multiplying the benefits of each type of agreement.

Chapter 4 turns to the present day. Rather than breadth, we now seek depth. We dissect the structure of the PTAs, examining some five dozen agreements by their various component parts, such as tariff liberalization, investment rules, and customs procedures. We arrive at four-fold conclusions:

- Most PTAs involve deep tariff liberalization, freeing 90 percent of products by the tenth year into the agreement. However, there are a number of outlier PTA parties (in general, developing countries) and product categories (particularly sensitive sectors include agriculture, textiles and apparel, and footwear) that feature prolonged tariff phase-outs and/or non-tariff barriers. Some countries also trail the general patterns when actual trade liberalized is being analyzed.

- Several PTAs contain product-specific rules that arbitrate market access as much as tariffs do, such as tariff rate quotas and rules of origin. These rules are as heterogeneous across PTAs as tariff liberalization schedules are, and tend to be particularly complex and restrictive in the most sensitive sectors.

- Many a PTA contains such mutually reinforcing provisions as tariff lowering, investment, services, competition policy, government procurement, and trade facilitation, and often spell out these rules with great precision. There are marked variations across PTAs in the coverage of trade-related disciplines; yet, the analysis also shows that PTAs tend to cluster into distinct "families" by the main world regions—Asia, Europe, and the Americas—and, in particular, by some global trade hubs, such as the United States, EU, and Singapore.

- Importantly, some of the PTA provisions can further trading with all of a country's trading partners. PTAs' services liberalization can improve the level of services provided in a country, which can boost the productivity of players engaged in trade in goods in general; improvements in customs procedures and trade facilitation mechanisms resulting from a PTA's customs chapter can further trade in goods with all the trading partners of PTA members.

The second part of this volume turns to interpreting the meaning of PTAs in the global trading system and international trade and production, and puts forth policy proposals for making sure PTAs are a more constructive force in the global economy.

Chapter 5 addresses the growing concerns that PTAs may fall short of complying with GATT Article XXIV, which sets out the conditions for the format of free trade agreements and customs unions, and goes on to examine the effects of PTAs on the unfettered flow of global trade. The chapter also proposes ways to enhance the complementarities between the PTA system and multilateral trade rules. There are three main conclusions.

- First, most of today's PTAs attain the most commonly used multilateral benchmarks for assessing their compliance with GATT Article XXIV. Trade agreements are often also "WTO+" in terms of incorporating a larger number and/or more specific provisions than the WTO Agreements do, and could as such be employed as incubators of, and laboratories for, global trade rulemaking. Yet, it is also the case that many a PTA also carries provisions that could potentially be classified as "other restrictive regulations of commerce" under Article XXIV, such as tariff rate quotas, special safeguards, and demanding rules of origin.

- Second, the academic jury is still out on PTAs' effects on global trade. While PTAs by and large take place in the context of open regionalism—simultaneous tariff liberalization at the regional and multilateral levels—some analysts argue that they can create frictions with the multilateral system and dissuade and distract countries from pursuing multilateralism. The more recent treatments involving product-level data on tariff liberalization in PTAs and incorporating other PTA provisions, such as rules of origin, have inaugurated a new era in capturing PTAs' economic effects, and offer the possibility of moving the debate on these arrangements forward.

- Third, an important new concept, "multilateralizing PTAs", has become the latest focal point of policy proposals to enhance compatibilities between PTAs and the global trading system, and to strive to advance toward global free trade by way of PTAs. Multilateralization can be pursued through global, regional, and case-by-case policies alike. While any multilateralization approach has its challenges, all approaches, when smartly sequenced and receiving the backing of the major trade agreement hubs, could revitalize and add value to the multilateral trading system. At the very least, they would help ensure that PTAs do not erode the gains of the past 60 years of multilateral trade liberalization.

Besides the complexities of the PTA–multilateralism interplay, there are growing concerns that the proliferation of PTAs is creating an unmanageable spaghetti bowl of rules that risks fragmenting the world trading system into hundreds of miniblocs. The PTA spaghetti could, in turn, generate new frictions and transactions costs for firms operating in multiple PTA theaters at once. Chapter 6 focuses on these concerns and puts forth ways of managing them.

We find that there are both theoretical and empirical reasons to believe that the PTA spaghetti does present problems and transactions costs for the member economies and companies operating in the agreements tangle. One solution to the PTA tangle—and perhaps the most feasible politically—is convergence, a process by which the various existing PTAs become connected to each other. Convergence was pursued in Europe in the late 1990s, when the various PTAs criss-crossing the old continent were brought together under a single, Paneuro area of cumulation of production; it is currently the focus of various country groupings in the Americas and Asia-Pacific.

We find that the prospects for convergence vary across subsets of PTAs and across economic sectors. There are clear PTA families centered around the United States, EU, and Mexico, in particular, wherein attaining convergence might be easiest. Any convergence drive would, however, require the members to define the scope of their effort and the stakeholders that would have to be involved, and, importantly, guarantee complementarities with the WTO system.

Chapter 7 brings together the various findings emerging from this book, and summarizes our policy recommendations for both unilateral and collective ways in which countries can deal with the system of PTAs in the most constructive fashion. Our main notion is that in the presence of the right designs and sound accompanying domestic, regional, and multilateral policies, PTAs can be conducive to global trade, further the development of multilateral trade rules, cut costs for global companies, and engender international cooperation in non-trade policy areas. The question in our view is not whether the system of PTAs has positive effects—it does—but, rather, under which conditions it does, and how its full positive potential can be harnessed.

We put forth five broad policy areas, both international and unilateral, that can help make PTAs an increasingly positive and complementary force in the global economy and politics:

- Designing PTAs. Trade agreements can be better designed. Most PTAs today are much more liberalizing and encompassing in product and issue coverage than were PTAs in the past. However, provisions governing sensitive sectors such as agriculture, textiles and apparel, and footwear evince pressures from import-competing interests. And several areas, such as investment and competition policy rules, could be crafted so as to enhance liberalization in these areas also in relation to non-member states.

- Building on PTAs. Working regionally rather than only nationally allows states to optimize their use of resources in the pursuit of growth, problem-solving, and development. Production of "regional public goods" is particularly compelling in light of the growing vulnerability of countries to issues that are beyond their unilateral control, such as financial crises and business cycles of their main trading partners, and negative cross-border externalities, such as pollution. Pooling resources at the regional level also makes business sense: countries can attain solutions and greater developmental outcomes with a smaller investment than they would make if acting alone. PTA partners can do much more to build upon their trade cooperation to induce integration in other policy areas—something that requires a conscious shift in policy thinking and implementation from national to regional.

- Connecting PTAs. The rapid proliferation of PTAs is splintering the global trading system, resulting in multiple overlapping PTAs. There are a number of concrete, practical steps for governments around the world to connect PTAs, such as through regional cumulation of production and some types of multilateral "rule caps" to control the proliferation of complex and restrictive trade rules.

- Implementing PTAs. An agreement is just the beginning of a long process of implementation. Many developing country PTAs still feature notable implementation deficits. Further, the fact that many countries belong to several PTAs at once and that any one agreement covers multiple issue areas, such as labor, sanitary standards, and the environment, poses new challenges for implementers in any country. Some of the key implementation gaps to be bridged include fostering capacities throughout governmental agencies to implement PTAs, creation of fluid inter-agency processes, as well as training the end-users—private sector players—to use PTAs.

- Complementing PTAs. While regional and global policies help, PTAs ultimately deliver for any one country only when buttressed by national policies and infrastructures conducive to trade. Lowered communications costs, improved transportation infrastructures, stable macroeconomic environments, and high-quality domestic institutions are some of the main factors that further economic actors' abilities to optimize the opportunities of hard-won market access. Trade agreements, like any other trade policy, must be accompanied by complementary policies that enable them to blossom.

PTAs are here to stay. Today, they are a global phenomenon that arbitrates the ways in which governments, politicians, companies, and individuals do business the world over. These actors can use PTAs in different ways— politicians to court business lobbies, governments for strategic purposes in international politics, businesses for cost-saving supply chains and efficiency-seeking investments. Making the most of PTAs is and should be, in short, in the self-interest of multiple national and global actors. It is hoped that the following chapters will provide a fresh framework for driving these interests in a more constructive fashion in the years ahead.

Part I

The Rise of Trade Agreements

2

Tides of Trade Integration

I. Introduction

Preferential trading arrangements (PTAs) have spread wildfire-like around the world in the past 20 years. Today, some 200 agreements have been notified to the WTO; the number is expected to soar to 400 by 2010. Virtually all countries are members of at least one agreement, and most countries belong to two or more agreements at once. The most prolific integrator, the United States, which up until the 1990s was reticent about forming preferential agreements, has in the span of a mere 13 years signed 14 agreements with partners in the Americas, Asia, and the Middle East; its North American Free Trade Agreement (NAFTA) partner Mexico sports 12 agreements, and Chile has entered into ten agreements, including with the United States and Mexico, respectively.[1] Singapore has been Asia's integrator juggernaut *par excellence*, having concluded 14 agreements in addition to being a member of the Association of South-East Asian Nations (ASEAN) Free Trade Area.

The European Union (EU), meanwhile, has adopted a distinct logic of integration, expanding to cover no fewer than 27 countries and thus swallowing up the manifold trade agreements it had formed with future members, such as the European Free Trade Agreement (EFTA) countries and East European nations. During its journey toward expansion, the EU signed dozens of agreements with non-member European countries. Yet today, the EU is also looking outward, having concluded trade agreements with the southern Mediterranean countries, South Africa, Mexico, and Chile, and aiming at further ones in the Americas and Asia, including with the ASEAN countries and India.

---

[1] The numbers refer to free trade agreements (FTAs) and customs unions only.

17

The inexorable rise of trade agreements in the past two decades is as indisputable as it is impressive. It has also gained growing attention from politicians and analysts alike. However, trade agreements have been a facet of the global economic landscape for decades and even centuries: their recent surge is but one, albeit forceful and qualitatively distinct, of the various trade agreement waves in world history.[2] And yet, most standard analyses on trade integration have focused on the past two decades only.

The purpose of this chapter is to employ new data to go beyond the PTA wave and describe the advance of international trade cooperation over the past 200 years. We base our analysis on the notion that the past can be a prologue: understanding the patterns of the past can provide insight into things present. Viewing the on-going PTA wave in the broader historical context of the rise and spread of different types of trade agreements—in essence, seeing PTAs as a subset of the trade agreements formed over the past two centuries—allows us to detect its unique features, and to propose policy recommendations that will help make trade agreements a positive force in the global economy.

The first section examines the waves of different types of trade agreements against the backdrop of broader trends in the global economy and the multilateral trading system, and explores the importance of these agreements in the member states' economies. The second section critically reviews the main political economy explanations for the ebbs and flows of cooperation in trade.

The main finding of this chapter is that today's trade agreement panorama is one of an unprecedented trinity of multilateral trade liberalization, comprehensive and liberalizing bi- and plurilateral trade agreements, and an expansion of world trade. Accentuating the significance of today's wave is the growing globalization of trade integration: virtually all countries belong to a trade agreement of some kind, all but one belong to a PTA, and most belong to several agreements simultaneously, while the bulk of countries—152 at the time of writing—are also members of the World Trade Organization (WTO). At the national level, these patterns have profound institutional and economic implications: all countries play by international trade rules of some kind, foreign trade overall has shot up in importance for the national economies, and much of that trade is conducted with a country's trade agreement partners. Trade agreements are here to stay and they can be hugely consequential in the global economy; this chapter endeavors to show how we got to this point.

---

[2] See Mansfield and Milner (1999) and Pollard (1974) for similar notions.

II. Trade Agreements Through Time

Countries have sought to eradicate barriers to each other's markets through ages. Ancient Greeks traded extensively around the Mediterranean basin and entered into several trade agreements in the region. In its efforts to ensure an adequate supply of grain for its citizens, Athens even entered into agreements with other states so that they would provide passage and favorable treatment to traders bound for Athens with grain. The Roman Republic of the fifth to the first centuries BC, whose economy lived off trade, entered into several commercial and political agreements with Carthage.

Fast-forwarding a good millennium, similar pressures were building up in Europe emerging from the Middle Ages. Initially, the new nation states of the continent were a patchwork of internal tolls and customs areas following the now sub-national, local jurisdictions. The centralization of political power in the 17th century was only gradually and often pains-takingly followed by the establishment of national customs unions that eradicated the barriers between local power centers.[3] Uniting under one monarch in 1603, England and Scotland managed to form a unified commercial union in 1707 through the Act of Union, which, together with another Act a year earlier, joined the two kingdoms into a single Kingdom of Great Britain. In France, it was the French Revolution that in 1790 allowed the internal barriers to be replaced by a single customs territory. In the future Germany, which was rife with customs frontiers, Prussia took the first step toward an economic union in 1808; this was followed by the formation of Zollverein, a customs union that implemented Prussia's external tariff, among most German states.

Trade agreements *among* the European sovereigns were also difficult to accomplish. The collapse of their colonial trade routes in the 1770s made Britain and France eager to open trade within the European continent. Britain was particularly intent on trade liberalization: Adam Smith provided an intellectual basis for free trade, while British manufacturers had a financial stake in it. The first tangible result was the 1783 Anglo-French treaty, which eliminated prohibitions and modestly reduced duties to bilateral trade. However, British trade negotiations with Poland, Prussia, Portugal, and Spain, among other important trade partners in Europe, proved less successful, and ground to a halt with the Napoleonic Wars. The hugely protectionist British Corn Law of 1815, imposed in part to

---

[3] See Irwin (1997).

hedge against the declining purchasing power of landlords and farmers, boded ill for tariff liberalization with the continental states.

The penchant for market opening among British manufacturers persisted, however. The 1823 Reciprocity of Duties Act paved the way for agreements with foreign governments for most-favored-nation (MFN) treatment on trade in goods and in shipping, and the Corn Laws were unilaterally repealed in 1846 as a result of the pressures of the Anti-Corn Law League, which argued for lower food prices and mobilized the industrial middle classes against the landlords. Perhaps not coincidentally, the United States passed the most liberal tariff to date the very same year, and Austria-Hungary, Spain, the Netherlands, Belgium, the Scandinavian countries, Switzerland, and Portugal brought their tariffs down in the late 1840s and 1850s.

However, it was the Anglo-French Cobden-Chevalier commercial treaty of 1860 that set the tone for a liberal trade order in Europe that would last through World War I. France abolished import prohibitions, and brought tariffs to 30 percent *ad valorem* or below—generally 10–15 percent—while Britain reduced the number of dutiable goods from 419 to 48, and lowered the wine tariff.[4] Most importantly, the treaty carried an MFN clause. This entailed that if either France or Britain negotiated further agreements with third parties, they would retain non-discriminatory access to each other's markets and receive no more unfavorable treatment than the third party.

The MFN clause of the Anglo-French treaty is widely seen as having helped trigger the subsequent rise of a network of trade treaties in late 19th century Europe. France formed agreements with Belgium in 1861, Zollverein in 1862, Italy in 1863, Switzerland in 1864, Sweden, Norway, Spain, and the Netherlands in 1865, and Austria in 1866. The MFN treatment enticed other countries to join, with tariff-lowering spreading throughout Europe. The main carrot for countries was to obtain as favorable treatment as Britain would get in the French market; Zollverein's joining the fray created similar incentives among the smaller states for a level playing field. In 1865, Britain, Belgium, Italy, and other states signed agreements with the Zollverein. By 1908, Britain would have agreements with 46 countries, Germany with 30, and France with some two dozen countries.

It was the logic of liberalization created by the expanding system of agreements that incentivized non-members to join. While the treaty network had two points of precariousness—it did not regulate members'

---

[4] See Irwin (1993) and Findlay and O'Rourke (2007).

external tariffs and the agreements formed in it generally expired after ten years, thus requiring renewals—its informality may have been what enabled countries to join it in the first place. Fueling the system were British economists disposed to free trade, France's industrialists keen on importing inputs at low tariffs, and German grain and timber exporters.[5]

The treaty network's importance was accentuated by the fact that the MFN clause was taken to include trade with the European colonies. French colonies adopted France's external tariff, thus in effect forming a customs union with their colonizer, while German, Belgian, and Dutch colonies had low tariffs. The 1884–5 Conference of Berlin, which divided Africa up among the European powers, made colonies in central Africa—Congo River Basin and adjacent territories—open to trade with all 14 European signatories on equal terms. In Asia, Britain defeated China in the Opium War of 1839–42 and went on to acquire Hong Kong, open five ports to free trade, and to set Chinese import duties at 5 percent *ad valorem* with the Treaty of Nanking in 1842. Japan liberalized its trade in 1858 as a result of US pressure.

The backdrop to the treaty network was *Pax Britannica*, European imperialism, and industrialization. The era also marked the onset of the Golden Age of globalization—a remarkable expansion in international trade, foreign direct investment, and migration flows, particularly between Europe and the New World, that are unparalleled even by today's standards—which was undoubtedly hurried into existence in part by the very tariff liberalization, along with the technological advances of the industrial era and the reduction of trade costs.[6] International specialization and intercontinental trade flows grew, with Europe, United States, and Japan exporting manufactured goods to Asia, Latin America, Africa, and Australia in exchange for foodstuffs and raw materials. The expansion of multilateral trade was buttressed by convertibility among national currencies. Anchored in the gold standard, the system of convertibility enabled countries to run trade deficits in some parts of the world and offset them with surpluses in others.

But tariff liberalization and globalization would peak in the late 19th century, and recede further in the inter-war era in reaction to the Great Depression and the onslaught of protectionism. One of the main drivers of the protectionist trade policies was countries' growing exposure to

---

[5] See Kindleberger (1975). Kindleberger sees free trade rooted in the general response to the breakdown of the European manor and guild systems. Governments coming under competing pressures for protectionism simply found it more efficient to swipe it away at once.

[6] See Findlay and O'Rourke (2007) and Clemens and Williamson (2004).

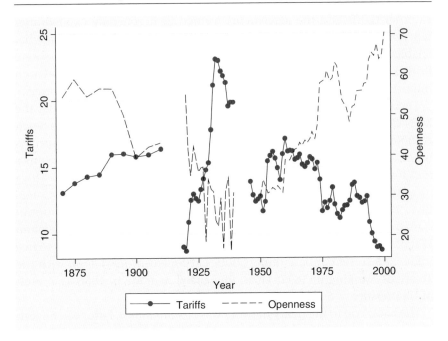

Figure 2.1 Tariffs and openness to trade around the world, 1875–2000

Note: Tariff data come from Clemens and Williamson (2004); for 1875–1949, they are simple averages for tariffs of 35 countries, and from 1950 onward, simple averages of tariffs for 182 countries (where available). The openness indicator is a simple average of trade/GDP data as collected by López-Córdova and Meissner (2005).

Source: Authors' calculations on the basis of Clemens and Williamson (2004).

international and intercontinental trade, which deepened domestic divisions among the winners and losers of trade.[7] Unlike in the past when trade politics was primarily a mercantilist struggle among governments and a tool for extracting rents, it was now a battle among domestic coalitions—and it was the losers who proved politically consequential. It would not be until the post-war era that globalization would make another appearance (Fig. 2.1).

The late 19th century is also the starting point for our data on 4,466 trade agreements and 370 PTAs (see Appendix 2.1 for details of the data). Figure 2.2 displays them, as formed annually during the period of 1875 to 2005, mapping out bilateral, plurilateral (here, 3–15 members),

---

[7] See Findlay and O'Rourke (2007) for an extensive treatment.

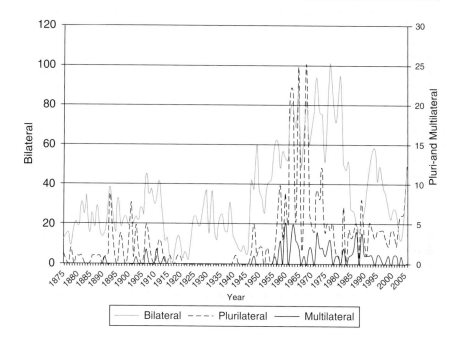

Figure 2.2 New trade agreements formed annually in 1875–2005, by type of membership

Source: Authors' calculations.

and multilateral (more than 15 members) agreements.[8] There are four distinct waves of bi- and plurilateral trade agreements: the first in the late 19th century, the second in the inter-war era, the third following World War II, and the fourth picking up in the 1980s. They are paralleled by multilateral agreements with the major exception of the inter-war era.

The agreements can be disaggregated into seven different types: general agreements that are about broad-based trade liberalization and often include such agreements as trade and navigation agreements in the early part of the data; sectoral agreements that are trade agreements limited to such areas as agriculture and textiles; agreements on certain trade rules such as standards or trademarks; trade and economic cooperation

[8] Data for 2005 include agreements that are in force, as well as agreements that are signed and agreements under negotiation. Note that what we here term as "agreements" range from convention to treaty, agreement, exchange of notes, protocol, final act, and amendment, among other types of binding legal instruments notified by the countries to the UN Treaty System.

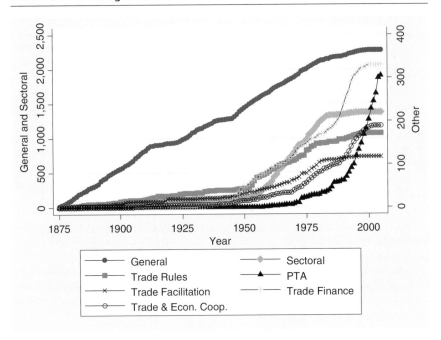

Figure 2.3 Cumulative trade agreements in 1875-2005, by issue area
Source: Authors' calculations.

agreements that stress broad-based economic collaboration among the partners; trade finance agreements such as post-war trade and payments agreements in Europe; and trade facilitation agreements, including agreements related to trade missions and other business facilitation (Fig. 2.3). The number of general trade agreements, which numbered nearly 2,300 or more than one-half of the agreements in the dataset by the turn of the millennium, dwarfs all other types of agreements. Sectoral agreements are a rather distant second, at about 1,400 agreements; there were nearly 200 PTAs by the end of 2000 and 370 by the end of 2005.

What are these agreements all about? And why did they rise (and fall) when they did? The first, pre-war trade agreement wave contains a number of bilateral agreements formed particularly by Great Britain, France, Italy, various Latin American states both with each other and with the United States, and a web of agreements woven by Zollverein.[9] These agreements

---

[9] See Pahre (2001), Mansfield and Milner (1999), Irwin (1993), and Pollard (1974) for further discussion.

were general in nature, often termed treaties of "commerce and naviga-tion" or "friendship and commerce". Their language is liberalizing, call-ing for national treatment in trade and shipping. For instance, the 1875 commerce and navigation treaty between the United States and Belgium stipulates

full and entire freedom of commerce and navigation between the inhabitants of the two countries, and the same security and protection which is enjoyed by the citizens or subjects of each country shall be guaranteed on both sides. The said inhabitants, whether established or temporarily residing within any ports, cities or places whatever of the two countries, shall not, on account of their commerce or industry, pay any other or higher duties, taxes or imposts than those which shall be levied on citizens or subjects of the country in which they may be; and the privileges, immunities and other favors, with regard to commerce or industry, enjoyed by the citizens or subjects of one of the two States, shall be common to those of the other.

The treaty also provides for reciprocal national treatment in naviga-tion, so that the counterpart's vessels would not pay any higher or other charges for "tonnage, pilotage, anchorage, buoys, light-houses, clear-ance, brokerage or, generally, other charges, whatsoever", than those that are required of the home country's shippers. And it notes that "any counterfeiting in one of the two countries of the trade-marks affixed in the other on merchandise, to show its origin and quality, shall be strictly prohibited".

Some treaties forged in Europe were more specific, enumerating a list of goods from the partner that would be free of tariffs, and specifying in detail such issues as transit dues, privileges related to stationing of vessel, tonnage dues. Portugal's treaty with the UK of 1914 specifies that "the contracting Parties also reciprocally undertake that no more favorable treatment shall be extended to the goods of any other foreign country in respect of importation, import duties, exportation, export duties, re-expor-tation, re-export duties, customs facilities, warehousing, transshipment, drawbacks, and commerce and navigation in general", while also detail-ing that "His Britannic Majesty's Government engage to recommend to Parliament to prohibit the importation into and sale for consumption in the United Kingdom of any wine or other liquor to which the description 'Port' or 'Madeira' is applied, other than wine the produce of Portugal and of the island of Madeira respectively". The treaty also contains a rather sophisticated dispute settlement mechanism.

These first wave trade agreements petered out with creeping global pro-tectionism. The most frequently cited culprit is the collapse of agricultural

25

prices in the late 1860s and 1870s.[10] With cheap grain imports flooding Europe from the New World and Russia, farmers' protectionist impulses overwhelmed the more liberalizing industrialists, shippers, shopkeepers, and financiers.[11] Indeed, Britain's imminent decline as the predominant global power can be attributed to international commodity trade integration.[12] British farmers' calls for tariffs set off a wave of protection in Europe: Prussia imposed the iron-and-rye coalition's favored tariff on agriculture and manufactures in 1879, and many other countries resorted to tariff hikes in the 1880s. Minor tariff wars broke out.

The expiry of the trade treaties compounded the protectionist drift, as renegotiation was beholden to protectionist sentiments. However, overall, the European tariff hikes were relatively moderate.[13] US Civil War tariffs in the 1860s were steeper, designed to cover the revenue demands of the war. The United States also remained outside the MFN system. In 1878, Canada raised tariffs on agricultural and industrial goods alike. Williamson (2004) reports a very pronounced rise in tariffs across Latin America—Latin America had the highest tariffs in the world from 1860 to the 1930s, mainly put in place to obtain government revenue[14]—across non-Latin European offshoots, and across the European periphery.

The liberalizing logic that had engulfed Europe in the mid-19th century waxed and waned. It would return in 1900, led by export lobbies and a growing intellectual disposition to free trade in Britain,[15] only to be broken down by, during, and after World War I. By 1913, France, Germany, Italy, Spain, Sweden, and Switzerland had increased their tariffs on manufactures—at times doubling them—notably from 1875 levels.[16] While not all countries raised tariffs, and while some even lowered them during the war, the liberal order ground to a halt, and the treaty network's *bilateralism-cum-MFN* logic dissipated. Trade was hurt, and hurt further by the surge in wartime transport costs.

In contrast to the first wave of trade agreements, in the inter-war era there was a wave of *bilateralism-sans-MFN*. The immediate post-war years

---

[10] See Irwin (1993) and Kindleberger (1975).

[11] See Gourevitch (1977) for a nuanced assessment of the potential determinants of protectionism during the era in Europe and the United States.

[12] O'Rourke and Williamson (1994).

[13] Irwin (1993).

[14] Williamson (2004) and Coatsworth and Williamson (2004a) explain that the Latin tariffs are driven by a complex set of political economy determinants, key among them the need for tariff revenue to wage intra-regional conflicts.

[15] See Kindelberger (1975) and Blattman *et al.* (2002).

[16] Findlay and O'Rourke (2007) based on Bairoch (1989).

saw various protectionist acts in Britain, while Central and Southeastern European countries failed to abandon the quantitative restrictions imposed during the war. Tariffs around the world rose in two stages.[17] The first stage was in the 1920s. The UK, the United States, and European countries increased tariffs following a decline in commodity prices—a policy that was halted only temporarily by the 1927 World Economic Conference— while Germany and the Eastern European countries imposed restrictions on foreign exchange transactions. The second stage in the 1930s was even more notorious, taking place when the onset of the Great Depression helped pull the world into a protectionist spiral.

The main factor driving the second stage of global closure was the US Smoot-Hawley tariff legislation of 1930, which was sparked off by an effort to protect American farmers against growing foreign agricultural imports. However, special interests took the tariff schedule revision beyond agriculture, securing protection also for industrial goods. When the dust settled, the United States had raised tariffs on more than 20,000 imported goods to record heights, and this in spite of protests from hundreds of economists. While in part caused by the Great Depression, the act exacerbated the slump, not least due to subsequent tariff increases in Canada, France, Italy, Spain, and Switzerland.

Tariff wars spiraled and most countries sported tariffs well above those of 1913 levels. Besides tariffs, quotas, import licenses, and exchange controls siloed world trade within formal and informal empires, the British Commonwealth bloc, the European gold standard bloc centered around France, and a Central European bloc built around Germany, which used discriminatory trade policies to carve out economic spheres of influence (Eichengreen and Irwin 1995; Kindleberger 1989). Portugal and France provided tariff preferences to their colonies, and Italy (with Austria and Hungary), Japan, and the Soviet Union created defensive trade blocs. In 1930, four Nordic and the three Benelux countries formed the Oslo group to counteract the effects of economic depression through trade and to reduce their dependence on Germany for export markets, and the Benelux countries formed their own bloc. In stark contrast to the heyday of the European MFN system, and despite various efforts to reinstate it, trade-diverting beggar-thy-neighbor policies took hold. World trade regionalized.

By 1931, tariffs on foodstuffs had shot up to 53 percent in France, more than 80 percent in Germany, and above 100 percent in Bulgaria, Poland,

---

[17] See Irwin (1993) for a discussion.

and Finland (League of Nations 1939). The growth of world trade between 1924 and 1929 was lost to the Depression, protectionism, commodity market disintegration, and the demise of the gold standard (Findlay and O'Rourke 2007). Between 1929 and 1932, manufactured goods trade dropped by 42 percent and agricultural trade by 13 percent. The World Economic Conference of 1933 proved ineffective in reversing the protectionist tide.

Countervailing pressures against protectionism would this time come from the New World. Liberalizing forces in the US Congress passed the Reciprocal Trade Agreements Act (RTAA) in 1934 to amend Smoot-Hawley by authorizing the US executive to negotiate alterations of up to 50 percent in existing import duties on a reciprocal basis.[18] The delegation of trade policymaking authority from the Congress to the president enabled the US State Department to initiate trade negotiations with several Latin American countries, in particular. By 1945 the United States had entered into 32 bilateral agreements under the RTAA with 27 countries; these cut rates by some 44 percent and covered a total of 64 percent of US dutiable imports (Jackson *et al.* 1984). Besides reciprocal trade agreements, our data also yield numerous commodity agreements formed by the United States, such as on the purchases of natural rubber with the Netherlands and France, respectively, and of exportable surpluses of rice produced in Brazil.

While our data in the 1930s are dominated by RTAA-powered agreements focused on item-by-item tariff cuts and a handful of other US agreements, the post-war era also witnessed a steady rise of different types of trade agreements, such as US agreements with a number of Latin American countries aimed at facilitating the work of "traveling salesmen" (here classified as trade facilitation agreements) and agreements for the protection of commercial and industrial trade marks (here, trade rules).[19] Sectoral agreements proliferated across such product categories as fuel lubricants, fish, and cheese among West European countries, such

---

[18] Hiscox (1999) argues that the RTAA did not cause US trade liberalization, but was merely symptomatic of the exogenous changes in party constituencies and societal preferences that shaped congressional votes to extend the RTAA authority and liberalize trade after 1945. See Destler (2005) for the most comprehensive and sweeping study of US trade policymaking in the 20th century.

[19] The former state, "Manufacturers, merchants, and traders domiciled within the jurisdiction of one of the high contracting parties may operate as commercial travelers either personally or by means of agents or employees within the jurisdiction of the other high contracting party on obtaining from the latter, upon payment of a single fee, a license which shall be valid throughout its entire territorial jurisdiction."

as Belgium, Denmark, Finland, Germany, Great Britain, Iceland, the Netherlands, Norway, Portugal, and Sweden, as well as between them and various East European states.

Much like the UK-inspired wave of liberalization around the world at the start of the 20th century, the United States was the locomotive of the global thrust toward free trade post-RTAA.[20] US preferential agreements were at first unable to spur global trade due to high external tariffs; trade creation was lost to trade diversion. Nonetheless, global trade started expanding rapidly in the late 1940s, rising well above pre-war levels by 1950. US exports and imports both more than quadrupled between 1950 and 1970 (Destler 2005), and, as Figure 2.2 suggests, the share in trade of world output doubled from some 30 percent after the war to above 60 percent in the 1970s. The underpinnings for a liberalizing post-war trade regime fell into place.

World War II only interrupted the integrationism. Much like the prior waves, the third, post-war wave was driven by Western Hemisphere and European states, but would over time come to incorporate developing countries throughout the world. And it would mark a return to the MFN principle. Yet, MFN would now become formal, and it would prove sustainable, as well as transformative, in global commerce.

The wave started off with the rise of what we here classify as trade finance agreements as well as trade and economic cooperation agreements within Europe and elsewhere in the world. The trade finance agreements formed in the late 1940s and 1950s were primarily bilateral trade and payments agreements in Europe and between European countries and countries in Latin America. The shortage of hard currency in post-war Europe hampered European countries' reconstruction efforts, which hinged on imports payable with dollars.[21] Bilateral agreements were geared to conserving hard currency while trading within Europe: some trade would be reduced to barter, with imports paid for with exports and no currency changing hands. The agreements also provided some leeway to cease trade with partners that exerted pressures on a country's hard currency holdings. The system was multilateralized with the creation of the European Payments Union capitalized by the United States under the Marshall Plan. The arrangement was aimed at suppressing prolific bilateralism through convertibility; the Bank of International Settlements was designated as the system's bookkeeper.

---

[20] See Blattman *et al.* (2002).
[21] See Oatley (2001) for an analysis of the European payments system.

The Soviet Union gave additional force to the third wave by forging numerous general trade agreements that stipulated most-favored-nation treatment and the establishment of Soviet trade delegations—entities in charge of fueling and administering Soviet trade—with countries around the world.

From the late 1950s onward, the third wave brought about sectoral agreements especially for agricultural commodities, meat, as well as cotton, wool and man-made fiber textiles, particularly between the United States and a number of developing countries. The agricultural agreements were formed under the Agricultural Trade Development and Assistance Act of 1954, which established the Eisenhower Administration's overseas food assistance program, Food for Peace. The purpose of the program was to combat world hunger and malnutrition, promote the development of agriculture, create and expand export markets for US agricultural products, and to foster private enterprise and democracy around the developing world. The trade and development aspect provided for concessional sales of agricultural products to friendly developing nations.[22]

The UK forged another quite important set of sectoral agreements with its grain suppliers, such as the United States, Romania, India, Australia, and Canada, in the context of the Kennedy Round push to reduce non-tariff barriers in global agricultural trade. In the agreements, the UK agreed to restrain domestic financial assistance to cereals production and to maintain a fair and reasonable balance between home production and imports, as well as to create a system of minimum import prices for the major cereals, cereal products, and by-products.[23]

Not all agreements had liberalizing intentions. The United States forged a number of agreements in the 1970s with Latin American countries to restrain the amount of US imports of meat, and with East Asian suppliers to limit textile imports. The latter agreements were a harbinger of the Multifiber Agreement that would come to regulate textile and garment trade around the world from 1974 until its 2004 expiration through quotas on developing country exports to developed countries.

---

[22] Under the Act, surplus bulk commodities purchased from the US would be monetized in the recipient country market, and income that was generated was to be channeled to support the objectives of the agreement between the US government and the recipient government. The concessional terms provided long-term credit of up to 30 years, with no minimum repayment for ten years, a grace period for payment of principle of up to five years at low interest rates.

[23] See Brunthaver (1965) for a thorough analysis of the agreement.

The third trade agreement wave took place within a consolidating multilateral and most-favored-nation framework—the establishment of the Bretton Woods institutions and the General Agreement on Tariffs and Trade (GATT), signed in 1948 by 23 countries,[24] and the ensuing multilateral trade rounds, Annecy in 1949, Torquay in 1951, Geneva 1956, Dillon 1960–1, Kennedy 1964–7, Tokyo 1973–9, Uruguay 1986–94, and Doha, which has run from 2001 to the present.

Formed to reduce tariffs and non-tariff barriers, GATT's first round yielded some 45,000 tariff concessions affecting some 20 percent of global trade. At the heart of the GATT system was non-discrimination. The agreement marked the formation of 123 bilateral agreements that were subsequently generalized via the MFN clause (Irwin 1995). However, the problem with the system was free-riding—countries would by way of the MFN clause ride on the preferences provided for in other countries' negotiations, while doing little themselves (Findlay and O'Rourke 2007). The Torquay Round mandated that the GATT negotiations be multilateral, and the Kennedy Round put multilateralism into practice. Multilateralizing reduced the free-riding problem, while also requiring mechanisms to reduce the coordination costs of arriving at agreements across the entire membership. However, as we shall see in Chapter 5, GATT Article XXIV also stipulated what has become a far-reaching exception to the MFN principle for customs unions and free trade areas.

While the first rounds, Annecy and Torquay, centered on tariff liberalization, the Kennedy Round opened a road beyond tariffs, delivering the Anti-Dumping Agreement and a section on development issues. The 1973–9 Tokyo Round created regulations, albeit mostly with a limited impact, to control the non-tariff barriers and voluntary export restrictions that had proliferated as a result of the blunting of the tariff instrument and the pessimism over the US economy.[25]

These years also brought about the renewal of various multilateral commodity agreements first launched in the 1930s and 1940s, such as for cocoa, coffee, tin, sugar, wheat, and olive oil. And they marked the rise of trade and cooperation agreements among developing countries through such fora as the Group of 77 (G-77) established in 1964 by 77 developing

[24] These were Australia, Belgium, Brazil, Burma, Canada, Ceylon, Chile, China, Cuba, the Czechoslovak Republic, France, India, Lebanon, Luxembourg, Netherlands, New Zealand, Norway, Pakistan, Southern Rhodesia, Syria, South Africa, the United Kingdom, and the United States.

[25] See Ray (1987) for an analysis of the determinants of non-tariff barriers in the post-war era.

countries and aimed at promoting the "southern" countries' collective economic interests on international economic issues. The rise of South–South agreements marked a departure from the Euro- and Americas-centric web of agreements for growing globalization of cooperation—a trend whose full force would nonetheless remain hampered by the Cold War and the Iron Curtain through the early 1990s.

The third trade agreement wave started dissipating with the oil shocks of the late 1970s and the economic downturn of the early 1980s. The US economy entered a severe recession in 1982, and the tightening of the money supply made interest rates soar. Latin America and Eastern European countries defaulted on the debts they had accumulated in the 1970s. The bad times would return in the late 1980s and early 1990s prior to the extensive and strong recovery starting in the spring of 1991.

This is also when the fourth, on-going trade agreement wave picked up. It would become a wave of intense regionalism, transcontinental bilateralism, and deep liberalization. And it would be paralleled by a globalization of the MFN principle and of the international economy.

The types of agreements that started to make their appearance in the third wave and surged particularly during the fourth wave were preferential trading arrangements (PTAs)—here, more than 300 bi- and plurilateral trade agreements notified to the GATT under Article XXIV or the Enabling Clause and some trade agreements that have not yet been notified, but which we here classify as PTAs.[26] PTAs are akin to general trade agreements. However, PTAs of the fourth wave have two properties that set them apart from general agreements: they are deeply liberalizing, and they are often highly comprehensive, covering such areas as services, investment, competition policy, and government procurement (Table 2.1). As such, they are the most hybrid of agreements, blending elements of sectoral agreements, agreements on rules, and often also trade facilitation and trade and economic cooperation agreements.

The trend toward more encompassing agreements has been paralleled by the growing comprehensiveness of multilateral agreements. During the

---

[26] WTO members are required to notify the regional trade agreements in which they participate to the WTO. By October 2007, the WTO reports that 111 FTAs and 13 CUs had been notified under GATT Article XXIV, which governs PTAs; 21 PTAs under the Enabling Clause, which governs developing country PTAs and imposes less stringent requirements on PTAs than does Article XXIV, and 49 services agreements under the General Agreement on Trade in Services Article V. We do not include services agreements in our analysis.

Table 2.1 Coverage of 25 trade disciplines in selected PTAs

	NAFTA	US–Australia	CAFTA	US–Peru	Chile–Mexico	MERCO-SUR–Chile	Mexico-Japan	Korea–Chile	EU–Mexico	EU–Chile	Japan–Singapore	Singapore–Australia	Thailand–Australia	ASEAN	COMESA
Agriculture															
Competition Policy															
Customs Procedures															
Dispute Settlement															
E-Commerce															
Environment															
Financial Services															
Government Procurement															
Intellectual Property Rights															
Investment															
Labor															
Market Access for Goods															
Non-Tariff Measures															
Other Measures															
Pharmaceutical and Medical															
Rules of Origin															
Sanitary & Phytosanitary Measures															
Services															
Special Regimes															
Technical Barriers to Trade															
Telecommunications															
Textiles and Apparel															
Trade Remedies															
Transparency															
Transportation															

Included as a chapter or section
Included as an annex or sub-section
Included as a side agreement

Note: Transportation in EU–Chile and EU–Mexico FTAs refers to chapters on international maritime services and transportation.

33

Dillon Round, GATT members' negotiations centered on tariffs; however, over time, the talks expanded to non-tariff measures, and by the Uruguay Round, covered tariffs, non-tariff measures, rules, services, intellectual property, dispute settlements, textiles, and agriculture. The on-going Doha Round deals with trade in goods and services, tariffs, non-tariff measures, anti-dumping and subsidies, regional trade agreements, intellectual property, environment, dispute settlement, and trade facilitation. Given the expansion in WTO membership, most countries today are subject to these disciplines, not only at the regional but also at the multilateral level (Fig. 2.4).

What are the various PTAs all about? We strive to get to the bottom of this question by employing a broader classification of PTAs than most analysts in order to draw contrasts among the different types of preferential agreements, and analyze a total of 370 PTAs. Figure 2.5 displays a stylized typology of PTAs—including free trade agreements that free tariffs on nearly all products between members, such as NAFTA, the EU–Mexico and Chile–Korea FTAs; customs unions (CUs), which in addition to sharing the prop-

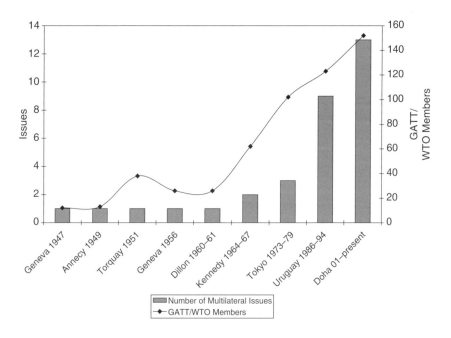

Figure 2.4 Growth in GATT and WTO membership and in the number of trade disciplines discussed at the multilateral level, 1947 to the present

Source: Authors' calculations based on WTO data.

erties of FTAs, strive to implement a common external tariff (CET), such as the EU, the Central American Common Market (CACM), and the South African Customs Union (SACU); FTA accession; CU accession; preferential arrangements, which are here primarily multi-member developing country schemes that provide some form of (more limited) preferential treatment, such as the Latin American Integration Association (LAIA) and the Global System of Trade Preferences (GSTP) among the Group of 77 members; non-reciprocal preferential arrangements, which are generally tariff preferences provided by developed countries to developing countries; economic areas, which are Latin American bilateral agreements formed under the LAIA umbrella and which tend to go beyond trade liberalization; and partial scope agreements, which are strictly about trade only and subject only a subset of product categories to tariff liberalization, and again include primarily bilaterals among LAIA members (see Appendix 2.1 for details of the data). FTAs and CUs are generally the most encompassing of PTAs in terms of products subjected to liberalization, reciprocal liberalization, and comprehensiveness of coverage of trade-related issues alike. The

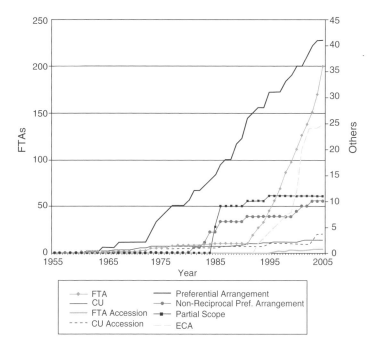

Figure 2.5 Cumulative PTAs in 1960–2005, by main types
Source: Authors' calculations.

pattern is even more pronounced when only PTAs notified to the WTO and that are in effect today are taken into account.[27]

The PTA wave started with the formation of the European Community in 1958 and expanded with such agreements as the European Free Trade Area (EFTA) among the Scandinavian countries, Austria, Switzerland, Portugal, and the UK in 1960, CACM in 1961, the Andean Pact in 1969, the Economic and Monetary Community of Central Africa of 1964, and the Bangkok Agreement between Bangladesh, India, Sri Lanka, the Republic of Korea, and Laos in 1977.

Also emerging were non-reciprocal schemes, such as the EC's Lome Convention for African, Caribbean, and Pacific (ACP) states in 1975; SPARTECA, Australia and New Zealand's preferential scheme for Pacific island nations in 1981; and the US Caribbean Basin Initiative (CBI) that went into effect in 1984. These agreements were based on the era's "trade not aid" development thinking, and provided the beneficiaries with broad-based access to the providers' markets. The GATT's Enabling Clause was what permitted such non-reciprocal treatment in global trade.

The proliferation of PTAs from the 1990s onward took off with the formation of sub-regional, aspiring customs unions around the world, such as the Southern Common Market (MERCOSUR) forged in 1991 between Argentina, Brazil, Paraguay, and Uruguay with the aim of fostering peace and democracy in a region that in the past had oscillated toward authoritarianism; ASEAN among the rapidly developing Southeast Asian countries; the South African Development Community (SADC) anchored around the locomotive economy of South Africa; significant revision of the CACM, Andean Community, and Caribbean Community, all in the early 1990s; and the consolidation of the European Union, including the launch of the Single Market in 1993 (Box 2.1). The wave of PTAs was subsequently transformed into prolific intra-regional bilateralism in the post-Cold War era with the formation of various bilateral FTAs between the EU and the Eastern European states emerging from the Soviet bloc and the numerous agreements criss-crossing the Americas. Most recently the PTA wave has acquired a transcontinental quality, with pairings such as the United States and Morocco, Mexico and Japan, and Chile and the European Union having recently entered into free trade agreements.

One of the putative reasons for the trend toward PTAs is the realization of the complementarities that PTAs provide among such disciplines as trade,

---

[27] Note further that FTAs would dwarf other agreements were a log scale not employed.

Box 2.1 PTA PATHWAYS IN THE 1990S: FROM INTRA-REGIONAL BLOCS
TO TRANSCONTINENTAL BILATERALISM

Countries in different world regions have had distinct PTA pathways along the four main "stations"—intra-regional blocs, intra-regional bilateral PTAs, continental megablocs, and transcontinental PTAs—over the past two decades (Fig. 2.1). In the Americas, the typical PTA path has been from intra-regional blocs—to a megabloc (FTAA), followed by intra-regional bilateral agreements and, subsequently, trans-continental trade agreements. The first PTAs were intra-regional aspiring customs unions—the Andean Community, Caribbean Community (CARICOM), Central American Common Market (CACM), Southern Common Market (MERCOSUR). The 1994 Miami Summit of the Americas launched the 34-country negotiations for the Free Trade Area of the Americas (FTAA), which was to merge these schemes and NAFTA under a single umbrella. The FTAA process was paralleled by some bilateral agreements, particularly between Mexico and other regional economies, but it was the stagnation of the FTAA talks in 2003 that "regionalized" the quest for bilateral FTAs. Among the most recent highlights are the US–Central America–Dominican Republic FTA (DR–CAFTA) and the MERCOSUR–Andean Community FTA signed in 2004, and the culmination of the US–Colombia, US–Peru, US–Panama, and Chile–Peru FTA negotiations in 2006.

Many countries of the Americas have also moved toward transcontinentalism, seeking in particular to establish a foothold in Asia's fast-growing trade agreement panorama. In 2003, Chile and South Korea signed the Asian country's first compre-hensive bilateral FTA, and in 2005, Chile concluded negotiations for a four-partite FTA with Brunei Darussalam, New Zealand, and Singapore. An FTA between Chile and China—the East Asian economy's first extra-regional FTA—went into effect in October 2006, and in November 2006 Chile became the second country of the Americas to reach an FTA with Japan. The United States and Singapore reached one of the first agreements of Singapore's now extensive network of trade agreements in 2003, and the US–Australia FTA entered into force in 2005.

The Mexico–Japan Economic Partnership Agreement (EPA), Japan's first extra-regional free trade agreement, also took effect in 2005. The same year, Peru and Thailand signed a bilateral FTA, while FTAs between Taipei, China on the one hand, and Panama and Guatemala, on the other, took effect in 2004 and 2006, respectively. Panama concluded FTA negotiations also with Singapore in 2006. Trans-Pacific agreements are poised to expand: the United States has concluded negotiations with Korea, and Malaysia and Chile have announced their intentions to pursue FTA negotiations.

Countries of the Americas have also been reaching across the Atlantic for agree-ments with the European Union (EU). Mexico launched an EPA with the EU in 2000, as did Chile in 2003. In May 2006, the EU and CACM countries announced the launch of comprehensive Association Agreement negotiations, while the EU–CARICOM talks have entered the final phase. The EU and the Andean Community have explored the opening of Association Agreement negotiations, and nego-tiations continue between the EU and MERCOSUR. And besides the trans-Pacific and trans-Atlantic fronts, ties have been forged between the Americas and other regions, such as between MERCOSUR and India, and between the United States and selected Middle Eastern countries. In the extra-regional sphere, five countries of the Americas—Canada, Chile, Mexico, Peru, and the United States—have pursued closer ties with the region in the context of the Asia-Pacific Economic Cooperation (APEC) forum founded in 1989.

European countries have a distinctive PTA pathway—yet one which is also culminating in transcontinental agreements. Western European countries have combined the construction of a megabloc with intra-regional bilateral agreements. The launch of the European Economic Community (EEC) in 1957 was a watershed; by 1968, the EEC had liberalized all intra-regional trade. The parallel smaller EFTA bloc also freed trade in the 1960s, and forged FTAs with the EEC that opened bilateral trade in 1973. By the early 1980s, the EEC claimed 12 members, expanding further to 15 in 1995 by absorbing three of the EFTA members, Austria, Finland, and Sweden. The EU and EFTA formed the European Economic Area (EEA) in 1994. At about the same time, virtually all Eastern European states freed from the Soviet yoke had begun forming FTAs with the then European Union as well as with each other, producing an extensive FTA network criss-crossing the old continent.

The EU has since expanded to incorporate no fewer than 27 members, and also pursued the so-called Euro-Mediterranean Association Agreements with various southern Mediterranean countries, forged extra-regional ties with South Africa, Mexico, and Chile, and set its sights on the Asian trade agreement market. Europe's integration, in short, took place from "inside out", with the member countries prioritizing comprehensive consolidation (and expansion) of the intra-regional market over extra-regional excursions.

The Asia-Pacific region is a more nascent player on the global trade agreement chessboard, but is currently surging as the region with greatest trade agreement activity in the world. For their part, Asian countries started out with a megabloc, the APEC forum created in 1989, and the Southeast Asian countries pursued a plurilateral scheme with the 1992 establishment of the ASEAN Free Trade Agreement (AFTA). However, the regional economies have in recent years moved rapidly to weave a web of FTAs both within and beyond the region. This represented the first formal step toward a more tightly integrated region.

Today, many Asian countries—first and foremost Singapore, South Korea, Japan, and China—have also set out to pursue bilateral FTAs. Indeed, the recent proliferation of FTAs in Asia-Pacific can be seen as the most notable development in the region's trading panorama in recent years. There have also been proposals for plurilateral FTAs in the Asia-Pacific region. China has entered into an FTA with ASEAN, and Japan is exploring a similar deal. Further ASEAN plurilateral initiatives include a proposal for an ASEAN–India economic partnership, and a recent decision to convert the long-running trade cooperation between ASEAN and Australia and New Zealand into a genuine FTA. The most ambitious current proposal is to form a multimember Free Trade Area of the Asia-Pacific (FTAAP).

African countries had their first experience of integration with their colonizers in the late 19th century, but have in the post-colonial era created a number of intra-regional PTAs, in particular, including the Common Market for Eastern and Southern Africa (COMESA), the Economic Community of West African States (ECOWAS), and the South African Development Community (SADC). In the Middle East, the foremost bloc is the Gulf Cooperation Council; many of the regional economies have abandoned inter-regionalism, forging FTAs with the United States that are envisioned to converge into the US–Middle East Free Trade Agreement (MEFTA).

investment, and services, and the likely reduction in bargaining costs compared with the situation where each of these different areas was negotiated separately. PTAs also expand opportunities for issue linkages and give and take in negotiations, for instance with tariff lowering abroad reciprocated by services liberalization at home. Indeed, the relative reduction in sectoral agreements and agreements on trade rules since the 1980s may well be related to the proliferation of PTAs, comprehensive trade agreements that subsume sectoral matters and multiple trade rules. A further, oft-cited reason is competition among developing countries for foreign direct investment: PTAs help attract investors through being a signal of credible, steady economic policies and by virtue of providing protection for investment.

It is FTAs that have surged in recent years. This in part evinces a drive for more comprehensive and reciprocal liberalization than is achievable in partial scope agreements, and a push by developed country exporters to open markets in, rather than provide unilateral preferences to, rapidly growing emerging markets. The rise of FTAs also reflects efforts by developing countries to lock in the preferences of non-reciprocal schemes via reciprocal agreements, as well as growing questioning in the trade policy world about the effectiveness of non-reciprocal agreements for the intended beneficiaries: lack of reciprocity has come to be seen as potentially counterproductive in postponing tariff liberalization and its associated efficiency gains in the beneficiary countries.

The rapid rise of FTAs as the preferred integration vehicle also stems from the real and perceived ease of forging them as opposed to customs unions, which require harmonization of external trade policies and overall more extensive negotiations.[28] Moreover, CUs are generally formed among geographically adjacent countries and as such may be inferior to FTAs as conduits of increasingly transcontinental supply chains.[29] Yet, given that partial scope agreements and non-reciprocal arrangements have also yielded to FTAs, the data are indicative of the world-wide drive to forge truly liberalizing and encompassing trade agreements.

The fourth trade agreement wave is taking place in an increasingly consolidated and globalized MFN system. The Uruguay Round of 1986–94 was the most ambitious round to date, aiming to go well beyond tariffs and non-tariff barriers to launch the liberalization of services, investment,

---

[28] See e.g. Crawford and Fiorentino (2005).

[29] There is an extensive line of studies on the determinants of the choice between an FTA and a customs union, and, more generally of the determinants of the institutional framework for trade agreements. For an overview, see e.g. Winters (1996).

intellectual property, as well as the previously relatively untouched (and protectionist) sectors, textiles and agriculture. The Round culminated in a comprehensive agreement among the 128 GATT members and the establishment of the WTO as a multilateral body to oversee the global trading system among 75 of them. The remaining 52 GATT members rejoined the WTO in the following two years. The on-going Doha Round was launched in 2001, and has seen attempts to broaden the issue coverage of the multilateral rounds to issues such as investment and trade facilitation (Box 2.2).

Box 2.2 PRIMER ON THE DOHA ROUND

Seven years after the conclusion of the Uruguay Round and the creation of the WTO, in November 2001 the WTO member governments agreed to launch a new trade round in Doha, Qatar, and to work on the implementation of the existing agreements. Purporting to focus particularly on furthering the prospects of developing countries in the global trading system, the new round was dubbed the Doha Development Agenda.

The Fifth Ministerial Conference in September 2003 in Cancún, Mexico, was a turning point. Strong disagreements broke out on agricultural issues, including cotton, and ended in deadlock on the "Singapore issues"—investment, competition policy, transparency in government procurement, and trade facilitation—that had been under negotiation since the WTO Singapore Ministerial in 1996.

The WTO's General Council meeting in August 2004 decided to drop all but one Singapore issue, trade facilitation, from the Doha negotiations agenda in order to propel the talks forward. However, the members subsequently missed deadlines for concluding the talks in the face of disagreements between the EU and United States on the one hand, and a number of developing countries spearheaded by Brazil, India, China, Argentina, and South Africa, on the other. The main points of contention are US agricultural subsidies and EU agricultural tariffs, and non-agricultural market access and services liberalization in the major emerging markets. The July 2006 talks in Geneva failed to reach an agreement about reducing farming subsidies and lowering import taxes; a year later, negotiations broke down in Potsdam following an impasse between the United States, the EU, India, and Brazil.

Econometric estimates of the benefits that Doha would deliver are unequivocally positive, although the magnitude remains contested and depends on the assumptions that are made. The estimates of the direct impact for world welfare range from $168 billion to $287 billion a year.[30] However, studies in general do not take into account the dynamic effects that trade liberalization could induce, which are difficult to quantify, but that could potentially be very large. There are also marked differences across countries in the gains that they would achieve as well as the positive effects of trade liberalization on poverty reduction. For instance, Mexico, a country with plenty of market access to its main trading partners and a relatively open domestic market except for MFN peak tariffs in such areas as agriculture and textiles, would attain more limited gains than would Brazil, Thailand, or Indonesia (Ivanic 2006).

---

[30] See Polaski (2006) for the former and Anderson *et al.* (2006) for the latter.

The multilateral trade rounds helped propel cuts in tariffs and expand trade around the world. Average tariffs have plunged from nearly 25 percent in the 1930s to well below 10 percent today; as shown in Figure 2.1, trade as a result has surged to represent some 70 percent of global GDP. Industrialized countries have liberalized much more forcefully than developing countries; tariffs in North America and Europe have declined from more than 30 percent in the 1930s to below 4 percent today.[31] Developing countries, besides acceding to the GATT system later on, continued to be somewhat, and in many cases very, protectionist through the early 1980s—Argentina's tariffs on manufactures were 141 percent in the early 1960s, Brazil's 99 percent, and Pakistan's 93 percent.[32]

The intellectual tide against infant industry protection had decisively turned and macroeconomic reforms in many troubled, debt-laden developing countries prescribed trade liberalization, among other remedies. China, India, Pakistan, and Latin American countries' tariffs, non-tariff barriers, and quantitative restrictions have come down in the past three decades. Another further putative contributor to trade policy changes was the end of exchange controls in many parts of the developing world. While barriers to trade would persist, by the turn of the millennium most of the world's population lived in open and liberalizing economies.[33]

The multilateral dynamics and liberal economic ideas have thus changed the environment for trade agreements and preferential agreements, in particular. The earliest PTAs of the 1960s in Latin America and in African and South Asian countries emerging from colonialism were grounded on import-substituting regionalism and their members' state-led industrialization policies, and were thus protectionist vis-à-vis the rest of the world. Except perhaps for CACM, intra-regional liberalization in developing country schemes was uneven and half-heartedly implemented. In contrast, more recent PTAs are not only more liberalizing internally; they are formed against the backdrop of much more extensive multilateral liberalization by the member states.

Indeed, membership of the GATT/WTO system has expanded following the Uruguay Round to encompass several major economies. Mexico joined prior to the round in 1986, a host of East European countries in the 1990s, China in 2001, and Saudi Arabia in 2005. At the time of writing,

---

[31] See Findlay and O'Rourke (2007) for construction of data.

[32] See ibid. for construction of data.

[33] See Anderson and Neary (2005) and Kee *et al.* (2006) for an analysis of tariff protection in 2000–4.

152 countries are WTO members and another 30, including Russia, are in the process of acceding. This, in turn, means that unlike in any trade agreement wave in the past, most countries today have become members of *both* the regional and multilateral trading systems. In fact, all but one WTO member, Mongolia, are also PTA (and CU and/or FTA) members. This in principle is promising: the bulk of countries around the world should have a stake in the success of both preferential and multilateral trade integration. Furthermore, WTO agreements and preferential schemes involving developed countries, in particular, are also increasingly thoroughly implemented and enforced.[34]

Geographic Fault Lines of Trade Integration

The above discussion shows that the waves of trade cooperation differ in the types of agreements that they contain, and the extent to which they are multilateralized, or embedded in the MFN principle. However, the waves also differ quite dramatically by their geographic scope.

Historically, there has been a marked contrast between the long-standing formal trade cooperation by states in Europe and the Western Hemisphere, on the one hand, and the more recent ascendance of global cooperation by Asian states and post-colonial Africa, on the other (Fig. 2.6). The patterns are similar, even if more recent, for PTAs; while the European integration spree made the continent the source of dozens of agreements starting in the early 1990s, PTAs have started to engulf countries in Asia, Africa, and the Middle East in the latter part of the 1990s.

Intra-regionalism has been the traditional driver of European and Western Hemisphere countries' trade agreements: more than 50 percent of European countries' agreements and nearly 30 percent of agreements formed by countries of the Americas are intra-regional (Fig. 2.7). In contrast, the figure is only 10 percent in Oceania and below 5 percent in the Middle East.

That states in regions with few agreements have tended to sign agreements primarily with extra-regional partners may simply indicate the real or perceived futility of investing resources in forging intra-regional agreements, should that come at the expense of extra-regional ties.[35] This is certainly the case in trade, where the dynamism and size of the intra-regional market shape the incentives to form agreements. However, it

---

[34] See De Lombaerde *et al.* (2008) on implementing PTAs.
[35] The patterns are similar even if the data are weighted by the overall number of states within the region.

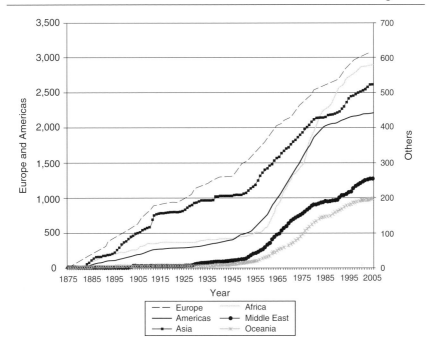

Figure 2.6 Cumulative trade agreements by world region, 1875–2005
Source: Authors' calculations.

may also be the case that states in these regions will start focusing on the intra-regional market for trade agreements only after connecting with key extra-regional partners, such as their former colonizers. And yet, intra-regionalism is not expanding in any region we have analyzed, and may even be receding. This further indicates that today's main trend is bilateral transcontinentalism, rather than consolidation of regional blocs—quite unlike during the era of intra-regionalism a generation ago in Europe and the Americas, in particular.[36]

If extra-regional agreements are increasingly important, who collaborates with whom in the extra-regional sphere? Figure 2.8 looks at each world region's extra-regional trade agreement portfolios in 1875–2005, revealing four trends.

[36] These findings coincide with two recent empirical contributions that focus on a more limited sample. Crawford and Fiorentino (2005) find that PTAs are increasingly formed between partners that are not geographically contiguous. Baldwin (2006) concludes that the boundaries of the "Big-3" blocs, were they to consolidate, would be "fuzzy" and "leaky" due to the proliferation of transcontinental bilaterals.

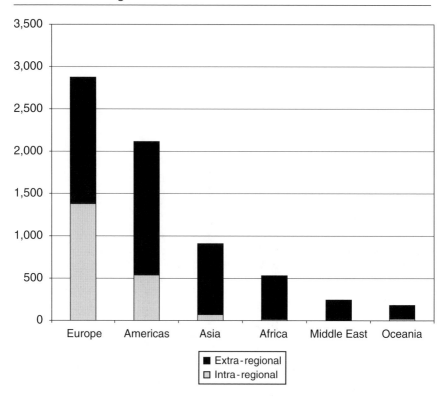

Figure 2.7 Extra- and intra-regional trade agreements in 1875–2005, by world region
Source: Authors' calculations.

The first is the predominance of Europe and the Americas as the main extra-regional partners for each world region, including for each other. In 1875–1913, the countries of the Americas made up more than 40 percent of all Europe's extra-regional agreements; by 1946–80, the figure exceeded 60 percent. Meanwhile, European countries made up more than 80 percent of all extra-regional trade agreements pursued by the countries of the Americas and Asia through World War II, and by African countries until World War I.

Second, countries of the Americas are particularly meaningful partners for all regions in the post-war era, largely because of the numerous agreements pursued by the United States around the world during the period. Third, there is a marked ascendance of the importance of Asia in the extra-regional trade ties of particularly the Americas, Middle East, and Oceania

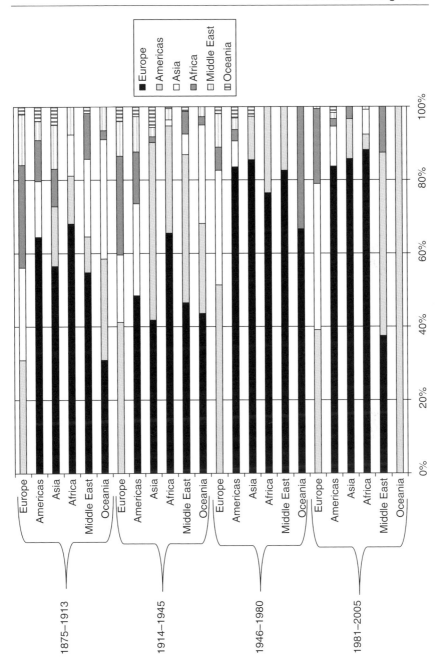

Figure 2.8 Extra-regional partners of world regions in 1875–2005, by period
Source: Authors' calculations.

over time, not unlikely due to the region's emergence as a major global economic power center and production hub, which accentuates the partners' interests in locking in market access gains and reducing costs in supply chains. And fourth, perhaps the main overall finding is the growing heterogeneity in the extra-regional partnerships for each region: rather than having one key extra-regional partner, each region seeks agreements with all of the other regions. Trade agreement "portfolios" have diversified and globalized—again likely not coincidentally with the globalization of production.

There are key countries—the United States and the large Western European countries—driving many of the regional trends (Appendix 2.2, Table A2.3). In fact, the traditional great powers form a distinct "global club" of trade cooperators: not only are they the most prolific trade cooperators *per se*, but most of their agreements are formed with each other. The results also indicate that the gravity model variables—high income levels, small bilateral distances, common borders, common languages, and other shared cultural affinities, all of which should increase bilateral trade—appear to play a role in the choice of trade cooperation partners, much as they do in arbitrating trade. Indeed, Baier and Bergstrand (2004) run a gravity model to show that this indeed is the case. Rich proximate countries trade as well as cooperate more with each other than do poor distant ones.

These main bilateral partnerships recur even when the data is analyzed in distinct, shorter periods of time. However, when a limited sample focused on the past decade only is examined, the "clubbishness" of the great powers yields to agreements between them and East European countries, as well as developing countries from Africa, Asia, and Latin America. In particular, trans-Atlantic and trans-Pacific agreements have been gaining ground, perhaps in search of intra-industry trade. It appears that traditional gravity parameters may to an extent be trumped by other variables, such as international and domestic institutional factors. Such variables as technology—the lowering of global communications costs—and a potential saturation of the regional trade agreement market in some regions could also have contributed to the search for more distant and perhaps unexpected partnerships.

Figure 2.9 summarizes the globalization of trade integration by providing a sequential network visualization of the spread of agreements and partnerships in five benchmark years in the past 130 years. The thickness of the lines denotes the number of pairwise agreements; the size of the bubbles indicates the number of agreements that a given country has. The system of trade agreements is increasingly complex and marked both by a diversification of hubs' partnerships and by the rise of linkages between the traditional spokes.

(a) 1900

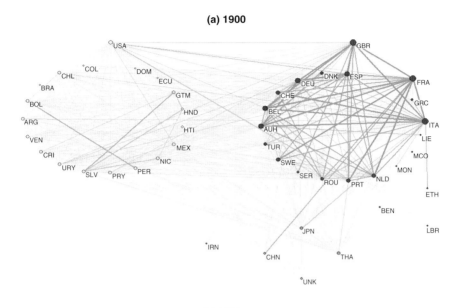

(b) 1930

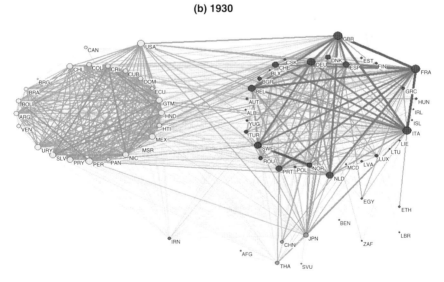

Figure 2.9 Trade agreements in 1900, 1930, 1960, 1990, and 2005
Source: Authors' calculations.

(*Continued*)

(c) 1960

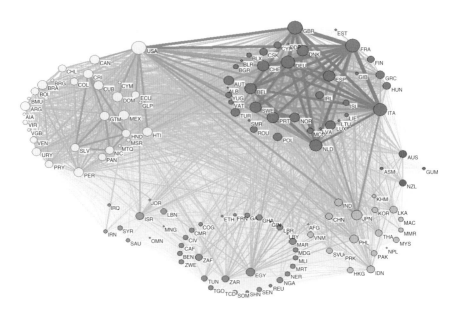

(d) 1990

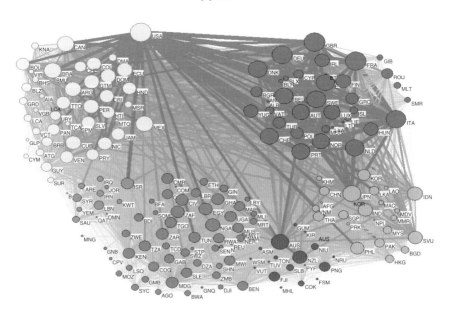

Figure 2.9 (*Continued*)

(e) 2005

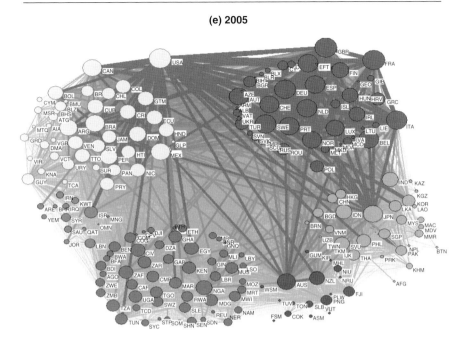

Figure 2.9 (*Continued*)

Trade and Agreements

World trade grew faster in the second half of the 20th century than at any time in history. Exports and imports grew by more than 10 percent in 1960–2006—some 15 percent in 1960–79, and 7 percent in 1980–2006—and notably above the 3.5 percent average annual growth before the World War I (Fig. 2.10). Economic policy and technological changes, such as decreases in air freight and sheer speed of transportation, contributed to the surge in trade, and the overall revival in globalization.

The growth of trade surpassed output growth in every world region. In practically all economies, the share of trade over GDP surged markedly in the second half of the 20th century—from some 20 percent to 100 percent in Japan, 40 to above 80 percent in Canada, 60 to 80 percent in Western Europe, 35 to about 60 percent in Latin America, 50 to 70 percent in sub-Saharan Africa, 10 to 20 percent in the United States (Findlay and O'Rourke 2007).

Also the composition of trade evolved in two fundamental ways. The first concerned the rise of intra-industry trade and, more generally, trade

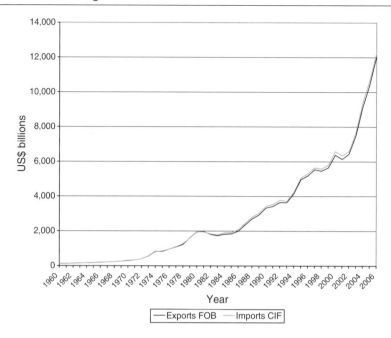

Figure 2.10 Growth of world trade, 1960–2006
Source: IADB calculations based on IMF DOTS.

in manufactures, which unraveled the pre-war specialization global commerce. This was not merely occurring in trade among developed countries—such as Japan sending cars to the United States and vice versa—but, rather, developing countries became a part of the pattern: industrialization in the developing world increased the share of manufactures in total trade from developing to developed countries more than six-fold, from some 10 percent in the 1950s to nearly 70 percent by the end of the century (Findlay and O'Rourke 2007). Another major change in global trade was the growth of trade in services. Services in US trade more than tripled from the pre-war era to 2000 (from 8 percent in 1913 to 28 percent in 2000).

What role may trade agreements—and PTAs, in particular—have played in the expansion of world trade? And does the spread of trade agreements mean that they are more relevant economically, and so for a greater number of countries?

These questions are hard to ascertain with precision, as capturing the amount of trade that has historically entered under preferential treatment (as opposed to MFN or other regimes) would require a country-by-country analysis, a virtual impossibility due to data constraints. However, a cursory glance at the data allows us to establish two facts: the bulk of world trade today is conducted among countries with at least one common bi- or plurilateral trade agreement, and the share of world trade among partners in common FTAs and CUs, the most liberalizing of agreements, has increased quite dramatically to about one-half of global trade from about a tenth in the 1960s.

These patterns hold in each world region (Fig. 2.11). The consolidation and expansion of the European integration process implies that more than 60 percent of regional countries' trade is now among countries belonging to a common FTA or CU. The conclusion of NAFTA in the Americas caused regional trade flowing between FTA partners to triple virtually overnight. Africa's intra-regionalism and some extra-regional agreements, such as those between the EU and the southern Mediterranean countries and South Africa, respectively, have recently increased the trade between FTA partners also in that continent. Asia at the time still had a limited share of trade within FTAs; the recent conclusion of manifold agreements among

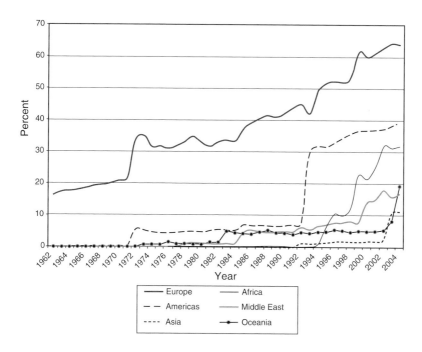

Figure 2.11 Trade among FTA and CU members as a percentage of total intra-regional trade in 1962–2005, by region

Source: Authors' calculations.

such trading powers as Japan and Thailand, and China and ASEAN, is bound to alter the picture significantly.

These patterns have direct implications for member states. For one thing, trade *per se* is of growing importance in most national economies. While in the 1980s trade represented some third of the surveyed economies' GDPs, by 2005 the figure for most countries was above 60 percent. With the accession of new members to the web of trade cooperation and the formation of multiple overlapping agreements, the importance of trade agreements has grown in many countries' trade. For instance, whereas in 1985, only one country, Ireland, had more than 80 percent of its trade with its FTA and CU partners (and mainly European Community), by 1995 this set had expanded to four countries—Mexico, Andorra, Austria, and Sweden—and by 2005 incorporated nine countries.[37] Figure 2.12 displays the 15 countries with the greatest number of signed FTAs and CUs as of 2005, and the share of their trade with PTA partner countries as a proportion of their total trade. It is quite safe to conclude that trade among partners to a common reciprocal preferential agreement makes up the lion's share of the trade flows of numerous countries around the world.

III. Why Trade Agreements?

Today's trade agreement network is thick and global. We have already discussed some reasons behind the differences between the types of agreements, such as agricultural agreements in the 1950s and 1960s that can be traced back to US domestic and foreign policy objectives, and the rise of PTAs in the 1990s, which in part reflects attempts to gain a preferential edge in an increasingly liberalized world. We have also hypothesized as to the reasons why trade agreements are increasingly transcending regional boundaries and being forged among countries across the oceans. Some reasons may include saturation of the intra-regional market for trade agreements, particularly in Europe and the Americas, and the multi-nationalization of production linkages and globalization of supply chains that demand transcontinental trade liberalization.

But what accounts for the historical ebbs and flows of trade agreements? Why did the various waves begin, and why did they recede?

---

[37] Note that the set of countries changes due to changes in the volume of their trade flows with trade agreement partners.

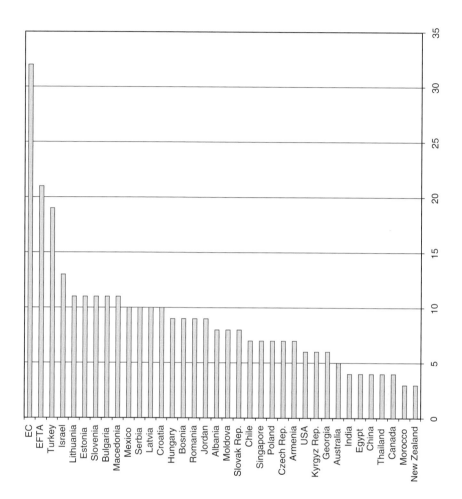

Figure 2.12 FTAs, CUs, and CU accessions in force through 2005, by country

Note: The figure lists the world's most prolific integrators—countries with at least three FTAs or CUs through 2005. EU and EFTA are here treated as countries. The many agreements signed by the Eastern European countries reflect their agreements with the EU as well as with each other; these agreements were submerged in the EU in 2004 and 2007. The Eastern European countries' accession to the EU is also counted as an agreement. In the meantime, the EU agreements here include all the agreements that became submerged in the EU, as well as the EU's bilateral agreements with the southern Mediterranean countries, Chile, Mexico, and South Africa, but excludes accessions to the EU. The post-2005 figure includes agreements that are notified to the WTO.

These questions have troubled political economists for decades. The short and common answer is that there is unlikely to be a "one size fits all" explanation; rather, the various interpretations may gain currency in some epochs and also vary from country to country. That the agreement waves contain qualitatively highly different agreements likely also entails that they are driven by different factors. Moreover, the theoretical strands are not necessarily mutually exclusive: while global dynamics may push countries in one direction, ultimately trade policy change tends to be rooted in the domestic micro-foundations of interest group pressures filtered through national political institutions.

For instance, the rise and fall of the European treaty network has been widely attributed to ideas and interest groups alike—the rise in intellectual backing for free trade and British manufacturers' interest in open markets with continental Europe and subsequently similar pressures for liberalization among traders around Europe, and the precipitous decline in agricultural prices, which hurried farmers to call for protectionism. However, the wave might never have taken place, or been as forceful, without the systemic push toward agreement formation engendered by MFN treatment.

The second, inter-war wave can be explained by domestic protectionist pressures coming from those experiencing a hard landing amid the depression. Indeed, the ups and downs of trade cooperation have to a large extent reflected prevailing economic conditions, and also represented a form of policy response to them. But another reason was surely also strategic: the rise of the beggar-thy-neighbor policies and web of defensive agreements provided incentives for countries to form their own defensive blocs as insurance policy (Eichengreen and Frankel 1995). The strategic calculus was transformed into a liberal one following the push of export lobbies and enlightened policymakers, led by Cordell Hull, in Washington.

Political Economy of the Rise of PTAs

The puzzle of the origins of PTAs has given rise to a particularly extensive literature. Mostly focused on CUs and FTAs, these explanations can be divided into domestic-level theories centered on pressures exerted by interest groups, such as exporters and investors, and "system-level" theories that focus on international dynamics as pushing countries to form trade agreements.[38]

---

[38] The literature is huge and while we cannot cover it all, we strive to highlight some representative studies. For more exhaustive literature reviews, see e.g. Winters (1996), Baldwin (2008), and Bhagwati (2008).

The earlier works were rather stylized models with strong assumptions about the incentives of decision makers. In a classic work, Grossman and Helpman (1994) construct a model where policymakers' utility function is composed of campaign donations and social welfare. Interest groups put forth donation contracts, or "contribution schedules", that specify how large a campaign contribution will be made for a given policy stance, such as the formation of an FTA.[39] Interest groups that are adversely affected by their country's remaining outside an FTA will promise contributions to policymakers in exchange for gaining membership in an FTA. An FTA emerges when its benefits to exporters exceed the aggregate losses that the FTA would impose on the welfare of the average voter and on the profits of import-competing industries.

Similar pressures can emanate from investors. One prominent argument is that holders of cross-border "specific assets"—investments that involve large sunk costs, such as cross-border oil pipelines or manufacturing plants in another country—would be keen to lobby for PTAs as legal guarantees of the integrity of their assets (Yarborough and Yarborough 1992). Similarly, the specter of a PTA can incentivize investors to make sunk investments in their own country's export sector, thus effectively compelling their government to go for the agreement (McLaren 1997).

Still others have focused on the incentives facing firms of different sizes for a PTA. In a novel contribution applying the new trade theory, Milner (1997a) argues that particularly large firms should prefer PTAs as the first-best trade policy option as a tool for realizing PTA-wide scale economies and locking in the regional market.[40]

Trade agreements inherently require two to tango, and thus are subject not only to domestic politics, but to international politics as well. Borrowing from Robert Putnam's (1988) two-level games, which involve strategic interactions both between two governments and between each of the two governments and its respective domestic constituency, Grossman and Helpman (1995) argue that two factors create an auspicious scenario for an FTA to be launched: a relative balance in the potential trade between

---

[39] As such, the model purports to capture the real-world "compacts" forged between interest groups and policymakers; the latter will be rewarded if they choose policies that benefit a donating interest group.

[40] For new trade theory, see e.g. Helpman and Krugman (1985). Others have argued that the rationale for developing countries to pursue a CU is independent of scale economies. See e.g. Krishna and Bhagwati (1997). In their model, a developing country CU yields only constant costs. However, any subset of countries can always form a welfare-enhancing CU while also maintaining the same level of industrialization as they achieved through protectionism.

the two countries (which entails similar incentives for the PTA), and the PTA's offering enhanced protection for most sectors vis-à-vis the rest of the world (so as to be supported by import-competing firms). Maggi and Rodriguez-Clare (2007) work along similar lines, developing a model where governments may be motivated to sign a trade agreement both by the standard terms-of-trade externalities and by the desire to commit vis-à-vis domestic industrial lobbies; the greater the domestic political incentives for a PTA, the deeper the agreement that results. Haggard (1997) also links domestic distributive politics to distributive bargaining at the international level. However, he claims that the processes and the bargaining agenda leading to PTA formation are to a great extent shaped by the domestic politics of the major powers, such as the United States, in the prospective PTA area. The preferences and strategies of powerful actors are, in turn, shaped by the domestic distributional conflicts stemming from the expected effects of trade policy.

The more purely systemic theories of PTA formation might be divided into three main categories. The first two link the rise of PTAs to the travails of the global trade regime. One argument advanced by those skeptical of trade agreements is that countries form them during episodes of lack of momentum in the on-going multilateral talks as a tool to hedge against the lack of liberalization, and/or to pressure other countries to move forward at the multilateral level. For instance, countries may "go regional" when sensing a decline in a global hegemon, e.g. the United Kingdom in the 19th century and the United States in the 20th and 21st centuries. The hegemon provides most of the global public good of a multilateral trading system, and its decline will result in a "specter of systemic closure" that countries will strive to avert by way of preferential agreements.[41]

Another argument relates to collective action problems in the multilateral trading system: the growth of WTO membership and of the issues that trade negotiators deal with at multilateral level leads to a proliferation of policy preferences in various policy areas, and thus augurs poorly for the prospects of decision-making in the multilateral system—which, after all, is based on unanimity, whereby everyone has to agree before anything is agreed, and single undertakings, whereby nothing is agreed

---

[41] See e.g. Kindleberger (1989) and Mansfield (1998). Lake (1988) breaks new ground by arguing that even if a hegemon is absent, a handful of great powers can collectively substitute for a hegemon and keep the system running.

before all is agreed.[42] The sluggishness of the multilateral rounds arguably compels countries to advance liberalization by going regional with like-minded partners: given their narrower membership, bilateral and small plurilateral trade agreements can hypothetically often be concluded faster than multilateral rounds, and are also more conducive to the consensuses necessary to attain meaningful broad-based and deep liberalization. This could particularly be the case in the absence of a hegemon or a "K-group" that can internalize some of the costs of running the multilateral system.

The second systemic approach sees PTAs as the result of the success, not the failure, of multilateral trade liberalization. One argument is that countries form trade agreements during multilateral talks in order to hedge against preference erosion resulting from impending multilateral liberalization. Freund (2000) argues that multilateral tariff reduction enhances the incentives to form a PTA and increases the likelihood that it is self-enforcing, so that each round of multilateral tariff reduction should lead to a new wave of PTAs.[43] A complementary view advanced by Ethier (1998) holds that multilateral liberalization makes trade flow among "natural" trade partners—generally, geographically proximate states with distinct factor endowments—which, in turn, encourages export lobbies to call for the formation of trade agreements with those partners. A more refined argument is that this outcome depends on the outcomes of multilateral bargaining. According to Bagwell and Staiger (1997), if multilateral trade rules allow for full internalization of benefits, countries can reach their "efficiency frontiers", and a PTA has nothing to add. But if MFN tariffs fail to yield efficiency gains, PTAs may have a role to play and PTAs can be optimal trade policy strategy.

The influence of the multilateral trading system on trade agreements is far from clear-cut.[44] Also the extent of the influence is questionable. Indeed,

---

[42] See e.g. Summers (1991), Kahler (1995), and Laird (1999).

[43] This argument is an extension of the simpler idea of "natural trading partners", whereby the larger pre-trade agreement trade volumes and lower transportation costs between PTA members, the likelier a PTA will be welfare-improving—so that it is natural to form a reciprocal trade agreement between geographically close neighbors for which transportation costs are low. See Wonnacott and Lutz (1989), Summers (1991), Krugman (1993), and Frankel *et al.* (1995). Bhagwati and Panagariya (1996) and Krueger (1999) argue that neighbors are not necessarily natural trading partners. Freund (2000) shows that in a model with economies of scale in transport, PTA members reach a higher welfare level under their arrangement than if they were to pursue multilateralism. Frankel *et al.* (1995, 1997) and Frankel (1996) also find that when inter-continental transportation and business costs increase relative to intra-continental ones, regional integration is better for welfare.

[44] Things get even more complicated in the further, complementary and rich line of scholarship that examines the effects of PTAs on the multilateral trading system; we will discuss this in Chapter 5.

the third main systemic approach views the fortunes of the multilateral system as less relevant for the rise of PTAs than the dynamic generated by the proliferation of PTAs. Under Baldwin's (1993, 2006) domino theory, the proliferation of trade agreements gives outsiders incentives to form new PTAs, or to join existing ones, lest they see their market access edge erode in international markets and/or in order to guarantee the integrity of unrecoverable, sunk investments.[45] Its cousin, the competitive liberalization theory, holds that countries compete in forming PTAs as tools to compete for investment.[46]

To be sure, PTAs can confer various non-traditional gains above and beyond trade that give an impetus to their formation. One of the better known ones might include the so-called lock-in theory, whereby reformist interests particularly in emerging markets seek PTAs with major developed countries as lock-in devices that signal to international investors the country's resolve not to renege on its economic reforms.[47] The argument has attracted support, particularly given the comprehensiveness of today's integration agreements, which contain numerous built-in policies for the members to bring their respective domestic legal and regulatory frameworks onto a par with the requirements of the integration agreements. It has been widely cited as applicable to Mexico in the context of NAFTA: joining a large developed economy in a legally binding, complex agreement with commitment from competition policy law to investment rules, reduced Mexican policymakers' room for maneuver and ability to backtrack from legislative and regulatory changes related to the agreement.

Besides domestic policy credibility, PTAs can deliver international bargaining power, insurance against external shocks or trade wars, and coordination among the members.[48] Indeed, a substantial line of literature sees trade agreements as a function of broader foreign policy and national security considerations (Mansfield 1998; World Bank 2000; Schiff and

---

[45] Yi (1996) was one of the first to formalize the domino logic using cooperative game theory with and without considering supply constraints. Haveman (1992), Syropoulos (1999), and Melatos and Woodland (2007) develop extensions including asymmetric nations. See Baldwin (2008).

[46] See Bergsten (1996) for the competitive liberalization hypothesis. Evenett (2007) finds limited empirical support for this. Freund (2000) argues that first-mover advantages may act against expansion of PTAs: if sunk costs such as distribution network costs are incurred on entering into a PTA, incumbent members pay lower marginal costs than new entrants because the former pay only the production cost.

[47] Ferrantino (2006) finds that trade agreements do not yield major improvements to developing countries' institutions—yet are better at the task than multilateral agreements are.

[48] See Whalley (1996) and Fernandez (1997).

Winters 2003). For instance, the Central and Eastern European countries' application for EU membership was undoubtedly motivated by a desire to strike a strong relationship with the West amid concerns about the future of Russia. The Gulf Cooperation Council was created in part to stave off the potential threat of regional powers such as Iran and Iraq, while ASEAN was partly motivated by a perceived need to stem the spread of communism in Southeast Asia (World Bank 2000). Whalley (1996) argues that the foundation of the European Economic Community in 1957 stemmed in part from a desire to foster the Europeans' international bargaining power relative to the United States.

The literature on PTA formation is huge and there is a kernel of truth in each of the main approaches. Ultimately, it is domestic politics and interests that in any country have an impact on how an agreement is negotiated and that lie behind the initial push for an agreement. However, international dynamics cannot be overlooked, either. The decline of the British hegemon and the rise of protectionism around the world is widely linked to the 1930s flurry of defensive trade agreements. In the early 1990s, the rise of such major schemes as APEC, ASEAN, EU bilaterals, as well as NAFTA—a watershed for the United States and Canada, countries traditionally disposed to multilateralism over regionalism—may in part have been caused by concerns about the lack of momentum in the multilateral sphere, and used as tools to threaten countries with discrimination unless they relented and liberalized at the multilateral level. Conversely, the multilateral Kennedy and Tokyo Rounds can be seen in part as arising from a US-sponsored consensus to pre-empt discrimination resulting from the consolidation of the European integration process (Bergsten 1998).

The domino theory is compelling, particularly in today's environment. The on-going expansion of the web of preferential treatment does provide powerful incentives for countries to enter the PTA game, lest they lose their market access edge. In short, there may be herd behavior at play. The PTA system may have grown too large for any country to ignore, and the only way not to lose out is to get enmeshed in the system.

And yet, arguments that view trade agreements as the result of successful liberalization at the multilateral level are also compelling in light of the proliferation of trade agreements in the wake of the Uruguay Round. It is likely hard to deny that the growing openness and globalization, along with the increasingly intricate cross-border private sector ties, would have something to do with countries' decision to provide clearer rules for trading and investing and deepening liberalization with some of their main trading partners. Sub-regionalism, the entry point for many countries into trade agreements, may subsequently have propelled countries to deepen their relationships with key bilateral partners because of the learning-by-doing gained from negotiating regional agreements. In other words, the post-Uruguay Round wave of sub-regional agreements may have been egged on by multilateralism, while the subsequent wave of intra- and inter-regional bilateral trade agreements may have been pushed along by the rise of sub-regionalism. This was followed by the onslaught of herd behavior. It is very plausible that countries around the world saw these different ways of liberalizing and integrating as complementary rather than as substitutes (Box 2.3).

Box 2.3 WHY A MULTIPOLAR TRADE LIBERALIZATION STRATEGY?

For many emerging markets, the flurry of trade agreements was part of the major macroeconomic reforms enacted after the economic turmoil of the 1980s. Trade liberalization was one of the main components of the reform packages, and most countries implemented it unilaterally in addition to participating in multilateral trade rounds and pursuing regional agreements. Overall, these processes can be seen as complementary and aimed at fostering the countries' global competitiveness through improved market access, allocation of resources, attractiveness for foreign investment, and opportunities for regional scale economies. This strategy provides further, increasingly important advantages:

- *First-mover advantages* in the world of expanding trade agreements. The multi-tiered strategy provides for agility in seeking to seize the various opportunities for deep economic integration emerging around the world. Any one country's trade policy options depend to an extent on strategic interactions among the other countries. Early integration can enable a country to gain an edge in new markets and to attract foreign investment. Conversely, failure the grasp the arising opportunities would result in remaining outside of the web of agreements and the economic "insider benefits" they can confer.

- *Fallback options* that the regional economies can activate in virtually any scenario of global trade policy—that is, should any one policy front yield sub-optimal outcomes. Multilateral talks may become protracted or result in "minimalist" outcomes, rather than delivering a substantial, deep agreement. Trade agreements can be insurance policy against the failure of obtaining market access through other means. And countries that have secured access to their major markets by way of trade agreements have less to lose in global talks, which can strengthen their bargaining positions.

- *Flexibility* for adjusting to the changing competitive advantages and demands of global markets. Global production and trade patterns are evolving at an unprecedented speed, and the variety of products traded in global commerce has grown notably in the span of a couple of decades. Changes in technology and reduction of transportation costs—not to mention the rise of electronic commerce and the growing importance of trade in services—will accentuate the speed of change in the world economy. The multi-tiered strategy allows for agility in exploiting today's niches that might have not existed yesterday.

- *Synergies* between the tiers. Regional and global trade rules are essentially about the same disciplines. Thus, understanding, negotiating, and implementing agreements on either front will yield positive externalities to these processes on the other front. For instance, negotiating liberalization in services trade at the WTO would undoubtedly improve the government's capacity to negotiate the services chapter in a trade agreement. Or, implementing trade agreement-mandated trade facilitation measures—such as modernizing customs procedures or providing a single window for exporters to handle paperwork—would deliver immediate benefits to the country's trade with *all* of its trading partners, not only the trade agreement partner.

- *Positive externalities.* Engagement at multiple trade policy levels can help produce further positive externalities in the form of regional and global public goods. One simple public good potentially resulting from international negotiations is intangible: mutual trust and willingness to engage in further cooperation. However, there can be more specific externalities. The dynamic effects of trade agreements can yield such regional public goods as scale economies and increases in the productivity of firms. Moreover, trade agreement partners can be expected to have incentives to provide further regional public goods to facilitate their trading relationship, such as solid regional infrastructure networks—something that they might not realize in the absence of trade agreements. At the global level, participation in multilateral trade negotiations opens up a host of opportunities to tap into the global public goods, such as access to the WTO dispute settlement mechanism.

A Narrow Passage: Politics of Trade Agreements

The decision to join a trade agreement is ultimately a political one, and trade politics are playing out each day around the world. By entailing trade liberalization, trade agreements create a set of winners and losers, driving deep wedges in any country's political arena. While the investors and exporters can be a formidable lobby in favor of trade liberalization, import-competing industries and industries potentially subject to outsourcing often muster an even fiercer counter-lobby.

Trade policy battles are often manifested in black and white in trade agreement texts in the form of long tariff phase-out schedules, stringent rules-of-origin requirements, complex instruments such as tariff rate quotas, non-tariff measures, and tough labor rights regulations (aimed in part at reducing the competitive edge that countries with low labor costs have compared with those with high costs), and even in the form of exclusions of products from trade agreement liberalization. To be sure, in contrast with agreements of the 1980s, today's trade agreements generally exclude fewer, if any, products, and are overall more liberalizing.

Yet, some of these instruments, so complex and non-transparent that they have been dubbed "hidden protectionism", may be the price that free-trade advocates will have to pay in order to secure the ratification of their agreements.

The politics surrounding US FTAs epitomize the contentiousness of trade liberalization. The oft-cited case is NAFTA: it was only after the side agreements on labor and environment were presented by the Clinton Administration that the US Congress relented and approved the agreement.

In CAFTA, one of the factors fueling ratification were textile rules of origin, which struck a compromise between protectionists and free traders: they were stringent enough to help protect US textile producers from Central American competition, yet flexible enough for US apparel industry and retailers to get low-cost supplies free of tariffs from the region. The passage of the US–Korea FTA is being jeopardized on both sides of the Pacific by Korea's reticence to open its market to US beef for alleged safety reasons. Perhaps the main insight arising from observing a series of trade battles around the world is that the passage of one agreement does not mean that the next one will be politically easier: indeed, the fact that import-competing lobbies can become increasingly squeezed by each consecutive agreement (and other, uni- and multilateral trade liberalization) may according to many trade theorists only galvanize them to work harder to kill the next agreement.[49]

The politics of trade are contentious not only because of the winners and losers created by trade opening, but because of numerous other alleged effects of trade, such as economic inequality, outsourcing, job churn, and migration. While trade, much less trade policy, is seldom the key reason for these problems,[50] it is easy to blame; trade policy is thus increasingly intertwined with vexing public policy issues. Even the most staunch and experienced pro-free traders are today turning into advocates of efforts to address the putative problems of trade—to balance "free trade" with "fair trade"—as a way to avert a backlash against trade.[51]

And yet, the fact that trade agreements are negotiated and in general passed—and the very fact that protectionism has yielded rather than increased around the world—may evince the jelling of increasingly

---

[49] For endogenous tariff formation, see e.g. Findlay and Welisz (1982), Mayer (1984), Magee (1989), Grossman and Helpman (1994), and Olarreaga and Soloaga (1998).

[50] See e.g. Lawrence (2008).

[51] See e.g. Scheve and Slaughter (2007), Aldonas et al. (2007a), Drezner (2006), and Lawrence (2008).

coherent investor and exporter lobbies in favor of liberalization. In the classic argument, consumers, the most numerous of potential lobbies and those with plenty to gain from trade liberalization in the form of lower prices and greater variety of goods, are too numerous and dispersed to constitute a weighty lobby, but, rather, stumble into collective action problems. If it is the case that concentrated interests prevail over dispersed ones, the main enabler of the proliferation of trade agreements may be a growing concentration of interests in favor of liberalization around the world, perhaps particularly among industries keen on seeking scale economies useful in the rough and tumble of global competition.[52] These interests have an increasingly important tool in their arsenal—namely the argument that the now-global race to integrate only compounds the urgency to form trade agreements in order to retain a beachhead in foreign markets. Credit for the survival of the free-trade mantra is certainly also due to the vocal opponents of protectionism in ivory towers, think-tanks, and other pro-trade hubs of economic analysis in around the world.

IV. Conclusion: What Future for Trade Agreements?

Trade integration has metamorphosed over the past 200 years. The 19th-century wave of trade agreements was dominated by the European treaty system based on the MFN treatment and general, liberalizing trade and navigation agreements. The second wave rose against the backdrop of the unraveled MFN system and started off with trade-diverting agreements in the depression-torn global economy, yet regained its liberal momentum with a push from the United States. The third wave took place in the context of the rise of a formal and genuinely global MFN system, incorporated hosts of developing countries, and was marked by the formation of a wide range of different types of trade agreements, such as sectoral and trade facilitation agreements.

The on-going wave is different again. Its trademarks are deeply liberalizing and comprehensive agreements, and the globalization of trade integration—the abandonment of intra-regional integration schemes among geographically proximate countries for bilateral transcontinental agreements. And it is buttressed by an unprecedentedly

---

[52] See Milner (1988) for theoretical grounds for export lobbies' growing influence on trade policy. For a recent treatment of the effects of scale on exports, see Van Biesebroeck (2005).

deep, comprehensive and globalized multilateral trade liberalization, a strong revival of globalization, and the heightened salience of trade even in the largest economies around the world.

What can these patterns from the past tell us about the future of international trade and integration? Perhaps three main implications can be highlighted.

First, some of the most fertile periods of proliferation of trade agreements have taken place amid multilateral trade negotiations and conclusion of multilateral agreements. It is thus not necessarily the case that trade agreements will proliferate only during, or because of, lack of progress at the multilateral level. Should the historical record be a guide, it could be argued that trade agreements would proliferate even more should a meaningful multilateral opening materialize: a breakthrough in Doha may not stem the trade agreement tide. After all, there are incentives for preferential agreements as long as they provide a preferential edge. Moreover, incentives for trade agreements can transcend preferences: strategic and foreign policy objectives and the fact that trade agreements go well beyond trade can provide a powerful stimulus for trade cooperation even in a system of free global trade.

Second, the latest wave of trade integration should assuage concerns about the prospect of the trade agreement constellations crystallizing into distinct continental megablocs, one in Asia, one in the Americas, and one in Europe, that would risk "siloing" the global trading system into three cones, and which, according to some analysts, would be the worst possible outcome to the global trading system.[53] Indeed, it seems that the formation of exclusive intra-regional blocs was a more pressing prospect a century ago than it is today. To be sure, the EU has certainly consolidated a continental bloc since creating the EEA in 1994 with the EFTA countries, and harmonizing rules of origin in its bilateral agreements with the East European countries in the late 1990s. However, efforts to build the Free Trade Area of the Americas stalled in 2003, while the APEC forum has

---

[53] Various theoretical studies have found the prospect of continental "megablocs" highly problematic. Perhaps the most oft-cited study is Krugman (1993), which finds that welfare actually *falls* as the number of blocs falls. Krugman divides the world into distinct geographical units, each of which is specialized in the production of a different good that is demanded symmetrically by all units. Each bloc has internal free trade but poses an optimal tariff on non-bloc imports. In terms of welfare, the best outcome of bloc formation is many such blocs; three blocs is the worst outcome. Stein (1994) finds that a stable equilibrium is two blocs—26 out of 30 countries in one large bloc and four in the other. However, Deardorff and Stern (1994) show that a given bloc will continue to grow until it encompasses the whole world, and that world welfare increases monotonically with the size of the blocs.

fallen short of a genuine, region-wide FTA. The idea of the Free Trade Area of the Asia-Pacific (FTAAP), which might include both Asian and Western Hemisphere countries, has, however, recently gained some traction.[54]

While there are credible efforts to knit PTAs together in the Americas and Asia, an issue we will discuss in Chapter 5, countries that formed such broader integration areas would necessarily be much more connected to the rest of the world than they would have been just a decade ago, both by virtue of belonging to multiple trade agreements and due to being members of the WTO. Rather than converging into blocs, the system of trade agreements is de-converging, decentralizing, and flattening. Centrifugalism is for now defeating centripetalism.

Moreover, the expansion of somewhat unlikely marriages between even small countries across the oceans also to an extent refutes the claims that the proliferation of trade agreements will give rise to global trade hubs connected to multiple spokes, a scenario that could prevent the full utilization of economies of scale that would result from the spokes being connected to each other. The bi-polar Euro- and Americas-centric world of trade agreements of the early 20th century has yielded to an unruly megalopolis whereby prior spokes are becoming linked to each other and in some cases becoming new hubs. Singapore, Mexico, Chile, China, and Thailand may be such examples. With everyone playing the game, the system of global trade integration has globalized.

To be sure, hub formation is a moving target and marked by some back-and-fro movement, with old hubs consolidating even as new ones arise. The traditional trade hub stalwarts still appear to hold sway when the agreements are weighted by trade: given that many new trade agreements are between smaller developing countries, their economic significance has yet to match the gravitas of such agreements as NAFTA or the US–Korea FTA, for instance. Overall, however, corridors devoid of agreements between spokes are increasingly bridged by new agreements.

The third and particularly important implication of past patterns is that the unique properties of the latest, on-going wave arguably entail higher risks and rewards than those of any other wave in the past. The rewards are five-fold:

- *Openness.* By virtue of belonging to multiple, liberalizing PTAs and having freed trade both unilaterally and at the multilateral level, countries around the world are more open than arguably at any time in history.

---

[54] See e.g. Bergsten (2007).

Openness provides countries with market access around the world, furthers national competitiveness, boosts productivity by selecting out inefficient industries, and expands the options and opportunities for the development of trade and investment ties around the world.

- *Comprehensiveness.* Today's trade agreements are highly comprehensive, which provides for important synergies across such disciplines as trade, investment, and services, and also furthers the transparency and sophistication of the rules guiding and governing international trade and investment. Moreover, by virtue of their sophistication and precision, PTAs in particular can also serve as laboratories for new global trade rules.

- *Globalization.* That international trade integration is increasingly globalized, with even small and distant countries forming agreements with each other, can help avert systemic siloing and provides opportunities to realize scale economies and carve out global production networks.

- *Multi-tiered integration.* The latest trade agreement wave has expanded against a backdrop of deepening multilateral integration, and many observers see important complementarities between the two levels. The trade agreement network can serve as a stepping stone to multilateral trade liberalization, training countries to negotiate and adjust to free trade at the global level and galvanizing export lobbies the world over. Similarly, the multilateral trading system and now-global MFN framework can bring out the best in trade agreements, as they are likelier to create trade in the context of open regionalism, with simultaneous liberalization at the regional and multilateral levels.

- *Insurance policies.* The global trading system today has multiple insurances against the type of protection that has engulfed the world in the past. One form of insurance is the GATT system: while it bears a resemblance to the European treaty network of the 19th century, it arguably provides better guarantees for sustained momentum for global free trade. For one thing, the multilateral agreements reached during the various trade rounds bind countries' external tariffs, whereas the treaty system allows all countries to set their own external tariffs. Second, GATT has no expiration, whereas the treaties of the 19th century generally expired after a decade and were thus subject to periodic renewals. Third, GATT Article XXIV regulates preferential agreements, while the treaty network had no such overarching governance or monitoring mechanism. And fourth, the GATT system is inherently and increasingly global. There are further insurances against protectionism, including the WTO's renowned dispute settlement mechanism, increasingly organized and well-entrenched export and producer lobbies around the world, strong intellectual backing for free trade, and the fact that most states have much more at stake in the fortunes of the global trading system and of their trading partners than at any time in the past.

However, the current wave of trade agreements also carriers some significant risks, particularly in light of the growing exposure of national economies to international trade and investment:

- *Potential friction with the multilateral trading system.* Multilateral trade liberalization is seen by virtually all economists as the first-best and most welfare-enhancing trade policy option. While PTAs are often being viewed as a second-best alternative to global liberalization and also something that can provide opportunities for advances at the global level, some more pessimistic observers view them as an instrument that may be incompatible with, and act counter to, the multilateral trading system. A chorus of economists argues that frictions between the rules of, and countries' loyalties to, "regional" and global systems may cause trade agreements to be a stumbling block for global free trade, entrenching protectionist lobbies, diverting attention and energy from multilateral trade talks, and lowering incentives for multilateral agreements.

- *Balkanization of the global trading system.* While the prospect of exclusive regional megablocs is eclipsed by the rise of transcontinentalism, the proliferation of trade agreements risks balkanizing the global trading system. A splintering of the global trading system into multiple overlapping agreements could increase the transactions costs of governments and companies dealing on multiple trading fronts simultaneously. Moreover, the system may lead to a self-perpetuating dynamic: even the most prolific integrator countries will end up facing discrimination and preference erosion with a growing number of trade partners, which may provide them with incentives to form new agreements. In the extreme, a network of overlapping agreements, particularly if not embedded in a liberalizing global trading system, may yield some of the same negative outcomes as the beggar-thy-neighbor policies of the 1930s.

- *Fragility of openness.* Trade cooperation at any level is fragile: as seen in prior eras of integration, economic hard landings and popular disenchantment with trade, even if unmerited, can translate into a slow-down in liberalization or outright protectionism around the world, particularly if and when gripping the leading trade powers. The fierce trade policy battles waged around the world evince the brittleness of the pro-trade majorities and awaken fears of a backlash against globalization. While the global trading system has multiple ways of insuring against a systemic collapse into protectionism, it is still beholden to the decisions of nation states and their domestic politics. A retreat from an open trading environment would be a blow to the global economy, the prosperity of nations, and also to the prospects for other forms of cooperation among countries that trade can help support. The liberalization and globalization of trade integration cannot thus be taken for granted, while turning our backs on them could have hugely devastating consequences.

The important rewards of the current wave accentuate the salience of managing these risks. Indeed, the past trade agreement waves dissipated in good part because policies that would have managed the risks were either not present (such as multilateral rules governing preferential agreements) or not implemented (such as the 1933 failure of the World Economic Conference to halt the beggar-thy-neighbor dynamic). The main difference between the past and today is that the stakes in today's environment are higher: due to their openness and the importance of trade in their economies, countries, and a greater number of them, are more vulnerable to fluctuations in the global economy than arguably at any time in the past. Moreover, countries whose economies were traditionally rather unexposed to international trade, such as Brazil and the United States, are today much more integrated with and affected by the global economy.

Today's challenge, then, is to continue to nurture trade liberalization and seek complementarities across agreements, all the while striving for open regionalism by way of continued reduction of most-favored-nation tariff and non-tariff barriers around the world. It is the purpose of the next three chapters to diagnose the extent to which the risks of today's trade integration scenario are present, and to outline policies that can help manage these risks while furthering the rewards.

Summary of Data and Sources for Chapters 2 and 3

The dataset encompasses 13,458 international agreements in 1875–2005. Ninety-four percent of the agreements are bilateral (have two parties), while 5 percent are plurilateral (have 3–15 parties), and 1 percent are multilateral (have 16 or more parties). The sample contains a total of 251 states and overseas territories.[55] Their number varies over time given the entry and exit of states in the international system. The maximum number of states and territories per year is 219 (since year 2002), while the minimum is 70 (in 1875) (Fig. 2.1). The bulk of the data for states' lifespans come from Lake and O'Mahony (2004); the *CIA World Factbook* is employed to complement their data.

In our data, the European Union is treated as a state when it enters treaties as a unit (such as in the case of the EU-Mexico trade agreement); selected states, most prominently Russia and Germany, are coded as the same states as the Soviet Union and West Germany so as to detect patterns of interaction over time. However, East Germany exits the data upon German reunification, and the former Soviet Republics enter into the data upon the breakup of the Soviet Union.

The complete dataset examined here and in Chapter 3 consists of 24 domains of cooperation ranging from trade to investment, customs, infrastructure, and transportation, among other things (Table A2.1). The choice of domains is influenced by our effort to explore the interactions between trade agreements and other forms of cooperation. As such, the sample here centers on domains that could plausibly be related to trade integration relatively quickly.

As discussed in the text, trade agreements are here divided into seven discrete types: general trade agreements, trade agreements regulating certain trade rules such as sanitary standards, sectoral trade agreements formed in such areas as agricultural goods or textiles, trade facilitation agreements, trade finance agreements centering on such areas as claims and debts, trade and economic cooperation agreements (that

---

[55] The data contain both independent states and overseas territories, primarily due to the fact that many preferential trade schemes as well as other international agreements are formed between a colonizer state and its overseas territories. Further iterations can derive the choice of states from theory. For instance, a neo-realist formulation would limit the sample to independent states, while a neo-liberal model might cover a more comprehensive category of customs territories or other units. Also, in this version of the chapter, none of the agreements is assumed to have expired.

do not necessarily entail the removal of barriers to trade), and 370 "modern" preferential trading arrangements (PTAs)—bi- or plurilateral trade agreements notified to the World Trade Organization (WTO) plus a handful of such trade agreements that have not yet been notified but that are generally considered to be PTAs (Table A2.1). PTAs by definition have been concluded exclusively in the post-war era.

We employ distinct sources for modern PTAs, bilateral investment treaties (BITs), and other trade agreements and agreements in other domains of cooperation, respectively. Data on PTAs come from the WTO and Arashiro *et al.* (2005); the classification of PTAs into distinct categories draws on that source as well as the authors' classification, as described in the main body of this chapter. Data on trade agreements signed before World War I come from Parry (1969–81); trade agreements concluded in the inter-war era from Smith (1996), United Nations (UN) (1947), and the US State Department website; and on trade agreements other than PTAs formed in the post-war era from the UN Treaty Series Database, which encompasses more than 50,000 international agreements notified by UN members. Data on BITs are from the UN Conference on Trade and Development (UNCTAD). The data on all other agreements for the 1875–1919 era come from Parry (1981), and for 1920–2005 from the UN Treaty Series.

Besides classifying each agreement by its domain of cooperation, we code each agreement by four dimensions: year of signature, year of entry into effect, membership (or "exclusiveness", the total number of members), and scope (number of issue areas covered by the agreement). While not explored in depth here, the dimensions of cooperation agreements will be of analytical interest in further iterations—and contribute to the growing literature on *how* states structure their cooperation.[56]

Table A2.1 PTAs covered in the study, by type and year signed

Free Trade Agreements (FTAs)

European Free Trade Association (EFTA)	1960
Central American Common Market (CACM)–Panama	1960
EC–Overseas Countries and Territories (OCT)	1971
Iceland (EC)	1973
Norway (EC)	1973
Switzerland (EC)	1973
Bahrain–Jordan	1976
Papua New Guinea–Australia Trade and Commercial Relations Agreement (PATCRA)	1977
Syria–EC	1977
Australia–New Zealand Closer Economic Relations Trade Agreement (ANZCERTA)	1983
Economic Cooperation Organization (ECO)	1985

[56] A notable example is Koremenos *et al.* (2001), who explore the determinants and interplay of dimensions of international institutions, such as scope, flexibility, membership, and hierarchy. Among their hypotheses is that scope increases with the heterogeneity of members, which tends to increase with membership; and that states are likelier to enter into binding and long-term agreements when membership grows large. See also Pahre (2001). The rational design school was preceded by a ground-breaking study by Lake (1999), who problematizes the degree of hierarchy in international security relationships. In another important contribution, Goldstein *et al.* (2000) and Kahler (2000) examine the extent of "legalization" of international agreements and institutions.

Israel (EFTA)	1992
Turkey (EFTA)	1992
ASEAN Free Trade Area	1992
Poland (EC)	1992
Hungary (EC)	1992
Czech Republic (EC)	1992
Czech Republic (EFTA)	1992
Slovak Republic (EC)	1992
Slovak Republic (EFTA)	1992
Jordan–Libya	1992
Armenia–Russian Federation	1993
Kyrgyz Republic–Russian Federation	1993
Faeroe Islands–Iceland	1993
Faeroe Islands–Norway	1993
Bulgaria (EC)	1993
Romania (EC)	1993
Bulgaria (EFTA)	1993
Romania (EFTA)	1993
Central European Free Trade Agreement (CEFTA)	1993
Hungary (EFTA)	1993
North American Free Trade Agreement (NAFTA)	1994
Commonwealth of Independent States (CIS)	1994
European Economic Area (EEA)	1994
Common Market for Eastern and Southern Africa (COMESA)	1994
Baltic Free Trade Area (BAFTA)	1994
Georgia–Russian Federation	1994
Moldova–Romania	1995
Faeroe Islands–Switzerland	1995
Armenia–Kyrgyz Republic	1995
Kazakhstan–Kyrgyz Republic	1995
Israel–United States	1995
Armenia–Moldova	1995
Mexico–Colombia–Venezuela (G3)	1995
Mexico–Bolivia	1995
Mexico–Costa Rica	1995
Latvia (EC)	1995
Lithuania (EC)	1995
Estonia (EC)	1995
Slovenia (EFTA)	1995
Armenia–Turkmenistan	1996
Hungary–Turkey	1998
Slovak Republic–Turkey	1998
Estonia–Slovak Republic	1998
Lithuania–Turkey	1998
Czech Republic–Turkey	1998
Hungary–Israel	1998
Israel–Poland	1998
Croatia–Slovenia	1998
Israel–Slovenia	1998
Turkey–Estonia	1998
Bulgaria–Turkey	1999
Palestinian Territory (EFTA)	1999
Georgia–Kazakhstan	1999
Chile–Mexico	1999
Morocco (EFTA)	1999
Former Soviet Republics (FSR)	1999

(Continued)

Table A2.1 (Continued)

Free Trade Agreements (FTAs) (Continued)

Slovenia–(EC)	1999
Latvia–Poland	1999
Egypt–Morocco	1999
Egypt–Tunisia	1999
Faeroe Islands–Poland	1999
Algeria–Jordan	1999
Faeroe Islands–Poland	1999
Georgia–Turkmenistan	2000
South Africa (EC)	2000
Bulgaria–Macedonia (EC)	2000
Morocco (EC)	2000
Israel (EC)	2000
Israel–Mexico	2000
Mexico (EC)	2000
Turkey–Macedonia	2000
Hungary–Lithuania	2000
Poland–Turkey	2000
Slovenia–Turkey	2000
Latvia–Turkey	2000
Hungary–Latvia	2000
Serbia and Montenegro–Russian Federation	2000
Bosnia and Herzegovina–Croatia	2001
New Zealand–Singapore	2001
Sri Lanka–India	2001
Jordan–United States	2001
Armenia–Kazakhstan	2001
Macedonia (EC)	2001
Macedonia (EFTA)	2001
Mexico (EFTA)	2001
Estonia–Hungary	2001
Slovenia–Bosnia and Herzegovina	2001
Egypt–Iraq	2001
Israel–Romania	2001
Bulgaria–Israel	2002
Central American Common Market (CACM)–Chile	2002
Albania–Macedonia	2002
Canada–Costa Rica	2002
Japan–Singapore	2002
Jordan (EFTA)	2002
Croatia (EFTA)	2002
Croatia (EC)	2002
Jordan (EC)	2002
Bahrain–Thailand	2002
Jordan–Syria	2002
Bosnia and Herzegovina–Macedonia	2002
Bosnia and Herzegovina–Serbia and Montenegro	2002
Bulgaria–Estonia	2002
Bulgaria–Latvia	2002
Albania–Croatia	2003
Bosnia and Herzegovina–Turkey	2003
Croatia–Turkey	2003
Australia–Singapore	2003
Albania–Bulgaria	2003

Albania–Kosovo	2003
Albania–Romania	2003
Chile (EC)	2003
Lebanon (EC)	2003
Association of Southeast Asian Nations (ASEAN)–China	2003
Croatia–Lithuania	2003
Singapore–EFTA	2003
China–Macao	2004
China–Hong Kong	2004
Singapore–United States	2004
Chile–United States	2004
Chile–Korea, South (R)	2004
Albania–Serbia and Montenegro	2004
Albania–Moldova	2004
Albania–Bosnia and Herzegovina	2004
Australia–Thailand	2004
Egypt (EC)	2004
Chile (EFTA)	2004
India–Thailand	2004
ASEAN–India	2004
South Asia Free Trade Agreement (SAFTA)	2004
Bosnia and Herzegovina–Bulgaria	2004
Bosnia and Herzegovina–Moldova	2004
Bosnia and Herzegovina–Romania	2004
Bulgaria–Serbia and Montenegro	2004
Croatia–Moldova	2004
Croatia–Serbia and Montenegro	2004
Macedonia–Romania	2004
Moldova–Serbia and Montenegro	2004
Romania–Serbia and Montenegro	2004
Greater Arab Free Trade Area (GAFTA)	2004
Panama–Taiwan	2004
Australia– United States	2005
Jordan–Kuwait	2005
Jordan–Singapore	2005
Macedonia–Moldova	2005
Algeria (EC)	2005
Turkey–Palestinian Authority	2005
EFTA–Tunisia	2005
Thailand–New Zealand	2005
Turkey–Tunisia	2005
India–Singapore	2005
Japan–Mexico	2005
Caribbean Community (CARICOM)–Costa Rica	2006
Northern Triangle (Northern T)	2006
Mexico–Uruguay	2006
United States–Bahrain	2006
United States–Morocco	2006
Caribbean Community (CARICOM)–Dominican Republic	2006
Central American Common Market–Dominican Republic	2006
United States–Central America–Dominican Republic Free Trade Agreement (CAFTA)	2006
Morocco–Tunisia	2006
Turkey–Morocco	2006
Singapore–Korea	2006
Japan–Malaysia	2006
Panama–Singapore	2006
Korea (EFTA)	2006

(Continued)

Table A2.1 (Continued)

Free Trade Agreements (FTAs) (Continued)

China–Chile	2006
Albania (EC)	2006
Turkey–Syria	2007
EFTA–Lebanon	2007
Central European Free Trade Agreement (CEFTA) Enlargement	2007
EFTA–Egypt	2007
Chile–Japan	2008

Customs Unions

European Community (EC)	1958
Central American Common Market (CACM)	1961
Economic and Monetary Community of Central Africa (CEMAC)	1966
South African Customs Union (SACU)	1970
Malta (EC)	1971
Caribbean Community (CARICOM)	1973
Cyprus (EC)	1973
Andean Community	1988
Southern Common Market (MERCOSUR)	1991
Andorra (EC)	1991
West African Economic and Monetary Union (WAEUMU)	1994
Turkey (EC)	1996
San Marino (EC)	2002

FTA Accessions

(CEFTA) Accession (Slovenia)	1996
(CEFTA) Accession (Romania)	1997
(CEFTA) Accession (Bulgaria)	1999
(CEFTA) Accession (Croatia)	2003

Customs Union Accessions

Denmark (EC)	1973
Ireland (EC)	1973
United Kingdom (EC)	1973
Greece (EC)	1981
Portugal (EC)	1986
Spain (EC)	1986
Austria (EC)	1995
Finland (EC)	1995
Sweden (EC)	1995
Czech Republic (EC)	2004
Hungary (EC)	2004
Lithuania (EC)	2004
Latvia (EC)	2004
Estonia (EC)	2004
Cyprus (EC)	2004
Slovak Republic (EC)	2004
Slovenia (EC)	2004
Poland (EC)	2004
Malta (EC)	2004

Iceland (EFTA)	1970
EC 25	2004
EC 27	2007
Trans-Pacific Strategic Economic Partnership (SEP)	2007

Preferential Arrangements

South Africa–Mozambique	
South Africa–Malawi	1967
Costa Rica–Panama	1973
Protocol Relating to Trade Negotiations among Developing Countries	1973
Honduras–Panama	1974
Nicaragua–Panama	1974
Guatemala–Panama	1975
Bangkok	1976
Mano River Union (MRU)	1977
India–Bangladesh	1980
Latin American Integration Association (LAIA)	1981
India–Maldives	1981
Gulf Cooperation Council (GCC)	1983
Indian Ocean Commission	1984
Economic Community of Central African States (ECCAS)	1985
Mexico–Panama	1986
Nicaragua–Venezuela	1986
Dominican Republic–Panama	1987
Arab Maghreb Union (AMU)	1989
Trinidad & Tobago–Venezuela	1989
Global System of Trade Preferences (GSTP)	1989
Economic Community of West African States (ECOWAS)	1990
Egypt–Libya	1991
Laos–Thailand	1991
Egypt–Syria	1991
Namibia–Zimbabwe	1992
Melanesian Spearhead Group (MSG)	1993
India–Bhutan	1995
South Asian Association for Regional Cooperation (SAARC)	1995
South Africa–Zimbabwe	1996
Israel–Jordan	1996
Egypt–Jordan	1998
Egypt–Lebanon	1999
Southern Africa Development Community (SADC)	2000
Community of Sahel–Saharan States (CEN-SAD)	2000
East African Community (EAC)	2000
Bangkok Accession	2002
Cambodia–South Korea	2002
India–Nepal	2002
India–Afghanistan	2003
Pacific Islands Countries Trade Agreement (PICTA)	2003
MERCOSUR–India	2004

Preferential Arrangements (Non-Reciprocal)

Generalized System of Preferences (by various developed countries [Austria, Canada, European Communities, Denmark, Ireland, Finland, Japan, New Zealand, Norway, Sweden, Switzerland, United Kingdom, United States] to several developing countries)	1971

(Continued)

Table A2.1 (Continued)

Preferential Arrangements (Non-Reciprocal) (Continued)

South Pacific Regional Trade and Economic Cooperation Agreement (SPARTECA)	1981
LAIA Market Access 1 (Bolivia)	1983
LAIA Market Access 2 (Ecuador)	1983
LAIA Market Access 3 (Panama)	1983
Caribbean Basin Initiative (CBI)	1984
Caribbean-Canada Trade Agreement (CARIBCAN)	1986
African Growth Opportunities Act (AGOA)	2000
Everything But Arms	2001
Cotonou Agreement	2003

Economic Complementarity Agreements

Chile–Bolivia	1993
Chile–Venezuela	1993
Chile–Colombia	1994
Chile–Ecuador	1995
MERCOSUR–Chile	1996
MERCOSUR–Bolivia	1997
Chile–Peru	1998
Brazil–Colombia, Ecuador, Peru, Venezuela	1999
Argentina–Colombia, Ecuador, Peru, Venezuela	2000
Cuba–Argentina	2000
Cuba–Brazil	2000
Cuba–Uruguay	2000
Cuba–Bolivia	2001
Cuba–Chile	2001
Cuba–Colombia	2001
Cuba–Ecuador	2001
Cuba–Mexico	2001
Cuba–Paraguay	2001
Cuba–Peru	2001
Cuba–Venezuela	2001
Brazil–Mexico	2002
MERCOSUR–Peru	2003
MERCOSUR–Andean	2005
MERCOSUR–Colombia, Ecuador, Venezuela	2005
MERCOSUR–Mexico	2006

Partial Scope Agreements

Colombia–Guatemala	1984
Colombia–El Salvador	1984
Colombia–Costa Rica	1984
Guatemala–Venezuela	1985
Colombia–Nicaragua	1985
Honduras–Venezuela	1986
El Salvador–Venezuela	1986
Costa Rica–Venezuela	1986
Guyana–Venezuela	1990
Colombia–Panama	1993

Table A2.2 Descriptive statistics

Domain	Total No.	% of Total	Year Signed				Number of Parties			
			Mean	Std.Dev.	Min.	Max.	Mean	Std.Dev.	Min.	Max.
Trade	4,466	32.64%	1945	33	1875	2004	2.7	5.4	2	128
BIT	2,281	16.67%	1993	8	1954	2005	2.0	0.0	2	2
Air Transportation	1,386	10.13%	1965	13	1880	1995	2.7	6.2	2	121
Frontiers	928	6.78%	1932	40	1875	2003	2.4	2.8	2	55
Visas	854	6.24%	1964	18	1882	2000	2.1	0.6	2	11
Infrastructure	617	4.51%	1961	32	1875	2001	2.3	1.6	2	20
PTA Modem	370	2.70%	1994	10	1957	2005	4.1	6.9	2	78
Customs	316	2.31%	1952	33	1876	2001	2.5	2.9	2	35
Financial Assistance	302	2.21%	1967	22	1880	1992	2.1	0.5	2	8
Investment	288	2.11%	1966	27	1875	2002	2.6	5.6	2	78
Merchandise Transportation	240	1.75%	1926	39	1875	1997	2.7	3.3	2	34
Education Cooperation	223	1.63%	1961	25	1893	2003	2.5	2.5	2	20
Industrial Cooperation	208	1.52%	1970	24	1875	1994	2.7	3.6	2	40
Economic Assistance	153	1.12%	1960	18	1915	2003	2.2	1.0	2	9

(Continued)

Table A2.2 (Continued)

Domain	Total No.	% of Total	Year Signed				Number of Parties			
			Mean	Std.Dev.	Min.	Max.	Mean	Std.Dev.	Min.	Max.
Technical Assistance	136	0.99%	1970	11	1943	2003	2.0	0.1	2	3
Security	126	0.92%	1907	12	1876	1919	3.6	5.1	2	38
Rail Transportation	118	0.86%	1905	20	1875	1992	2.9	2.6	2	21
Energy	113	0.83%	1975	17	1913	1997	2.3	1.3	2	11
Immigration	107	0.78%	1940	35	1877	2003	3.9	8.6	2	63
Monetary Cooperation	71	0.52%	1942	32	1875	1965	7.4	3.9	2	26
Passenger Transportation	56	0.41%	7974	17	1891	1995	4.1	6.5	2	27
Weapons	45	0.33%	1972	13	1954	2002	10.6	24.8	2	112
Arms	43	0.31%	1946	34	1897	1985	5.1	7.8	2	27
Labor	39	0.29%	1906	11	1879	1919	2.3	1.8	2	13
Financial Cooperation	38	0.28%	1913	23	1882	1960	3.7	3.7	2	17
Nonproliferation	5	0.04%	1991	13	1968	2001	28.2	46.8	2	110

APPENDIX 2.2

Geography of Trade Cooperation

Table A2.3 displays in the first column the 20 main trade agreement hubs—countries with the largest number of trade agreements—in the period 1875–2005, and in the subsequent rows their ten main trade agreement partners (in terms of numbers of agreements). Column 1 refers to the ranking of the hub country in terms of the number of trade agreements; in the fourth column, "partner" refers to countries with which the ranked hub has the highest number of trade agreements. "No. T-Agrs." is the number of agreements between the hub and the partner; "% of State's Agrs." refers to the agreements with the partner as a percentage of the hub's total number of agreements; and "Reverse Rank" refers to the hub's ranking among the partner country's key trade agreement partners. Thus, the United States is the hub in most agreements, its main partner is the UK, with which it has a total of 62 agreements. These agreements represent 2.2 percent of all US trade agreements. The United States is the UK's third most important agreement partner (in terms of number of agreements).

Table A2.3 Twenty trade agreement hubs and their partners, 1875–2005

Rank	State	Total No. T-Agrs.		Top 10 Partners									
				1	2	3	4	5	6	7	8	9	10
1	United States	2,868	Partner	UK	Pakistan	India	Japan	Indonesia	Dominican Rep	Korean Rep	Brazil	Canada	France
			No. T-Agrs.	62	58	56	52	52	52	50	48	47	46
			% of State's Agrs.	2.2	2.0	2.0	1.8	1.8	1.8	1.7	1.7	1.6	1.6
			Reverse rank	3	1	1	1	1	1	1	1	1	11
2	United Kingdom	2,337	Partner	France	Italy	US	Germany	Spain	Netherlands	Belgium	Portugal	Denmark	Sweden
			No. T-Agrs.	85	66	62	59	57	55	55	51	51	50
			% of State's Agrs.	3.6	2.8	2.7	2.5	2.4	2.4	2.4	2.2	2.2	2.1
			Reverse rank	1	2	1	3	1	3	4	2	1	4
3	France	2,127	Partner	UK	Italy	Germany	Belgium	Netherlands	Sweden	Spain	Switzerland	Portugal	Denmark
			No. T-Agrs.	85	80	65	62	58	57	57	53	52	47
			% of State's Agrs.	4.0	3.8	3.1	2.9	2.7	2.7	2.7	2.5	2.4	2.2
			Reverse rank	1	1	1	2	2	2	2	1	1	4
4	Germany	1,944	Partner	France	Italy	UK	Sweden	Spain	Belgium	Netherlands	Switzerland	Austria	Luxembourg
			No. T-Agrs.	65	60	59	54	53	53	50	48	42	40
			% of State's Agrs.	3.3	3.1	3.0	2.8	2.7	2.7	2.6	2.5	2.2	2.1
			Reverse rank	3	3	4	3	3	6	5	3	1	4
5	Italy	1,915	Partner	France	UK	Germany	Belgium	Switzerland	Spain	Netherlands	Denmark	Sweden	Austria
			No. T-Agrs.	80	66	60	55	50	49	48	48	45	40
			% of State's Agrs.	4.2	3.4	3.1	2.9	2.6	2.6	2.5	2.5	2.3	2.1
			Reverse rank	2	2	2	5	2	4	6	2	6	4

6	Sweden	1,881	Partner	Norway	France	Germany	UK	Denmark	Italy	Netherlands	Switzerland	Spain	Belgium
			No. T-Agrs.	70	57	54	50	47	45	44	43	42	40
			% of State's Agrs.	3.7	3.0	2.9	2.7	2.5	2.4	2.3	2.3	2.2	2.1
			Reverse rank	1	6	4	10	3	9	7	5	8	8
7	Netherlands	1,798	Partner	Belgium	France	UK	Luxembourg	Germany	Italy	Sweden	Spain	Denmark	Switzerland
			No. T-Agrs.	70	58	55	54	50	48	44	44	39	38
			% of State's Agrs.	3.9	3.2	3.1	3.0	2.8	2.7	2.4	2.4	2.2	2.1
			Reverse rank	1	5	6	2	7	7	7	5	11	8
8	Denmark	1,776	Partner	UK	Italy	Sweden	France	Austria	Spain	Portugal	Norway	Germany	Switzerland
			No. T-Agrs.	51	48	47	47	42	41	40	40	40	39
			% of State's Agrs.	2.9	2.7	2.6	2.6	2.4	2.3	2.3	2.3	2.3	2.2
			Reverse rank	9	8	5	10	2	10	4	4	11	7
9	Belgium	1,700	Partner	Netherlands	France	Luxembourg	UK	Italy	Germany	Spain	Sweden	Switzerland	Denmark
			No. T-Agrs.	70	62	57	55	55	53	43	40	37	37
			% of State's Agrs.	4.1	3.6	3.4	3.2	3.2	3.1	2.5	2.4	2.2	2.2
			Reverse rank	1	4	1	7	4	6	7	10	9	12
10	Spain	1,700	Partner	UK	France	Germany	Italy	Netherlands	Switzerland	Belgium	Sweden	US	Denmark
			No. T-Agrs.	57	57	53	49	44	43	43	42	41	41
			% of State's Agrs.	3.4	3.4	3.1	2.9	2.6	2.5	2.5	2.5	2.4	2.4
			Reverse rank	5	7	5	6	8	6	7	9	15	6
11	Portugal	1,690	Partner	France	UK	US	Denmark	Sweden	Spain	Norway	Italy	Germany	Switzerland
			No. T-Agrs.	52	51	44	40	39	39	38	38	35	34
			% of State's Agrs.	3.1	3.0	2.6	2.4	2.3	2.3	2.2	2.2	2.1	2.0
			Reverse rank	9	8	11	7	11	11	5	13	13	11

(Continued)

Table A2.3 (Continued)

Rank	State	Total No. T-Agrs.		Top 10 Partners									
				1	2	3	4	5	6	7	8	9	10
12	Japan	1,588	Partner	US	UK	Italy	Netherland	France	Denmark	Belgium	Sweden	Spina	Germany
			No. T-Agrs.	52	41	39	34	33	31	31	29	29	29
			% of State's Agrs.	3.3	0.5	0.5	2.1	2.1	2.0	2.0	1.8	1.8	1.8
			Reverse rank	4	13	11	13	15	13	13	16	14	15
13	Switzerland	1,559	Partner	France	Italy	Germany	UK	Sweden	Spain	Denmark	Netherlands	Belgium	Austria
			No. T-Agrs.	53	50	48	45	43	43	39	38	37	36
			% of State's Agrs.	3.4	3.2	3.1	2.9	2.8	2.8	2.5	2.4	2.4	2.3
			Reverse rank	8	5	8	11	8	6	10	10	9	8
14	Canada	1,545	Partner	US	UK	France	Japan	Italy	Germany	Australia	Spain	Netherlands	Denmark
			No. T-Agrs.	47	32	27	26	26	26	26	25	25	25
			% of State's Agrs.	3.0	2.1	1.7	1.7	1.7	1.7	1.7	1.6	1.6	1.6
			Reverse rank	9	17	18	14	16	18	6	16	16	17
15	Norway	1,529	Partner	Sweden	France	UK	Denmark	Portugal	Germany	Spain	Italy	Switzerland	Netherlands
			No. T-Agrs.	70	46	41	40	38	38	36	33	31	31
			% of State's Agrs.	4.6	3.0	2.7	2.6	2.5	2.5	2.4	2.2	2.0	2.0
			Reverse rank	1	12	12	8	7	12	13	15	12	15

16	Austria	1,510	Partner	Germany	Denmark	France	Italy	UK	Sweden	Spain	Switzerland	Belgium	Netherlands
			No. T-Agrs.	42	42	41	40	37	37	37	36	33	32
			% of State's Agrs.	2.8	2.8	2.7	2.6	2.5	2.5	2.5	2.4	2.2	2.1
			Reverse rank	9	5	14	10	14	12	12	10	11	14
17	Mexico	1,494	Partner	US	Argentina	Brazil	UK	Japan	Peru	France	Italy	Netherlands	Dominican Rep
			No. T-Agrs.	42	29	28	26	26	24	24	23	22	22
			% of State's Agrs.	2.8	1.9	1.9	1.7	1.7	1.6	1.6	1.5	1.5	1.5
			Reverse rank	14	3	3	23	13	4	20	20	19	2
18	Brazil	1,488	Partner	US	Peru	Mexico	UK	Ecuador	Bolivia	Argentina	Paraguay	Colombia	Italy
			No. T-Agrs.	48	30	28	27	27	27	27	24	24	24
			% of State's Agrs.	3.2	2.0	1.9	1.8	1.8	1.8	1.8	1.6	1.6	1.6
			Reverse rank	8	2	3	22	2	2	4	2	2	18
19	Australia	1,475	Partner	US	UK	New Zealand	Germany	France	Canada	Sweden	Spain	Portugal	Japan
			No. T-Agrs.	34	32	30	26	26	26	24	24	24	24
			% of State's Agrs.	2.3	2.2	2.0	1.8	1.8	1.8	1.6	1.6	1.6	1.6
			Reverse rank	24	18	1	19	19	7	17	17	16	17
20	Luxembourg	1,353	Partner	Belgium	Netherlands	France	Germany	Italy	UK	Sweden	Switzerland	Denmark	Austria
			No. T-Agrs.	57	54	41	40	36	32	32	30	28	27
			% of State's Agrs.	4.2	4.0	3.0	3.0	2.7	2.4	2.4	2.2	2.1	2.0
			Reverse rank	3	4	13	10	14	16	13	13	16	15

3

Cooperating to Trade, Trading to Cooperate

I. Introduction

This volume opened with the historical speech by Winston Churchill in Munich following World War II, where he advocated trade integration as a "sovereign remedy" for building lasting peace between the war-ravaged European nations. The legendary pro-trade US Senator Cordell Hull was an avid preacher of the benefits of free trade, elegantly arguing that "Unhampered trade dovetail[s] with peace; high tariffs, trade barriers, and unfair economic competition, with war...". Empowered by the Reciprocal Trade Agreements Act (RTAA) of 1934, Hull was a key figure behind the spree of bilateral trade agreements the United States negotiated in the inter-war era as an escape valve for the 1930 Smoot-Hawley tariff.

Churchill and Hull are not alone: dozens of statesmen, politicians, and analysts have time and again seen trade integration as doing more for relations between nations than merely spurring the exchange of goods and services. A thousand years BC, the reclusive and controlling Spartan government would not allow trade with other countries for fear that Spartans would become exposed to foreign ideas. In the 1850s, British statesman Richard Cobden campaigned against the protectionist Corn Laws by arguing that free trade "unites" states, "making each equally anxious for the prosperity and happiness of both". The founding fathers of the European Community, Robert Schuman and Jean Monnet, argued that economic integration would make war "materially impossible" on the continent (Milward 1984). On the 1960 Democratic Party platform, President John F. Kennedy stated that "World trade is more than ever essential to world peace".[1] Fast-forward to the present day: upon signing the US–Central America FTA (CAFTA) in August 2005, President George W. Bush remarked that "CAFTA is more than a trade bill; it is a commitment among freedom-loving nations to advance peace and prosperity throughout the region".[2]

Alongside the notions about the benefits of trade for cooperation has emerged a set of reverse arguments viewing international cooperation as helpful and even necessary for trade integration to blossom. The previous chapter showed that wars and, less starkly, isolationist sentiments were in part to blame for the ruptures of international trade cooperation and the outright collapse of the waves of trade integration throughout the 20th century. There are few reasons why they would not lead to similar outcomes today; nurturing incentives for cross-border cooperation may thus be a potent and perhaps even necessary way to sustain constructive cooperation in trade. Politicians refer to the loyalties of allies when drumming up domestic support for a trade agreement with that country. In his State of the Union address in January 2008, President Bush himself, seeking support for an FTA with Colombia, stated that "Colombia [is] a friend of America that is confronting violence and terror, and fighting drug traffickers. If we fail to pass this agreement, we will embolden the purveyors of false populism in our hemisphere."

The point is that PTAs and trade agreements may have broader determinants and effects than are captured in the various political economy studies. Too often, trade agreements are analyzed as if arising in a vacuum on the international stage, or at best in some relationship or another with the multilateral trading system. Analysts seldom pay heed to the importance of placing trade in the broader context of global cooperation. This potentially curtails our understanding of the conditions that make trade agreements happen and work.

Are trade agreements virtuous agents of peace, trust, and cooperation between states?[3] Or is cooperation a necessary backdrop for countries entering into trade agreements—and, more generally, the handmaiden of further cooperation? Why might different types of agreements be linked—

---

[1] Spruyt (1994) argues that trade over the period 1000–1350 was the main factor behind the rise of European sovereign territorial states and city-states from the travails of feudalism: the expansion of trade compelled leaders of cities and towns to strengthen their defenses in order to protect their merchants and secure property rights.

[2] USINFOR, "Bush Signs Trade Accord with Central America, Dominican Republic", 2 Aug. 2005. <http://usinfo.state.gov/wh/Archive/2005/Aug/02-35199.html>.

[3] "Cooperation" refers here to the mutual adjustment of policies by two or more states. Trade integration refers here to cooperation in the domain of trade. International agreements are here understood as a subset of international institutions. We follow Koremenos *et al.* (2001: 762) in defining international institutions as "explicit arrangements, negotiated among international actors that prescribe, proscribe, and/or authorize behavior".

why, more generally, would cooperation beget further cooperation? Does the historical record bear out any of the theoretical hypotheses about the progression of cooperation?

The policy relevance of endeavoring to answer these questions is clear: should trade agreements have their putative beneficial effects, they would not only be a worthy goal for governments to pursue and, bluntly put, be more attractive sells to their constituents, but also be a catalytic force multiplier that can transform international relations. And should cooperation help pave the way to trade cooperation, it ought to be harnessed as another tool for freeing global trade. It would also mean that the outcomes of today's wave of integration hinge on a host of factors—many of which can be managed through smart international policies.

This chapter seeks to arrive at some such policy-relevant answers in two ways. First, it strives to gain insight into the waves of trade agreements mapped out in Chapter 2 against the broader contours of international relations. Second, this chapter will start developing empirical insights into the potential relationships between trade and cooperation by using a dataset of more than 13,000 trade and cooperation agreements formed in the past 130 years. Verifying such a relationship would require a broader effort than offered here; nonetheless, we hope to stimulate further empirical policy research into the effects of trade integration on international cooperation.

Our effort is humble: we do not even start attempting to describe, let alone explain, the ebbs and flows of international cooperation agreements; such a subject merits a collection of volumes. This chapter merely seeks to provide preliminary insights into one specific area of international relations, the nexus of trade and cooperation agreements.

The next section surveys the rich academic literature on the evolution of international cooperation in general, and trade cooperation, in particular. Section III examines the main trends in cooperation agreements, and discusses some of the potential sequences between trade and other cooperation agreements. Section IV concludes.[4]

II. Evolution of International Cooperation

Academics have long debated whether economics or politics drives economic integration. The common wisdom about the European integration

---

[4] This chapter draws on Estevadeordal and Suominen (2008).

process was that it was spurred by political motivations—the desire to tie the fates of European war-torn nations together through trade so as to render future wars unfeasible and, eventually, unthinkable. However, some more recent surveys of the process have placed economics in the driver's seat. Moravcsik (1998) argues that it was economic interdependence that was and has been the primary force compelling the European nations to integrate. European politicians in his account shrewdly pursued national economic advantage, exploiting asymmetric interdependencies with other nations and manipulating common institutional commitments. Similarly, many agreements, such as the North American Free Trade Agreement (NAFTA), have since their inception been seen as propelled by economic logic; Mexico's initiative to launch the agreement has been interpreted as a way for the country to solidify its integration into the global economy and to gain credibility for its domestic economic reforms.[5]

The point is that whether politics or economics propels integration, trade integration does not occur in a vacuum, but can be affected by a host of factors in relations between nations. The previous chapter discussed the potential impact of multilateral trade cooperation (and the lack of it) on the formation of bilateral trade agreements. A further causal factor might be prior wars, which can undercut the incentives and capacities of trade cooperation; another might be high economic interdependency, which can provide compelling incentives to liberalize and facilitate further through integration agreements; still another might be the existence of prior cooperation, which should help countries gain confidence in each other. Countries that frequently engage in conflicts have little trade with each other.

These arguments are nothing new, of course. Trade agreements and other forms of cooperation have long been hypothesized to be both path-dependent and endogenous to one another, rather than being spurred by exogenous forces alone. Economists have tended to follow Balassa's (1961) linear notion of the progression of regional trade integration from an FTA to a CU and further to a common market and potentially also a monetary union. Balassa theorized that freeing the movement of economic factors across national borders would create a demand for further integration both economically and politically, so that economic unions would naturally evolve into political unions over time. However, the theoretical grounds and empirical evidence remain thin on the sequencing of

---

[5] See e.g. Hufbauer and Schott (2005).

FTAs, CUs, and other types of trade agreements. Political economy studies by Maxfield (1990) and Frieden (1996), which focus on the progression from trade integration to monetary cooperation, and by Pastor (2001), which develops an agenda for furthering North American integration on the basis of the EU's integration experience, are some of the exceptions. More recently, scholars have sought to establish an empirical relationship between different *levels* of integration, namely whether regional trade agreements might help catalyze multilateral trade liberalization. The results, reviewed indepth in Chapter 5, are decidedly mixed.

Political scientists have produced a massive body of literature on the evolution of international cooperation, thus bringing political dynamics into the analysis of the evolution of economic integration. Balassa's scholarly predecessor and keen student of the then-European Economic Community, Ernst Haas, in 1958 argued that European integration would over time acquire its own logic, claim states' loyalties, and engender "spillovers"—further cooperation and integration in other issue areas. The inevitable setbacks in the European integration process in the following decades made some analysts discredit Haas's thesis. However, in the 1980s, neo-liberals led by Robert Axelrod (1984) gave sturdier theoretical bases for such notions of path-dependent integration. They established that repeated interactions between states, particularly when conducted within international institutions, can help overcome the Prisoner's Dilemmas inherent in international relations, and spur on cooperation thereby.[6]

Neo-liberals saw international institutions (agreements, laws, rules, and organizations alike) as intermediaries of international cooperation, as tools to help states overcome collective action problems, high transaction costs, and information asymmetries. Institutions of broad scope in particular can allow states to engage in logrolling, create issue linkages, and make contingent deals that provide for continuous tit-for-tat, alter the pay-offs that states can expect to receive from cooperating and reciprocating, and again incentivize states to keep playing the cooperative game.[7]

Institutions not only facilitate cooperation; they can also provide states with incentives to avoid short-term temptations to renege on their commitments or to free-ride on others. They do so by decreasing the lag in states' detecting each other's cheating, furthering states' ability to gauge each other's behavior, and providing enforcement and punishment

---

[6] See Axelrod (1984), Keohane (1984), and Oye (1986).
[7] See Koremenos *et al.* (2001) on the interplay of the various institutional features, such as scope and membership.

mechanisms. Indeed, institutions can shape some of the finer strategic aspects of cooperation, including states' beliefs about each other, the value of reputation, the subtleties of signaling, and the credibility of commitment.[8] For example, signals sent out by a state are most effective in changing the beliefs of others when such signals are credible; that is, when reneging on them would impose material costs on the deviant state.[9] A state reneging on their commitment to an international institution would likely incur the cost of precluding other states from cooperating with it ever again, and thus forgo the benefits of reciprocity. Institutions and existing cooperation can also reduce informational gaps about capabilities and make bargaining more transparent and cooperation more likely: when information is more complete, states engaged in a bargaining process are more aware of each other's reservation points, or exactly how far the other is willing to go in holding out when bargaining for a common agreement.[10] Both thus have a clearer sense of the bargaining range and also know the side deals that might induce the counterpart to expand that range.

Neo-liberals thus thought that prior agreements and other institutions can transform the anarchic international system of self-interested states into cooperation between similarly self-interested states. Until then, such notions had been debunked by neo-realists, spearheaded by Waltz (1972), who viewed states as being inherently suspicious of each other and cooperation between them as being fundamentally hampered by the specter of unbalanced, relative gains from cooperation and perennial cheating: any form of cooperation would have to be a mere short-term marriage of convenience, generally to oppose a common security threat.

Neo-liberals countered that in an environment populated by international institutions and common histories of cooperation, states are likelier to choose cooperative strategies and reciprocate than they are

---

[8] See e.g. Morrow (1992, 1994, 1999) and Fearon (1997). Many of the game-theoretic works of international cooperation build on Thomas Schelling's seminal (1960) work on international bargaining.

[9] Otherwise, intended recipients are likely to dismiss signals as cheap talk. However, in some circumstances, even cheap talk can be an effective signal (Crawford and Sobel 1982). This occurs when states' prior beliefs are that they are likely to have a high degree of common interest, and that they will be better off if they coordinate their actions rather than making independent choices.

[10] A fitting analogue is bargaining in a market: what makes the problem of finding an agreeable price difficult is that neither player knows the other's reservation point: thus, when making offers, each side must weigh the benefits of asking for a more favorable deal for oneself against the risk that the other side will reject the offer as unacceptable, and terminate the bargaining process.

in an environment devoid of institutions. While individually rational action by states could impede mutually beneficial cooperation, institutions expand time horizons and allow states to avoid short-term temptations to renege and thus realize the available mutual benefits. Constructivism, which departs from the rational choice-based theories altogether, goes even further, viewing the pay-offs from inter-state interactions as helping to merge states' preferences and identities with those of the collective—which, in turn, should render sequential cooperation near-automatic.[11]

The literature on the progression of international cooperation is too large and diverse to catalogue in a few pages. However, a glance at some of the main approaches shows both the seemingly insurmountable obstacles to cooperation—such as distributional concerns, enforcement problems, and uncertainties about counterparts' capacities to forego cooperation—and the heady prospects of sustained cooperation in the presence of incentives to reciprocate, long time horizons, and lowered informational gaps.

Perhaps the most common simple prediction arising from the vast range of theoretical approaches is that inter-state cooperation, once launched, may well improve the odds of further cooperation. However, its breadth notwithstanding, the literature has some gaps. For instance, although there is a vast body of literature examining why cooperation occurs in a given domain (such as trade),[12] studies do not usually problematize the choice of the domain (such as choice of trade over investment). Also less attention has been paid to the relatively greater frequency of cooperation in one realm over others. For instance, do states come together more often or more intensely in the area of trade than in, say, investment, and if so, why? Studies have also yet to fully explore the relationships between different domains of cooperation. One area where good progress has been made is on the relationship between trade and security cooperation, but the causality usually runs both ways.

Empirical assessments of these questions are also quite thin and largely limited to qualitative case studies.[13] Even though scholars have examined the effects of cooperation agreements on economic and political outcomes

---

[11] See e.g. Wendt (1992).

[12] For the determinants of trade agreements, see e.g. Yarbrough and Yarbrough (1992), Nye (1992), McLaren (1997), Milner (1997a, 1997b), Ethier (1998), Mattli (1999), and Mansfield and Rosendorff (2000).

[13] Koremenos (2003), using a large-sample study on the flexibility of agreements, is a promising exception.

in a number of domains (such as the impact of trade agreements on the likelihood of inter-state disputes or the effects of security alliances on trade flows),[14] less empirical attention has been paid to patterns of sequences of *agreements* and endogeneity of different types of agreements in relation to each other. To our knowledge, there are as yet no systematic and genuinely global mappings of international cooperation agreements. The static and dynamic relationships between the domains of cooperation, including the potential complementarity (or substitutability) between agreements formed in different domains, also awaits analysis.[15]

Yet, an examination of the sequences of international agreements is compelling in light of the proliferation of trade agreements and many other types of agreements around the world over the past few decades. An empirical examination of how agreements are related and sequenced is crucial to understanding both the determinants and outcomes of cooperation. Indeed, studies that have encountered causality between agreements in certain domains (such as trade) and outcomes (inter-state disputes) may suffer from an omitted variable bias should the causality travel through another, intervening agreement in another domain instead (a security cooperation agreement). Moreover, given that empirical studies have focused on relatively limited samples of states and domains, they risk selecting on the dependent variable, and, as such, supporting the authors' theoretical biases.

From the policy perspective, an improved understanding of the drivers and relationships between different types of agreements can help governments sequence their external agendas so as to obtain higher pay-offs from cooperation—and attain outcomes that are superior to those that can reached through unilateral policies alone. In the following, we strive to open one window—a potential link between trade and other cooperation agreements—into these issues.

---

[14] On the impact of trade agreements on disputes between states, see e.g. Mansfield and Pevehouse (2000). See also Russett and O'Neal (2001) for extensive research on economic interdependence and security. Haftel (2004) examines the effects of different types of regional trade integration schemes, such as schemes with a security policy component, on intramural conflict; however, the chapter is not about sequencing agreements in different domains, but, rather, of agreements with divergent dimensions. See e.g. Gowa and Mansfield (1993) and Gowa (1994) on security alliances and trade.

[15] The potential relationships between the dimensions and domains of agreements have also yet to be submitted to systematic empirical scrutiny. The few existing empirical studies that problematize the dimensions of agreements are not necessarily generalizable since they usually follow a case study format and focus on developed states.

III. Trade and Cooperation: Is There a Nexus?

How might trade cooperation and other forms of cooperation be connected? This section strives to offer a preliminary answer to these questions by employing the sample of trade agreements explored in Chapter 2, and 27 domains of cooperation ranging from investment, to customs, infrastructure, and transportation, among other things, for the period 1875–2002 (Chapter 2, Appendix 2.1).[16]

As in the case of trade agreements, European and Western Hemisphere countries have been the drivers of the rise of cooperation agreements (Fig. 3.1), and this due to their prolific and long-standing intra-regionalism. The key players behind the regional patterns are the traditional great powers —the United States and Western European states. They form a distinct global club of cooperators: not only are they the most prolific cooperators *per se*, but most of their agreements are with each other. It appears that "gravity model" variables—income, distance, common border, common language, and other shared cultural affinities—might play a central role in the choice of cooperation partners, much as they do in arbitrating trade volumes and choice of trade agreement partners.[17] Wealth and proximity are strong preconditions for cooperation.

In other regions, particularly Asia and Africa, cooperation followed the post-war era's surge in intra-regional cooperation and the rise of multilateralism. Indeed, multilateral agreements from the 1944 Convention on International Civil Aviation to the 1960s commodity agreements helped "globalize" global cooperation, enabling even poor and distant states— states that would seem unlikely to form a bilateral agreement—to cooperate with each other. Furthermore, much as in the case of trade agreements, the club of global cooperation among the traditional great powers is eroding. While the main players still dominate the overall system of cooperation—the United States and UK are party to some *half of all* agreements analyzed here—the past two decades in particular have seen a growing prominence of trans-Atlantic and trans-Pacific agreements, along with the proliferation of agreements between Western and Eastern European states in the post-Cold War era.

---

[16] The choice of domains is influenced by our effort to explore the interactions between trade agreements and other forms of cooperation. As such, the sample here centers on domains that could plausibly be related relatively quickly to trade integration.

[17] Baier and Bergstrand (2004) show that gravity variables also explain the selection into trade agreements.

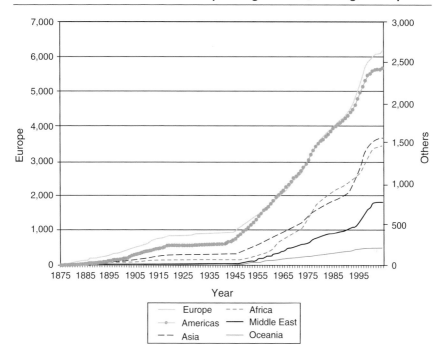

Figure 3.1 Cumulative cooperation agreements in 1875–2002, by region
Source: Authors' calculations.

Notwithstanding the similarities in the proliferation and geographical patterns between trade and cooperation agreements, one difference persists: the number of trade agreements is considerably higher than the number of agreements in any other domain of cooperation. Aggregating economic cooperation agreements under seven broad categories and comparing them to trade agreements shows that trade agreements dominate the data in nearly every era, followed by transportation, border issues, investment, economic assistance, and infrastructure agreements (Fig. 3.2). Only investment agreements outpace trade agreements in the last period explored here, 1981–2002, due to the strong rise of bilateral investment treaties (BITs) around the world in the 1990s. The dominance of trade is also clear in the top cooperators' "cooperation portfolios" (Fig. 3.3).

The high number of trade agreements is in part indicative of the fact that trade agreements hail back to the 19th century, whereas a couple of domains examined here, such as air transportation agreements, are nearly exclusively post-war domains. However, and less trivially, the

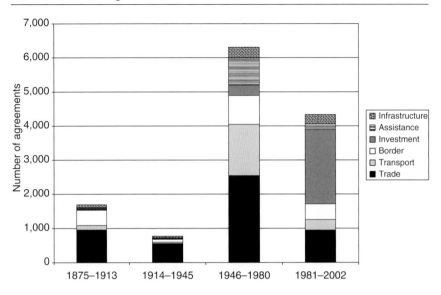

Figure 3.2 International agreements by domain, 1875–2002

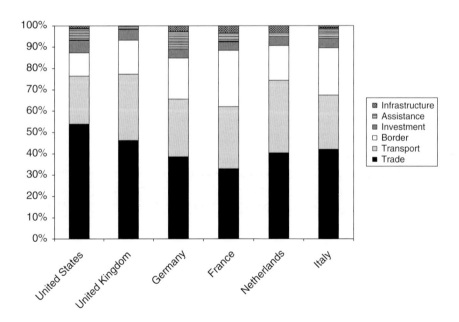

Figure 3.3 Shares of the main domains of selected states agreements in 1875–2002
Source: Authors' calculations.

outcome potentially also reflects six rather unique properties of trade agreements.

First, trade is potentially more divisible than many other domains: trade agreements can be forged on a single product (e.g. steel or textiles) and/or trade rule (e.g. standards). Indeed, Chapter 2 showed that sectoral agreements and agreements on rules make up almost one-third of the entire sample of trade agreements. As such, any pair of states may well have multiple agreements forged under the broader label of trade.

Second, to obtain pay-offs from expanded market access generally requires international cooperation. In contrast, governments arguably have a great many purely unilateral tools at their disposal to respond to domestic demands in the domains of, say, monetary or health policy.

Third, trade agreements can be made a "club good" through such instruments as most-favored-nation tariffs and restrictive rules of origin, which provides greater incentives for forming trade agreements than agreements that deliver pure public goods, such as air quality agreements, for instance.

Fourth, PTAs in particular often follow a relatively standard model, so that the domestic and international transaction costs of negotiating each successive agreement can be significantly lower relative to those of negotiating the first agreement.

Fifth, PTAs are often not only about trade, but also cover such areas as customs procedures, labor issues, and even transportation, and thus potentially have pre-empted the formation of stand-alone agreements in these areas, particularly in the post-war era. Investment is an exception, as many PTAs employ the parties' BIT as the set of rules that also applies to the PTA's investment chapter.

Sixth, as discussed in Chapter 2, multilateral trade agreements have not advanced as rapidly or been as deep as many WTO members would wish. This may well have induced many members to forge bilateral agreements alongside multilateral agreements to deepen market access gains and to regulate further areas of bilateral commerce. Similar dynamics may be in play in the area of investment, where the perceived inadequacies of multilateral agreements as well as domino effects—countries' fear of remaining outside the widening web of bilateral agreements—have generated a rapid proliferation of BITs. It may well be that in other areas of international cooperation, such as monetary issues, multilateral agreements are not similarly paralleled by bilateralism, which limits the spread of agreements.

Overall, trade agreements—and bilateral trade agreements in particular—might be easier to reach than agreements in other domains. Should this be the case, trade agreements could be considered a particularly likely first node in interactions between two states previously uninitiated in bilateral cooperation.

Are trade and cooperation agreements related? There are also at least three theoretical reasons to expect so. There are a number of reasons why trade agreements in particular could be a harbinger of future cooperation in other domains.

First, today's trade agreements are often more multifaceted than are many other types of international agreements, extending to such areas as competition policy, labor regulations, and intellectual property rights. As such, they could hypothetically open ample opportunities for states to engage in issue-linkages and log-rolling, which, neo-liberals would argue, would help states attain further cooperation agreements. Multi-faceted trade agreements can also reduce the need for compensatory schemes (Schiff and Winters 2002), which is positive because compensation could reduce the incentives of the likely net contributors to cooperate further in the first place.

Second, the positive effects and externalities of trade agreements, such as lowered barriers to trade and the potential for pooling production, can augment the policy salience of, and pay-offs from, regional rules and regulations, awakening latent domestic interests in the member states to demand further cooperative agreements.[18] A different causal chain traveling through the domestic arena is that trade agreements can help foster political reforms and institutions in the member states—something that NAFTA is seen as having done in Mexico, for instance—thus rendering the members increasingly attractive as future cooperation partners.

Third, trade agreements can also produce negative externalities, such as border congestion and air pollution, which, in turn, can give rise to demands for cooperation in other domains, such as for regional transportation networks or environmental protection (Devlin and Estevadeordal 2004). By eradicating border barriers, trade agreements can also accentuate the vulnerability of states to the transmission of external shocks. For

---

[18] For example, increased trade flows can generate demands for agreements aimed at cutting any remaining policy or other barriers hampering trade and raising trade costs, such as poor regulatory frameworks, cumbersome standards, and inefficient customs procedures. Furthermore, a trade agreement can induce the parties to have sunk assets—fixed costs or irreversible investments that are independent of output and that a firm must bear to operate and that cannot be recouped even if the decision to produce is later reversed—in a bilateral relationship. As such, it can spur demands for hedging against defection by the partner through further, more precise agreements between the member states.

instance, the synchronization of business cycles that tends to accompany trade integration will also synchronize economic downturns, and, as such, generate demands for economic surveillance and macroeconomic coordination. More generally, in the presence of economies of scale or inter-state externalities, market solutions to problems may be sub-optimal while regional cooperation can have marked pay-offs (Schiff and Winters 2002).

In general terms, then, trade agreements can be hypothesized to spur demand for a host of regional public goods (RPGs), which, given their public goods characteristics, require formal frameworks for regional cooperation—such as regional cooperation agreements (Estevadeordal *et al.* 2004).[19] If this were the case, the causal relationship between trade agreements and further cooperation agreements should be particularly strong when trade agreements are "productive"—when they live up to their promise of expanded trade flows and generate traffic, expanded market size, and synchronization of business cycles.

To be sure, there are also reasons for believing that cooperation can help states trade and forge trade agreements. As a practical matter, wars can severely interrupt trade flows even among friends if supply routes are cut off. There can also be strong incentives to cooperate in trade in the presence of a guaranteed trustworthy relationship. Political scientists have repeatedly shown that military allies are likely to trade more with one another than non-allies. Even sworn realists skeptical of the prospects of sustained cooperation note that trade can create security externalities, which countries want to internalize within their alliances.[20] Thus, while trade agreements can be the handmaiden of cooperation in other realms, they are likelier to take hold in an environment that is cooperative, or at least free from conflict.

Have trade agreements led to cooperation agreements? Does cooperation facilitate trade integration? How have the two forms of cooperation been sequenced and related over time?

Conceptually, progression or sequencing of trade agreements *per se*, and of trade agreements and other types of agreements, can take a variety of forms. Table 3.1 summarizes four main types of sequences—"deepening" (a series of agreements formed between states A and B in one domain such as trade), "demonstration" or "domino" sequencing (adoption of an agreement between C and D in the domain where A and B have an agreement); "expansion" (an agreement between A and C in the domain where A and B have an

---

[19] See Barrett (2007) for an extensive survey of global public goods.
[20] See, for instance, Gowa (1994).

agreement); and "spillover" sequencing (whereby A and B enter a sequence of agreements in different domains, such as trade and investment).

Here, we are primarily interested in spillover sequencing between trade agreements and other cooperation agreements, something that Ernst Haas discussed in his renowned work. Figure 3.4 takes a first look by mapping out the evolution of the two types of agreements over the past century.

Table 3.1 Types of sequencing of cooperation agreements

| | Round t | | Round t+1 | | |
States	Domain of Cooperation	States	Domain of Cooperation	Type of Sequencing
A,B	x	A,B	x	Deepening
A,B	x	A,B	y	Spillover
A,B	x	C,D	x	Demonstration
A,B	x	A,C	x	Expansion

Source: Authors.

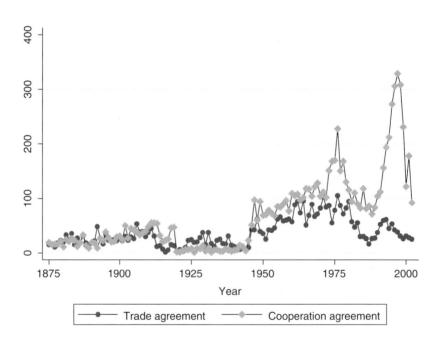

Figure 3.4 Trade agreements and other cooperation agreements around the world, 1875–2002

Source: Authors' calculations.

The patterns could be propelled by each of the four types of sequencing. However, in terms of spillovers, it shows that trade and cooperation agreements have fluctuated together over the course of the past several decades: surges in trade agreements are closely related to—and often appear to precede—surges in cooperation agreements. Patterns within Europe and the Americas, respectively, follow (and, to be sure, drive) global trends (Fig. 3.5).

Getting at the spillover effects requires a closer look at bilateral patterns. A simple look at the top 20 global cooperators' top ten trade and cooperation partners, respectively, for 1875–2002 suggests that particularly European states that cooperate most intensely with each other in the area of trade do so also in other domains of cooperation (Appendix 3.1). There is less such rank correlation in the case of the United States; this is potentially due to the nation's superpower status: the United States probably can and does maintain strategic relationships with a larger number of countries than any other country, selecting distinct and most appropriate partners in each realm of cooperation.

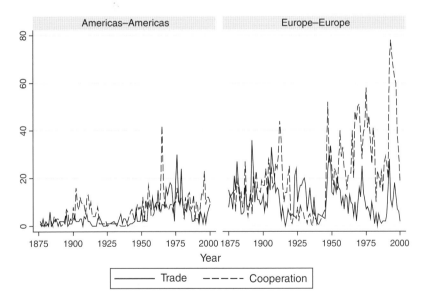

Figure 3.5 Trade and cooperation agreements in the Americas and Europe, 1875–2002

Source: Authors' calculations.

The European case is especially emblematic of the spillover effects: the advance of integration in one issue area has furthered cooperation across other issue areas across the region. The union was launched with the 1957 Treaty of Rome, which created the European Economic Community (EEC) aimed at creating a common market. In the 1960s, the-then European Community members stopped charging custom duties in intra-regional trade, and also agreed on a new topic—joint control over food production. The EU's regional policy was set in motion in the 1970s to channel funding to and generate economic activity in the poorer areas of the Community. In 1987, Community cooperation progressed further through the Single European Act, which provided for a vast six-year program aimed at the European Single Market carrying "four freedoms"—freedom of movement of goods, services, people, and money. The Single Market was finalized in 1993, and the EU's long-standing monetary integration efforts culminated in a common currency, the euro, in 1999, with 11 of the 15 members joining; Greece joined in 2001. The past two decades in particular have seen the rise of a multitude of further common and joint policies from fisheries to foreign and defense policies, from external trade to intra-regional transportation, from social issues and employment to environmental policies. The EU appears to have fulfilled Ernst Haas's 1950s vision.

The EU's experience of sequential accessions is also illustrative of integration by expansion. The Union was started by six founders—Belgium, France, Germany, Italy, Luxembourg, and the Netherlands. The first expansion took place in 1973 with the addition of Denmark, Ireland, and the United Kingdom; Greece joined in 1981, and Spain and Portugal a year later. Austria, Finland, and Sweden joined in 1995, and ten Central and Eastern European states in 2004. Bulgaria and Romania joined in 2007, raising the total membership to 27.

The EU stands apart in depth and breadth of integration issues built largely on trade integration, and also outrivals virtually any other group in the width of membership. A continent away in US–Mexico relations, trade and other forms of cooperation have also surged in parallel in the past century, albeit with less coordination and depth than in Europe. Trade relations between Mexico and the United States go back centuries, but were accentuated during the late 19th century. The two countries signed trade and cooperation agreements annually starting in 1895 through World War II (Fig. 3.6).

These agreements dealt mostly with consular issues, the regulation of employment of Mexican seasonal workers, and the traffic in illegal

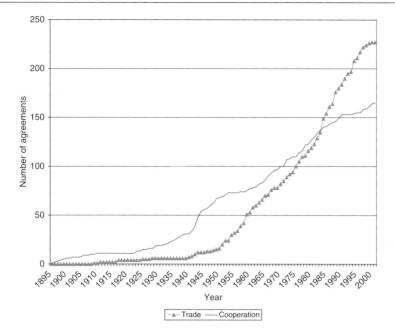

Figure 3.6 Cumulative bilateral trade and cooperation agreements between Mexico and the United States, 1895–2000

Source: Authors' calculations based on Mexican foreign ministry data.

substances between the two countries. Some of the first formal trade agreements were signed in 1942, the year Mexico entered the war, perhaps thanks to the US 1934 Reciprocal Trade Agreement Act, which authorized Washington to negotiate bilateral trade agreements with various countries. Opening vis-à-vis Mexico was useful for the United States, as the southern neighbor was an important supplier of raw materials, and, soon thereafter, oil, to a host of US industries.

The post-war era was marked by a steady stream of bilateral cooperation agreements, mostly on regulation of agricultural issues, employment of seasonal workers from Mexico, and cultural cooperation. Various trade agreements were signed as well, mostly on regulating the trade of cotton textiles and exports of beef. By the early 1990s, Mexico made up half of US trade with Latin America. In the wake of the Cold War, Canada, Mexico, and the United States set out to negotiate the North American Free Trade Agreement (NAFTA), which entered into force in 1994. NAFTA helped propel a number of further cooperation agreements across North America as well as between Mexico and the United States on issues ranging from environmental cooperation to satellite signal transmission and personal communication services along the border. Trade agreements appear to have propelled cooperation; cooperation, trade agreements.

In the meantime, the Asia-Pacific region has featured perhaps more incipient formal trade cooperation, owing to both the regional penchant for informal cooperation and to the long-standing relative openness to intra-regional trade. Indeed, while APEC had already been launched as a trade forum in 1989, it is cooperation in financial matters following the Asian financial crisis of 1997–8 that is often seen as a particular harbinger of the proliferation of intra-regional trade integration initiatives in the past few years.

In the aftermath of the turmoil, the ASEAN+3 grouping (ASEAN, China, Korea, and Japan) set out to pursue cooperation on issues ranging from macroeconomic risk management to monitoring of regional capital flows, fostering the banking and financial systems, and reforming the international financial architecture. May 2000 marked a milestone for the grouping with the signing of an ASEAN Currency Swap Agreement in Chiang Mai, Thailand. The Chiang Mai Initiative aims to expand the existing ASEAN Swap Arrangement in both financing and membership, and to create a new network of bilateral swap arrangements among the ASEAN+3 members.

Further key efforts toward regional financial cooperation have involved economic surveillance—carried out particularly through the ASEAN+3 Economic Review and Policy Dialogue introduced in May 2000—and the development of Asian bond markets. In 2003, ASEAN+3 established the Asian Bond Market Initiative to develop local currency-denominated bonds. The same year, the Executives' Meeting of East Asia Pacific Central Banks (EMEAP) announced the launch of the Asian Bond Fund (ABF). With an initial total of $1 billion, the ABF strives to expand bond markets through the purchase of dollar-denominated sovereign and semi-sovereign bonds issued in eight of the EMEAP economies. In December 2004, the EMEAP group announced the launch of the second stage of the ABF (ABF2) aimed at investment in sovereign and quasi-sovereign domestic currency bonds issued in the eight EMEAP markets.

These efforts provide a concrete basis for discussions on the potential formation of an Asian Monetary Fund, envisaged as a surveillance and supervisory mechanism and a potential supplementary source of support to the funds disbursed by the International Monetary Fund. An even more ambitious goal that has received broad-based support is the creation of a common unit of account, the Asian Currency Unit, possibly through the establishment of a basket of regional currencies. Further, more long-term cooperation initiatives include the East Asia Vision Group (EAVG), established in 1998 to promote the creation of the East Asian Community (EAC) and the East Asian Summit process.

While FTAs have spread in the Asia-Pacific space following financial cooperation, it is also the case that APEC progress has over the years expanded via spillover integrationism from the more purely trade-related issues to a host of themes, including energy and anti-terrorism. While APEC commitments are not binding and enforced as they are in the EU, their broadening into new issue areas nonetheless communicate similar patterns as in the old continent. And like the EU, APEC has expanded from 12 to 21 members, including three countries in Latin America and Russia. The forum is hugely popular and has had to impose a moratorium on membership twice. Overall, in Asia, it seems that trade and cooperation have progressed hand-in-hand over the years, perhaps more so than in Europe or the Americas, where trade cooperation often has been the impetus for other forms of cooperation.

IV. Conclusion

This chapter has sought to place trade agreements against the backdrop of broader trends in international cooperation, and to discuss ways in which trade and other forms of cooperation might be linked. We have elaborated on some reasons why trade agreements might propel further cooperation among the partner countries, and why cooperation can be conducive to trade agreements.

There are manifold theoretical grounds for believing that under the right conditions, two states can indeed break the Prisoner's Dilemma situations inherent in international relations and set out on a path to cooperate, as well as to sustain their cooperation. The historical narrative here is not so elaborate as to verifiably confirm this hypothesis, let alone call it a law of international politics.

However, we have shown that the global waves of trade agreements have tended to be closely related to surges in cooperation agreements. Moreover, there is preliminary evidence, particularly from Europe, to suggest that countries that cooperate most extensively with each other in the area of trade are each other's most favored partners also in other areas of cooperation. Perhaps the main insight arising from these patterns is that should trade agreements be building blocks for further cooperation around the world, their on-going spread of PTAs could translate into a new wave of cooperation agreements. Conversely, cooperative relations between nations may be necessary if not sufficient for fruitful trade relations and trade integration.

The literature on the causes and effects of international cooperation is huge and well beyond the scope of this chapter, as are policy prescriptions for furthering cooperation between nations. Further, linking trade and cooperation agreements is a complex econometric exercise due to the numerous causal and intervening variables that would have to be taken into account; this too is beyond the scope of this chapter. We have also focused here on the number and simple counts of agreements, rather than agreements' characteristics or qualitative features, such as scope and size of membership, and their effects on sequencing.

What can be ascertained, however, is the policy relevance of improved understanding of the patterns of cooperation, including the various types of sequences of cooperation that nations may undertake. Even more importantly, it ought to be stressed that analyzing international cooperation is ultimately meaningful only through an assessment of the *outcomes* of cooperation. Particularly central is to establish the conditions under which the proliferation of formal cooperation is "productive", or yields national, regional, and global public goods that states would be unlikely to attain through unilateral action. It is hoped that the dataset developed here will provide a start for such research.

APPENDIX 3.1

Table A3.1 displays in the first column the ten main trade agreement hubs—countries with the largest number of trade agreements—in the period 1875–2005, and in the subsequent rows their ten main trade agreements partners (in terms of numbers of agreements). The third column refers to the ranking of the hub country in terms of the number of trade agreements; in the fifth column, "partner" refers to countries with which the ranked hub has the highest number of trade agreements; "No. T-Agrs." to the number of agreements between the hub and the partner; and "% of State's T-Agrs." refers to the the agreements with the partner as a percentage of the hub's total number of agreements.

"C-Rank" refers to the partner's ranking in the hub country's list of main partner countries with which the hub has the greatest number of cooperation agreements. "No. C-Agrs." refers to the number of the cooperation agreements between the hub and the partner; "% of State's C-Agrs." refers to cooperation agreements with the partner as a percentage of the hub's total number of cooperation agreements. Thus, the United States is the hub with the greatest number of agreements, its main trade agreements partner is the UK, with which it has a total of 62 trade agreements. With its C-Rank of 1, the UK is also the United States' main cooperation partner; the two have 121 common cooperation agreements. Those agreements represent 3.5 percent of US cooperation agreements.

Table A3.1 The top ten trade hubs and their top ten trade and cooperation partners, 1875–2005

Top 10 Partners

United States — Trade: Rank 1, Total No. Agrs. 2,868; Cooperation: Rank 2, Total No. Agrs. 3,467

Partner	UK	Pakistan	India	Japan	Indonesia	Dominican Rep	Korean Rep	Brazil	Canada
T-Rank	1	2	3	4	5	6	7	8	9
No. T-Agrs.	62	58	56	52	52	52	50	48	47
% of State's T-Agrs.	2.2	2	2	1.8	1.8	1.8	1.7	1.7	1.6
C-Rank	1	53	63	5	62	17	45	18	2
No. C-Agrs.	121	27	20	58	20	45	29	45	83
% of State's C-Agrs.	3.5	0.8	0.6	1.7	0.6	1.3	0.8	1.3	2.4

United Kingdom — Trade: Rank 2, Total No. Agrs. 2,337; Cooperation: Rank 1, Total No. Agrs. 3,550

Partner	France	Italy	US	Germany	Spain	Netherlands	Belgium	Portugal	Denmark
T-Rank	1	2	3	4	5	6	7	8	9
No. T-Agrs.	85	66	62	59	57	55	55	51	51
% of State's T-Agrs.	3.6	2.8	2.7	2.5	2.4	2.4	2.4	2.2	2.2
C-Rank	1	4	3	2	13	5	6	7	9
No. C-Agrs.	174	116	121	122	58	86	82	71	67
% of State's C-Agrs.	4.9	3.3	3.4	3.4	1.6	2.4	2.3	2	1.9

France — Trade: Rank 3, Total No. Agrs. 2,127; Cooperation: Rank 5, Total No. Agrs. 3,141

Partner	UK	Italy	Germany	Belgium	Netherlands	Sweden	Spain	Switzerland	Portugal
T-Rank	1	2	3	4	5	6	7	8	9
No. T-Agrs.	85	80	65	62	58	57	57	53	52
% of State's T-Agrs.	4	3.8	3.1	2.9	2.7	2.7	2.7	2.5	2.4
C-Rank	1	2	3	4	7	10	6	5	14
No. C-Agrs.	174	163	152	149	88	65	94	118	54
% of State's C-Agrs.	5.5	5.2	4.8	4.7	2.8	2.1	3	3.8	1.7

Germany — Trade: T-Rank 4, No. T-Agrs. 1,944 · Cooperation: C-Rank 3, No. C-Agrs. 3,333

Partner	France	Italy	UK	Sweden	Spain	Belgium	Netherlands	Switzerland	Austria
T-Rank	1	2	3	4	5	6	7	8	9
No. T-Agrs.	65	60	59	54	53	53	50	48	42
% of State's T-Agrs.	3.3	3.1	3	2.8	2.7	2.7	2.6	2.5	2.2
C-Rank	1	4	2	10	16	5	3	6	15
No. C-Agrs.	152	106	122	58	47	95	121	82	52
% of State's C-Agrs.	4.6	3.2	3.7	1.7	1.4	2.9	3.6	2.5	1.6

Italy — Trade: T-Rank 5, No. T-Agrs. 1,915 · Cooperation: C-Rank 9, No. C-Agrs. 2,706

Partner	France	UK	Germany	Belgium	Switzerland	Spain	Netherlands	Denmark	Sweden
T-Rank	1	2	3	4	5	6	7	8	9
No. T-Agrs.	80	66	60	55	50	49	48	48	45
% of State's T-Agrs.	4.2	3.4	3.1	2.9	2.6	2.6	2.5	2.5	2.3
C-Rank	1	2	3	5	4	14	6	8	10
No. C-Agrs.	163	116	106	86	104	47	79	58	55
% of State's C-Agrs.	6	4.3	3.9	3.2	3.8	1.7	2.9	2.1	2

Sweden — Trade: T-Rank 6, No. T-Agrs. 1,881 · Cooperation: C-Rank 10, No. C-Agrs. 2,701

Partner	Norway	France	Germany	UK	Denmark	Italy	Netherlands	Switzerland	Spain
T-Rank	1	2	3	4	5	6	7	8	9
No. T-Agrs.	70	57	54	50	47	45	44	43	42
% of State's T-Agrs.	3.7	3	2.9	2.7	2.5	2.4	2.3	2.3	2.2
C-Rank	1	5	8	6	2	10	7	3	12
No. C-Agrs.	103	65	58	64	89	55	64	66	50
% of State's C-Agrs.	3.8	2.4	2.1	2.4	3.3	2	2.4	2.4	1.9

Netherlands — Trade: T-Rank 7, No. T-Agrs. 1,798

Partner	Belgium	France	UK	Luxembourg	Germany	Italy	Sweden	Spain	Denmark
T-Rank	1	2	3	4	5	6	7	8	9
No. T-Agrs.	70	58	55	54	50	48	44	44	39
% of State's T-Agrs.	3.9	3.2	3.1	3	2.8	2.7	2.4	2.4	2.2

(Continued)

Table A3.1 (Continued)

State	Main Domain	Rank	Total No. Agrs		Top 10 Partners								
	Cooperation	4	3,276	C-Rank	1	4	5	3	6	2	9	14	8
				No. C-Agrs.	147	88	86	102	70	121	64	49	66
				% of State's C-Agrs.	4.5	2.7	2.6	3.1	2.1	3.7	2	1.5	2
Denmark	Trade	8	1,776	Partner	UK	Italy	Sweden	France	Austria	Spain	Portugal	Norway	Germany
				T-Rank	1	2	3	4	5	6	7	8	9
				No. T-Agrs.	51	48	47	47	42	41	40	40	40
				% of State's T-Agrs.	2.9	2.7	2.6	2.6	2.4	2.3	2.3	2.3	2.3
	Cooperation	8	2,804	C-Rank	4	9	1	7	19	13	16	2	3
				No. C-Agrs.	67	58	89	63	39	46	42	84	77
				% of State's C-Agrs.	2.4	2.1	3.2	2.2	1.4	1.6	1.5	3	2.7
Belgium	Trade	9	1,700	Partner	Netherlands	France	Luxembourg	UK	Italy	Germany	Spain	Sweden	Switzerland
				T-Rank	1	2	3	4	5	6	7	8	9
				No. T-Agrs.	70	62	57	55	55	53	43	40	37
				% of State's T-Agrs.	4.1	3.6	3.4	3.2	3.2	3.1	2.5	2.4	2.2
	Cooperation	7	2,843	C-Rank	2	1	3	6	5	4	13	8	9
				No. C-Agrs.	147	149	109	82	86	95	47	66	53
				% of State's C-Agrs.	5.2	5.2	3.8	2.9	3	3.3	1.7	2.3	1.9
Spain	Trade	10	1,700	Partner	UK	France	Germany	Italy	Netherlands	Switzerland	Belgium	Sweden	US
				T-Rank	1	2	3	4	5	6	7	8	9
				No. T-Agrs.	57	57	53	49	44	43	43	42	41
				% of State's T-Agrs.	3.4	3.4	3.1	2.9	2.6	2.5	2.5	2.5	2.4
	Cooperation	13	2,143	C-Rank	3	1	9	8	5	6	10	4	12
				No. C-Agrs.	58	94	47	47	49	48	47	50	44
				% of State's C-Agrs.	2.7	4.4	2.2	2.2	2.3	2.2	2.2	2.3	2.1

4

Intricate Designs: The Architecture of Trade Agreements

I. Introduction

The first chapters of this volume explored the ecology of trade agreements through time. We identified four trade agreements waves, each more diverse than the previous ones. Each wave has taken place in a quite distinct multilateral trade policy environment and different global economic conditions. We have also found today's wave is marked by a convergence of multilateral trade liberalization, expansion of world trade, and, in particular, the forceful rise of comprehensive preferential trading arrangements (PTAs). Standing out among PTAs is the rapid proliferation of free trade agreements (FTAs) since the mid-1990s.

Despite the growing importance of PTAs in global commerce, very little is as yet understood about their architecture and, consequently, their full implications for the global economy. In fact, most studies on PTAs have operationalized them as a dummy variable, rather than disaggregating them into a more granular variable. This chapter strives to help fill some of the gaps. We analyze the structure of some 60 PTAs by their various key component parts, including tariff liberalization schedules, rules of origin, and investment, services, competition policy, and customs procedure provisions.

Our foremost purpose is to gain a deeper comparative understanding of the contents of trade agreements around the world. The data employed in this chapter is hoped to provide a basis for analyzing the determinants and ultimate economic effects of PTAs so as to facilitate decision-making about PTA formation and the best PTA designs.

The following section focuses on product-level data—tariff liberalization schedules, tariff rate quotas, and rules of origin—in 38 PTAs. The second section dissects some of the provisions in 60 PTAs' main texts, including services, investment, competition policy, and customs. Section IV briefly discusses the importance of implementing PTAs, while Section V concludes.

II. Sectoral Dynamics in PTAs

Preferential tariff liberalization is one of the most fundamental aspects of PTAs and a key driver of PTA formation. But how liberalizing are PTAs really? Do they free trade on all products and do so quickly, or is liberalization less comprehensive and prolonged?

We strive to answer these questions by analyzing the tariff liberalization schedules of 76 parties in 38 PTAs as grouped into intra-Asian, Americas–Asia, intra-Americas, Americas–Europe, and other (largely European and select US) agreements (see Appendix 4.1).[1] The agreements were chosen by employing three criteria—geographic diversity, relative importance in the partners' trade flows, and, simply, due to the relative methodological ease of coding the several thousand product lines in these agreements.

Figure 4.1 provides a starting point, showing the share of tariff lines liberalized by the partners in the 38 PTAs, mapping out the shares of national tariff lines that become subject to liberalization in year 1, years 2–5, years 6–10, years 11–20, and more than 20 years into the PTA. The three-letter ISO code of each country giving the concession (i.e. the importing country) precedes the arrow, while the code of the partner

---

[1] We draw in part on Estevadeordal *et al.* (2008), which is the first comprehensive and detailed survey of PTAs' market access provisions. There are some previous, more limited studies. The WTO (2002) carries out an extensive inventory of the coverage and liberalization of tariff concessions in 47 PTAs of a total of 107 parties. The data cover tariff treatment of imports into parties to selected PTAs, tariff line treatment as obtained from individual countries' tariff schedules, and tariff dispersion for a number of countries. Scollay (2005) performs a similarly rigorous analysis of tariff concessions in a sample of 18 PTAs. The IADB (2002) presents an exhaustive survey of market access commitments of PTAs in the Americas, while the World Bank (2005) carries out a more general mapping of the various disciplines in PTAs around the world. The tariff liberalization schedules were obtained from the Foreign Trade Information System at <http://www.sice.oas.org/> and some national sources, including websites. Some tariff data were obtained from Trade Analysis and Information System (TRAINS).

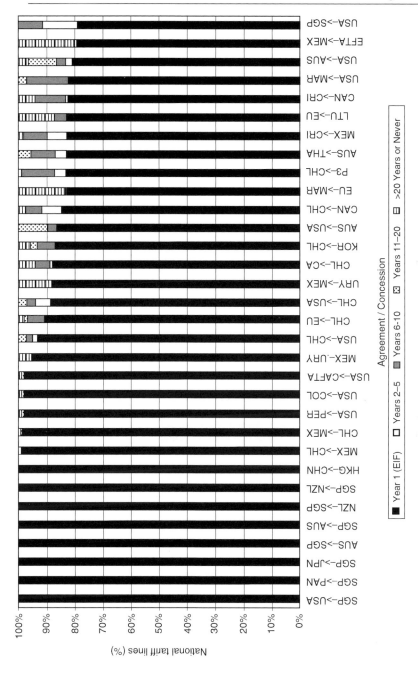

Figure 4.1 Percent of tariff lines' duty freed by selected PTA partners, by selected benchmark years

Source: IDB calculations.

(Continued)

Figure 4.1 (Continued)

country follows the arrow. Year 1 refers here to the year of entry into force.

The data are revealing of the share of tariff lines subject to backloaded liberalization—particularly marked in Morocco and South Africa's schedules in FTAs with the EU, and in the EU's schedule in the FTA with Lithuania, largely due to the persistent protection in the agricultural protocols. Agreements formed in the Americas and particularly those signed by the NAFTA members generally liberalize trade relatively fast, with some 75 percent or more of lines freed in the first year of the agreement. However, some of MERCOSUR's agreements have somewhat more backloaded liberalization, with a large share of lines being liberalized six to ten years into the agreements.

Asian PTAs stand out for being particularly frontloaded: they liberalize the bulk of the tariff universe in the first year of the PTA. This is in good part due to Singapore's according duty-free treatment to all products upon the entry into force of its agreements. Overall, although PTA partners vary markedly in the share of tariff lines subject to liberalization in years 1 and 5, the bulk of them liberalize 90 percent or more of tariff lines by year 10 of the PTA.

PTA members differ in how they pace tariff lowering: reciprocity does not proceed evenly. The parties' respective product coverages often diverge markedly in year 5, with some partners (such as Korea) liberalizing up to twice as many lines as their partners (such as Chile); however, the differences shrink considerably by year 10 (Figs. 4.2a and 4.2b). The wider gaps in concessions among a pair tend to be due to differences between more and less developed partners—a pattern that recurs in all regions.

Tables 4.1a and 4.1b provide further flavor to tariff lowering by numerically detailing the bilateral liberalization match-ups (share of liberalized tariff lines of total lines) in the Americas in 2007 and 2010. The black boxes indicate common customs unions; liberalization in these agreements can be seen as nearly complete.

The main finding is the extent of deep liberalization throughout the region: most FTA members had already liberalized more than four-fifths of the tariff items to their partners in 2007; some of the newer FTAs will attain this level by 2010. To be sure, liberalization in the Southern Cone (MERCOSUR)–Andean agreement, which is an amalgam of bilateral agreements between the groups' members, is only incipient, reaching about a fifth or a quarter of tariff lines by 2010.

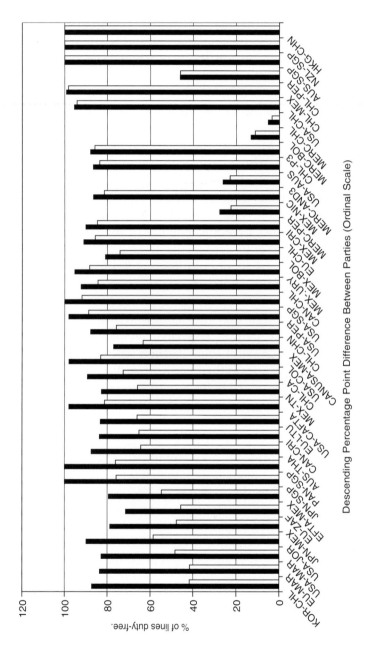

Figure 4.2a Reciprocity of concessions: year 5

Source: IDB calculations.

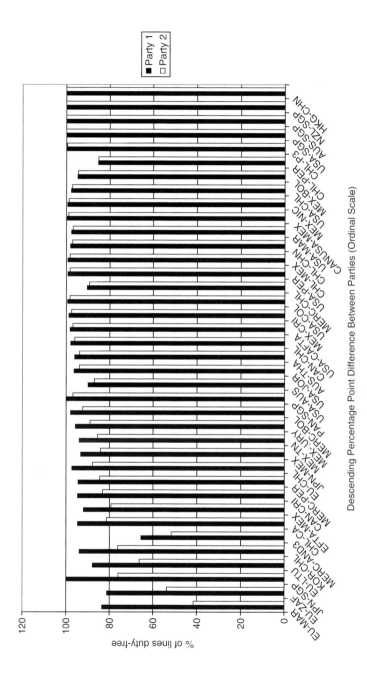

Figure 4.2b Reciprocity of concessions: year 10
Source: IDB calculations.

Table 4.1a Americas liberalization state of play, 2007

Country giving preference ↓ / Country receiving preference →

	Avg. Mfn	ARG	BOL	BRA	CAN	CHL	COL	CRI	DOM	ECU	GTM	HND	MEX	NIC	PAN	PER	PRY	SLV	URY	USA	VEN
ARG	9.7	X	97.9	■		98.0	12.2			15.9						4.7	92.4				12.3
BOL	8.2	92.4	X	92.4		98.0	33.9			28.3			96.7			20.2	92.4				n.a.
BRA	10.8	97.9	97.9	X		98.0	33.9			28.3						20.2	■				27.4
CAN	6.5				X	97.9		83.6												98.8	
CHL	6.0	97.7		97.7	97.3	X	96.8	94.9		96.7			98.3			85.2	96.1	94.1	97.7	94.3	
COL	11.9	10.9	25.6			95.7	X		98.0				90.7				21.0	98.3	25.0	76.0	
CRI	6.3				65.2	82.5		X	98.0		■	■	97.6	■	X			■		71.7	
DOM	8.7						98.3	98.3	X		98.3	98.3		98.3				98.3		76.5	
ECU	11.2	21.6	22.0			91.6				X							19.4		21.2		n.a.
GTM	5.9							■	98.0		X	■	76.0	■				■		79.7	
HND	5.9							■	98.0		■	X	63.0	■				■		74.4	
MEX	13.1	97.7				99.3	95.8	98.8	97.5		93.9	83.3	X	99.4		15.5		93.6	95.4	99.8	99.8
NIC	5.9							■	97.5		■	■	98.8	X	X			■		71.5	
PAN	8.6														X						
PER	9.9	10.4	■	9.8		85.1	95.8			■			15.5		X	X	9.1		59.4	77.6	n.a.
PRY	8.8	97.9	97.9	■		96.3	14.8		98.0	15.0						15.5	X			9.1	
SLV	6.2		97.9			79.1	12.1		98.0		■	■	76.1	■		65.3		X		77.8	
URY	9.3	97.9				98.0	12.1		97.9	11.4			88.4			65.3	98.0*	97.9	X		
USA	5.7				98.0	95.5	98.0*	97.9	97.9		97.9	97.9	98.8	97.9		98.0*		97.9		X	
VEN	12.0	8.7	n.a.	10.9		95.5	n.a.			n.a.			99.8				10.0		9.0		X

Notes: includes only customs unions (black cells) and free trade agreements (gray cells), not unilateral preferences.

Numbers in cells show percentage of total national tariff lines duty-free in 2007.

n.a. = not available at this time

* Signed but not yet entered into force as of 12/31/2006. Assuming entry into force in 2007.

Avg. Mfn is the average MFN tariff for 2005, or the most recent year available. Source of Tariffs data: TRAINS, FTAA Hemispheric Database.

Source: IDB calculations.

Table 4.1b Americas liberalization state of play, 2010

Country giving preference / Country receiving preference

Country giving preference	Avg. Mfn	ARG	BOL	BRA	CAN	CHL	COL	CRI	DOM	ECU	GTM	HND	MEX	NIC	PAN	PER	PRY	SLV	URY	USA	VEN
ARG	9.7	X	97.9			98.0	30.9			29.6			97.5			27.9	92.4		92.4		27.3
BOL	8.2	92.4	X	92.4													97.9				n.a.
BRA	10.8	97.9	97.9	X		98.0	53.2			45.5						36.0					43.0
CAN	6.5				X	97.9	94.6	95.2					99.3							98.8	
CHL	6.0	97.7		97.7	97.3	X	96.8	94.6		n.a.			99.0			95.7	96.1	94.1	97.7	94.3	
COL	11.9	18.4		48.8	83.2	95.7	X						90.7				36.5	98.3	41.7	76.1*	n.a.
CRI	6.3				82.5			X	98.0				98.2							76.3	
DOM	8.7							98.0	X		98.3	98.3		98.3						82.4	
ECU	11.2	26.0		26.7		n.a.				X							19.5		22.5		n.a.
GTM	5.9								98.0		X		90.1							83.4	
HND	5.9								98.0			X	76.1							80.7	
MEX	13.1	98.4	98.4		99.3	99.3	95.8	98.9	97.5		97.5	86.9	X	99.4				97.4	95.4	100	
NIC	5.9								98.0				98.8	X						79.8	
PAN	8.6														X					n.a.*	
PER	9.9	11.3				95.7										X	9.6			77.8*	n.a.
PRY	8.8									30.2						29.4	X		64.7		28.7
SLV	6.2												90.1					X		84.6	
URY	9.3									36.9			88.4			78.8			X		30.5
USA	5.7						98.0*	98.0	98.0		98.0	98.0	100	98.0	n.a.*	98.0*		98.0		X	
VEN	12.0	18.9		25.4						n.a.						n.a.	24.7		21.4		X

Notes: includes only customs unions (black cells) and free trade agreements (gray cells), not unilateral preferences.
Numbers in cells show percentage of total national tariff lines duty-free in 2010.
n.a. = not available at this time
* Signed but not yet entered into force.
Avg. Mfn is the average MFN tariff for 2005, or the most recent year available. Source of Tariffs data: TRAINS, FTAA Hemispheric Database.

117

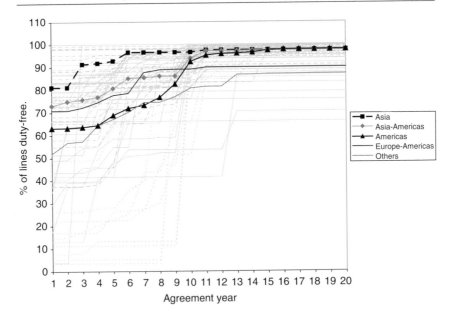

Figure 4.3 Evolution of duty-free treatment in selected PTAs
Source: IDB calculations.

Figure 4.3 goes beyond the snapshots to display the dynamic, year-on-year liberalization trajectories of the 76 PTA parties over 20 years, as well as the respective averages of the five regional groupings.[2] Agreements between the Americas and Asia and those within Asia feature the fastest and most extensive liberalization; in the case of Asia, the data are affected by the predominance of Singaporean agreements. Overall, PTAs in general free more than 90 percent of tariff lines within 10 years. However, a small number of agreements contain phase-outs even after year 20—although the number of products subject to prolonged phase-outs is quite small.

What of liberalization in "real time"? Where is liberalization across PTAs today, and where can we expect it to be in, say, two decades? Most PTA members have liberalized more than four-fifths of the tariff items to their partners; some of the newer agreements will attain this level by 2010 (Fig. 4.4). Overall, Asian (primarily Singaporean) agreements and the advance of tariff liberalization in Asia–Americas agreements entail

---

[2] The entry into force dates differ between agreements, thus the actual years of a given benchmark (e.g. agreement year 10) differ as well.

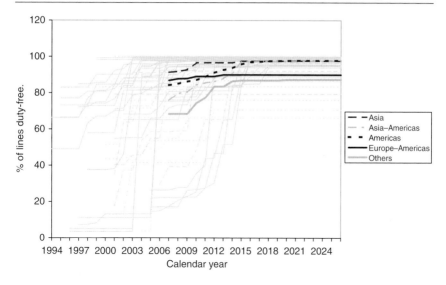

Figure 4.4 Evolution of duty-free treatment in selected PTAs, 1994–2026
Source: IDB calculations.

that they will have freed more than 95 percent of tariff lines by 2015. Liberalization is also quite advanced in the Americas; the regional average is pulled down by the MERCOSUR–Andean agreements, where liberalization will reach about a fifth or a quarter of tariff lines by 2010.

Not all product lines are freed even after the 15th year, and herein lies the main political economy question of scholars of trade agreements— what accounts for the lags and gaps in liberalization? Unsurprisingly, agriculture is one of the main laggards (broken lines in Fig. 4.5). Agricultural products are in each region more protected than are industrial products. On average, PTAs liberalize only 61 percent of tariff lines in agriculture by year 5 and 78 percent by year 10, while reaching duty-free treatment for 77 and 94 percent of industrial goods by the same points in time.

The Asia–Americas average sees a meaningful, though smaller, jump in agricultural liberalization in year 10. This is primarily due to increases in China's concession to Chile and Panama's to Singapore. In Asia, the jump is less substantial and comes earlier. This is mainly due to increases in coverage in the China–Hong Kong schedule in year 3. PTAs in the Americas take off in agricultural liberalization in year 10, gradually converging with Asian agreements. This is largely due to very large jumps (of the order of 60 percentage points or more)

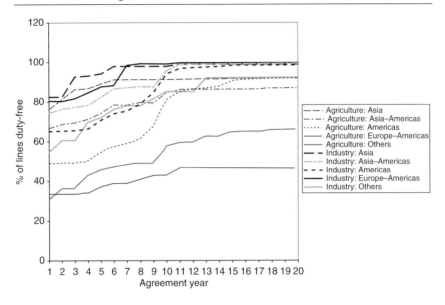

Figure 4.5 Evolution of sectoral duty-free treatment in selected PTAs

Source: IDB calculations.

in agricultural duty-free coverage in the MERCOSUR–Bolivia and MERCOSUR–Chile agreements, as well as smaller increases in coverage in Mexico–Nicaragua and Mexico–Costa Rica FTAs and the representative average Central American countries' schedule in CAFTA vis-à-vis the United States. Peru's agricultural concession to MERCOSUR also increased substantially that year.

Agricultural chapters in PTAs feature the least liberalization and also the highest dispersion of liberalization across PTAs, which indicates that these chapters are particularly protected in some PTA parties' schedules. Liberalization is also slow: on average, PTA parties liberalize fewer than 60 percent of tariff lines in some chapters—dairy produce (ch. 4) and sugars, cocoa, and cereals (17, 18, and 19, respectively), and footwear (64)—by the fifth year of the agreement, and only some 65 percent or less by year 10. To be sure, on average, parties liberalize more than 80 percent of tariff lines in the bulk of chapters by year 5 and more than 90 percent of tariff lines in most chapters by year 10. The fastest and deepest liberalization is effected in such non-sensitive products as ores (ch. 26), fertilizers (31), pulp of wood (47), and some base metals (81).

The results indicate that most "action" in the extent of liberalization occurs in agricultural, textile, and apparel products. Notably, there is significant movement in the textile chapters between the 5- and 10-year benchmarks; by the same measure, dairy and sugar show little additional liberalization. The differences across parties dissipate by year 10; the persistent variation in agriculture is due largely to the EU's agreements where liberalization is postponed—at times in perpetuity, as is the case, for example, for certain live animals, meat, dairy, and sugar products originating in South Africa in the EU–South Africa PTA.

Simply measuring the share of liberalized tariff lines fails to capture the full effects stemming from the exclusion of sensitive products from PTAs if those products are covered in a very small number of tariff lines. We shed light on this question by introducing two alternative methods of exploring the depth and speed of liberalization in PTAs: liberalization statistics examined above as weighted by trade at the hormonized

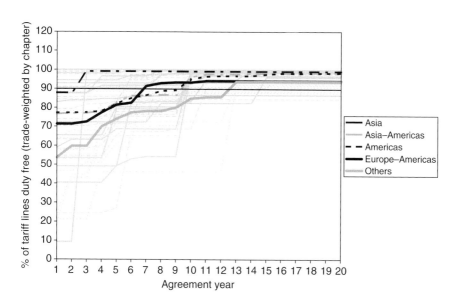

Figure 4.6a Trade-weighted evolution of duty-free treatment in 23 PTAs
Source: IDB calculations.

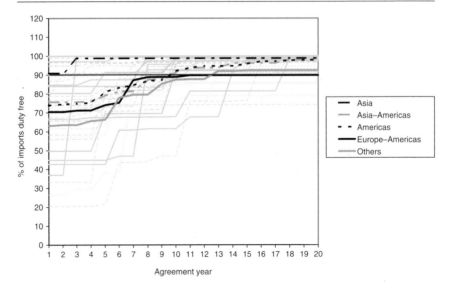

Figure 4.6b Evolution of duty-free imports in 19 PTAs
Source: IDB calculations.

system (HS) chapter level (Fig. 4.6a), and the actual percentage of total trade (imports) from the PTA partner that is liberalized (Fig. 4.6b), find strong general similarities with the unweighted data. To be sure, none of these calculations captures the extent of *potential* trade between partners. Sectors with backloaded liberalization also tend to feature the highest tariffs, which means that they could also generate the greatest pay-offs from liberalization.[3]

Qualifying Market Access: TRQs and Rules of Origin

Besides tariffs, PTAs contain numerous rules, such as non-tariff measures, special safeguards, tariff rate quotas (TRQs), and demanding rules of origin (RoO), that may significantly qualify the market access provided by tariff liberalization. Agreements involving countries of the Americas use TRQs frequently in agriculture; there is also some TRQ incidence in textiles (Fig. 4.7).

---

[3] The set of agreements is more reduced—23 and 19 PTAs, respectively—due to methodological issues related to linking the trade data with the tariff line data.

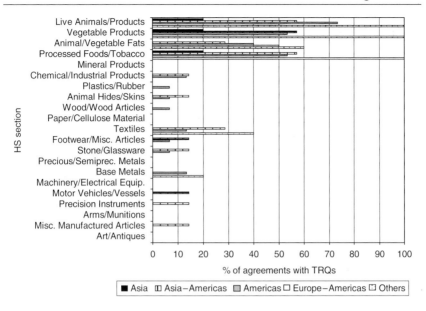

Figure 4.7 TRQ incidence in 34 PTAs, as a percent of regional PTAs by sector
Source: IDB calculations.

Most agreements also contain exceptions in agriculture, whereby they fail to liberalize all products, rather subjecting a handful of products to rules that imply infinite liberalization (such as forever-expanding tariff rate quotas). Some agreements also exclude some key products from PTA negotiations. Overall, exceptions and exclusions are employed in PTAs in nearly all products and so in most regions, with countries of the Americas and the EU's agreements driving much of the action (Fig. 4.8).

Figure 4.9 provides an example of the operation of exceptions in CAFTA. Arrows point to markets where imports are subject to exclusions; arrows with two points denote reciprocal exclusions. Some exceptions involve TRQs, most notably in sugar for the United States, fresh onions and potatoes for Costa Rica, and white corn for El Salvador, Guatemala, Honduras, and Nicaragua. CAFTA also perpetuated existing exceptions to preferential treatment between Central America and the Dominican Republic, as well as within Central America. A single oval denoting Central America as a whole illustrates the exclusions in intra-Central America trade in sugar and coffee, as well as between Central America as a whole and the Dominican Republic (in beer, alcohol, sugar, coffee, tobacco). The Central America-wide

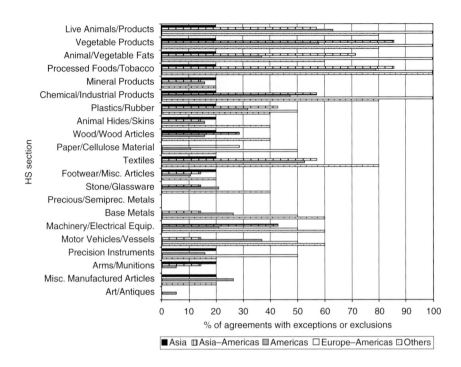

Figure 4.8 Incidence of exceptions and exclusions in 38 PTAs, as a percent of regional PTAs by sector

Source: IDB calculations.

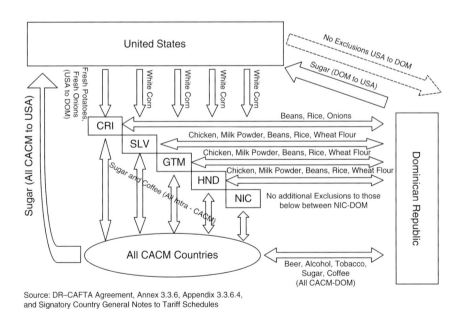

Source: DR–CAFTA Agreement, Annex 3.3.6, Appendix 3.3.6.4, and Signatory Country General Notes to Tariff Schedules

Figure 4.9 Exceptions to tariff liberalization in CAFTA

Source: IDB.

exceptions to tariff elimination are supplemented by country-specific exceptions (such as in chicken, milk powder, beans, rice, wheat flour between Honduras and the Dominican Republic).

Rules of origin can also arbitrate the trade-creating potential of PTAs. Indeed, RoO are widely considered "hidden protectionism", an obscure and opaque trade policy instrument that can work to offset the benefits of tariff liberalization.[4] The economic justification for RoO is to curb trade deflection—to avoid products from non-PTA members being transshipped through a low-tariff PTA partner to a high-tariff one. As such, RoO are an inherent feature of free trade agreements (FTAs) where the member states' external tariffs differ as the members wish to retain their individual tariff policies vis-à-vis the rest of the world (ROW). RoO are also widely used in customs unions (CUs), either as a transitory tool in the process of moving toward a common external tariff (CET), or as a more permanent means of covering product categories where reaching agreement on a CET is difficult, for instance due to large tariff differentials between the member countries. Thus, basically all PTAs contain rules for establishing the origin of goods.

RoO in effect set up walls around PTA members that prevent them from using some inputs in a final product. This can limit the access of member country producers to inputs from the rest of the world, as well as input providers' sales to the PTA region. When rules are more restrictive, the walls are higher, and efficient allocation of resources is even more difficult. Since a failure to meet the RoO disqualifies an exporter from the PTA-conferred preferential treatment, RoO can and must be seen as a central market access instrument reigning over preferential trade. When rules of origin are restrictive and intra-PTA final goods' producers lack access to globally cheapest inputs, their utilization of PTA preferences is dampened.[5]

How restrictive are preferential rules of origin? Estevadeordal (2000) Suominen (2004), and Estevadeordal, Harris, and Suominen (2007) measure the restrictiveness of RoO through two main indices (see Appendix 4.2), finding that EU, Mexican, Chilean, US, and selected Asian agreements

---

[4] Most prominently, RoO can be employed to favor intra-PTA industry linkages over those between the PTA and the rest of the world, and, as such, to indirectly protect PTA-based input producers vis-à-vis their extra-PTA rivals (Krueger 1993; Krishna and Krueger 1995). As such, RoO are akin to a tariff on the intermediate product levied by the country importing the final good (Falvey and Reed 2000; Lloyd 2001).

[5] See Suominen (2004) and Estevadeordal and Suominen (2008).

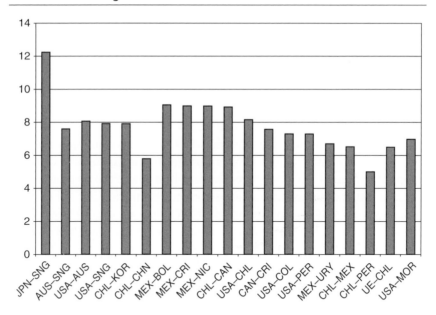

Figure 4.10 Restrictiveness of rules of origin in selected PTAs
Source: Estevadeordal, Harris and Suominen (2007).

sport some of the most restrictive RoO (Fig. 4.10).[6] However, it is also the case that US agreements have become less restrictive over time: NAFTA is more restrictive than the US–Chile PTA of 2004, which is more restrictive than the 2005 CAFTA, which is more restrictive than the US–Peru and US–Colombia PTAs negotiated in 2006 (Box 4.1).[7] Indeed, unlike the straitjacket RoO model that the EU uses in all of its PTAs, agreements in the Americas are marked by a diversity in RoO that suggests not only political economy forces but also accommodation to PTA-specific idiosyncrasies. The regional countries have also employed such measures as short supply clauses to help producers adjust to shocks in the availability of intra-regional inputs.

Table 4.2 catalogues the sectoral restrictiveness of RoO across the PTAs analyzed in tariff liberalization statistics. The data reveal that agricultural products and textiles and apparel are marked by a particularly high

[6] To be sure, real, effective restrictiveness depends on factors beyond the RoO regime text, namely on the input pool and the geographical pool of supplies. The wider these are, the less the effective restrictiveness is likely to be. See Estevadeordal, Harris, and Suominen (2007).
[7] See Suominen (2004), Estevadeordal and Suominen (2006), and Estevadeordal, Harris, and Suominen (2007).

Box 4.1 PTAs EVOLVE: CONSIDER US RoO REGIMES

While RoO regimes may carry hidden protectionism, an examination of their evolution over the past few years in the Americas gives cause for optimism. First, the more recent RoO regimes based on the NAFTA model—namely, the US–Chile free trade agreement and CAFTA—incorporate simpler, more practical, and less restrictive product-specific rules of origin than NAFTA. This evinces a trend toward market-friendly rules of origin in the hemisphere.

Second, the RoO regime of the hemisphere's most remarkable agreement in terms of trade flows, NAFTA, has been under a liberalization process.[8] The Working Group in charge of the rules of origin review process has completed two phases of RoO simplification covering such sectors as alcoholic beverages, petroleum/topped crude, esters of glycerol, pearl jewelry, headphones with microphones, chassis fitted with engines, photocopiers, chemicals, pharmaceuticals, plastics and rubber, motor vehicles and their parts, footwear, copper, various textiles products, cocoa preparations, cranberry juice, ores, slag and ash, leather, cork, feathers, glass and glassware, copper and other metals, televisions and automatic regulating or controlling instruments among other things.

Third, the various regimes designed after NAFTA are fairly similar vis-à-vis each other, in both the types of rules of origin specified and their level of restrictiveness. This can help reduce any potential transaction costs for NAFTA-model adherents that export under preferential terms to two or more NAFTA-model PTAs. NAFTA's review of its rules of origin may engender further compatibilities between regimes, paving the way for diagonal cumulation linking NAFTA-model free trade agreements.

Fourth, the NAFTA model has now been adopted in numerous free trade agreements. The current adherents will thus find it fairly easy to negotiate, adopt, and implement future free trade agreements. Should the FTAA come to carry NAFTA-type rules of origin, the costs of adjusting to its RoO regime would be low for a good part of the hemisphere.

Finally, negotiators of trade agreements based on the NAFTA model have proven willingness to revise existing RoO regimes to make them more flexible, as evinced by the declining restrictiveness of successive US agreements. This demonstrates a commitment to keep PTAs in step with changes in technology and the globalization of production, and potentially also marks a growing role for export interests in setting trade policy.

More generally, the precision of the NAFTA-model rules of origin is superior to the vaguely defined and subjective rules of origin of the past. Precision provides clarity and certainty to traders and customs alike. Because the NAFTA regime is based on the change in tariff classification, it provides a fairer, more transparent, and more easily verifiable RoO model than regimes based on value content, which paradoxically can be hard to meet in countries with low production costs and are difficult to implement in the face of fluctuations in exchange rates and changes in production costs. Precise rules of origin do not need to be restrictive rules of origin; the NAFTA review process may well yield rules of origin that are both precise and flexible.

---

[8] See <http://www.international.gc.ca/trade-agreements-accords-commerciaux/agr-acc/nafta-alena/tech-rect.aspx?lang=en&menu_id=35&menu=>.

Table 4.2 Average restrictiveness of rules of origin, by HS section, selected PTAs

Section	Japan–Singapore	Mexico–Bolivia	USA–Chile	USA–Singapore	Chile–Korea	Australia–Singapore	Chile–Mexico	Chile–China
1. Live Animals	16.0	8.8	8.7	8.6	10.5	7.0	8.4	8.0
2. Vegetable Products	16.0	8.0	8.2	7.9	8.4	7.0	8.0	8.0
3. Fats & Oils	16.0	13.9	13.6	13.6	11.0	7.0	8.1	8.0
4. Food. Beverages & Tobacco	15.6	10.4	9.3	8.5	8.2	7.0	8.5	6.5
5. Mineral Products	14.0	8.6	5.3	5.4	7.5	7.0	8.6	5.7
6. Chemicals	10.3	6.1	3.2	3.1	4.0	7.0	5.0	5.6
7. Plastics	11.0	8.8	6.9	3.6	4.1	7.4	8.7	5.6
8. Leather Goods	15.3	8.8	7.9	7.5	6.9	9.1	9.9	5.0
9. Wood Prod.	14.6	6.7	6.0	6.1	6.1	7.0	7.0	5.9
10. Pulp & Paper	7.7	8.0	8.6	6.2	6.4	7.0	7.6	5.9
11. Textile & App.	4.9	16.0	16.1	16.3	14.9	9.9	3.0	6.0
12. Footwear	13.1	12.3	11.2	9.7	12.0	9.2	12.3	5.5
13. Stone & Glass	12.6	9.8	9.1	9.3	10.0	7.1	10.0	5.3
14. Jewelry	14.0	10.6	9.0	9.0	9.4	7.6	9.4	5.0
15. Base Metals	11.6	9.7	8.4	7.6	8.0	7.1	9.1	5.3
16. Machinery & Electric Equipment	16.0	5.9	6.0	5.9	6.1	7.1	5.8	5.2
17. Transportation Equipment	15.9	7.1	6.0	6.4	4.2	7.6	4.7	5.2
18. Optics	15.8	6.2	4.8	5.3	5.1	7.1	6.4	5.0
19. Arms & Ammunition	6.5	6.3	6.1	6.5	5.6	7.0	6.3	6.0
20. Misc. Merchandise	12.0	6.9	6.5	6.6	6.0	7.2	6.7	5.5
21. Works of Art	16.0	8.0	4.0	5.4	6.0	7.0	8.0	5.0

Source: Estevadeordal, Harris and Suominen (2007).

restrictiveness score in each regime, which is consistent with Estevadeordal (2000), Suominen (2004), and Harris (2007) in that the restrictiveness of RoO is driven by the same political economy variables that arbitrate the level of tariffs particularly in the EU and the United States.[9]

Besides their restrictiveness, the complexity of RoO regimes renders their administration by receiving customs and sending country's origin certification entities an unwieldy process. Figure 4.11 replicates the instructions of the South African Revenue Service's flowchart on "How to Apply Rules of Origin". The administrative costs of RoO stem from the procedures required for ascertaining compliance with the RoO regime. They are essentially book-keeping costs—the paperwork and costs for the exporter of certifying the origin—and the costs incurred by the partner country's customs upon verification of origin. These costs can be considerable even in regimes where the exporter and self-certify origin. Cadot *et al.* (2002) disentangle NAFTA's non-RoO and RoO-related administrative costs, finding the latter to approximate 2 percent of the value of Mexican exports to the US market.

In sum, the exercises here have revealed both similarities and differences across PTAs in tariff-line level commitments:

- The overall set-up of tariff liberalization programs varies notably across agreements. Agreements differ from each other in the number of product groups that are subjected to liberalization, as well as in the final year of liberalization: in some cases all tariffs are eliminated upon the entry into force of the agreement, while in others, tariff provisions are spread over transition periods as long as 20 years.

- PTA members differ in their tariff reductions trajectories. Some parties use a linear trajectory, while others employ a non-linear trajectory that often involves some backloading, with larger reductions left to the latter part of the transition period. In some cases a grace period is provided before the reductions begin.

- Most PTA partners liberalize 90 percent or more of their trade-weighted tariff lines as well as their imports from their PTA partners by the tenth year into the PTA. However, again, there are a number of exceptions, particularly among developing countries: for instance, one PTA party

---

[9] To be sure, the "real" or effective restrictiveness depends on the availability of efficient input supplies in the PTA member countries. After all, if the RoO walls are high yet the PTA zone is very large, the restrictive RoO will pose less of a problem for producers in accessing efficient inputs than when the PTA zone is very small and domestic inputs are hard to come by.

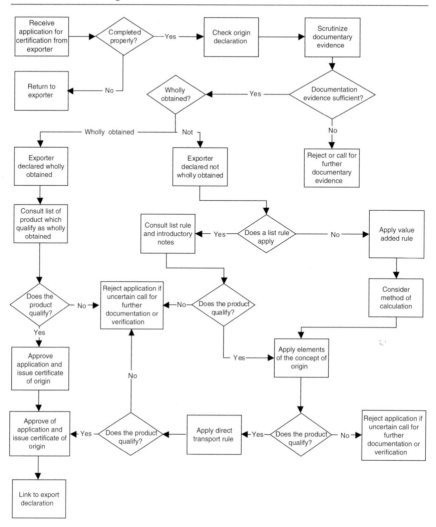

Figure 4.11 Instructions for Certifying the Origin of Goods, South African Revenue Service

Source: South African Revenue Service.

fails to liberalize even 60 percent of its trade-weighted tariff lines by year 10, and three PTA parties free fewer than 80 percent of their imports from their respective partners by year 10. Moreover, the sensitive sectors—particularly agriculture and textiles—lag behind the pace of liberalization in other sectors across nearly all agreements.

- Many PTAs contain rules, such as tariff rate quotas and rules of origin, that arbitrate market access as much as tariffs do. These rules are as heterogeneous across PTAs as tariff liberalization schedules are, and tend to be particularly complex in the most sensitive sectors.

III. Trade-Related Rules in PTAs

Tariff liberalization is but one, albeit a central, part of PTAs. The various other PTA provisions, such as rules governing investment, trade in services, competition policy, and intellectual property rights, all affect the effective access of traders, service providers, and investors in the PTA market. They also work with tariff reductions to arbitrate the ultimate overall economic effects of, and dynamic gains from, trade integration. For instance, services and investment liberalization can compound the gains provided by tariff liberalization. Moreover, many PTA provisions, such as customs procedures trade facilitation, while boosting trade among PTA partners, are inherently good for trade between PTA members and all their trading partners. Competition policy provisions can do the same when helping to transpose non-discrimination principles to national competition policy frameworks.

Here, we supplement the tariff liberalization statistics by providing a comparative description of the *coverage* of 17 investment, 29 services, 24 competition policy, and 15 customs procedure provisions in 61 PTAs.[10]

A stylized visualization of PTAs' coverage of the four disciplines is revealing of the variation (Fig. 4.12). US agreements are clearly the most encompassing across the four disciplines, while Asian agreements and some agreements among South American countries are thinner. The following four sub-sections elaborate on each discipline in turn.

Investment rules are a key component in numerous PTAs. Indeed, one of the key motivations cited particularly for developing countries entering into PTAs was to attract foreign direct investment (FDI) by adopting measures to liberalize investment across economic sectors and to protect investors.

The most important effects on foreign direct investment would likely occur when a PTA eliminates restrictions on foreign capital inflows through national treatment provisions in cases where the host government discriminated against foreign investors in the past, or if the pre-existing

---

[10] For further disciplines and analysis, see e.g. Estevadeordal *et al.* (2008) and Baldwin *et al.* (2007).

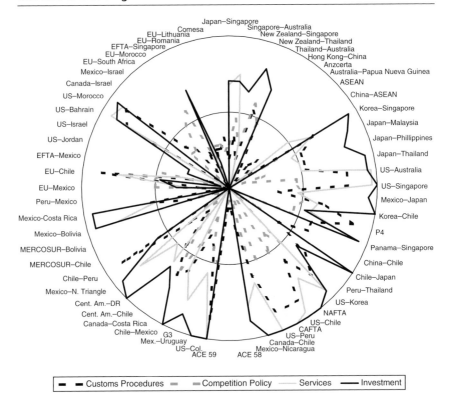

Figure 4.12 Coverage of selected PTA provisions in 60 PTAs
Source: Authors' calculations.

barriers to inward FDI were considerably high. Similarly, a PTA's establishment of dispute settlement provisions could also boost FDI, particularly in North–South schemes when the Northern country is willing and able to enforce investment-encouraging club rules, such as a dispute settlement mechanism (Winters 2000).

FDI inflows could also be increased by the PTA's elimination of requirements on foreign affiliates to satisfy certain export targets, or guaranteeing strong investor property rights that reduce the risk of expropriation (Blomström and Kokko 1997). To be sure, they could be incentivized by preferential tariff treatment. Indeed, there is interaction between tariff liberalization and relaxation of investment rules. For instance, numerous Asian vehicle producers located plants in Mexico post-NAFTA to take advantage of the low production costs and ready preferential access to

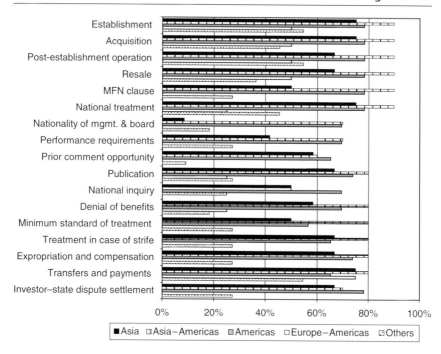

Figure 4.13 Coverage of selected provisions in investment in 60 PTAs in selected regions
Source: Authors' calculations.

the US market. In an econometric study, Estevadeordal, López-Córdova, and Suominen (2006) find that tariff preferences by the United States and reductions in Mexican restrictions on foreign investment were among the key factors propelling FDI to Mexico under NAFTA.

How do PTAs deal with investment? The more recent PTAs' investment chapters in particular tend to be encompassing, extending to such areas as MFN treatment, national treatment, transparency, denial of benefits and restriction of transfers, nationality of management and board of directors, performance requirements, expropriation, and investor–state disputes (Fig. 4.13).[11] All PTAs forged by the three NAFTA members with their respective partners in the Americas are comprehensive,

---

[11] An FTA's investment provisions are coded when there is an investment chapter in a PTA or when the PTA refers to a bilateral investment treaty as the agreement applicable to the PTA. When no such reference is made, a zero value is assigned (even if the PTA partners were connected via a BIT).

applying the four modalities of investment—establishment, acquisition, post-establishment operations, and resale.[12] They cover such disciplines as MFN treatment, national treatment, and dispute settlement, and most also address transparency, denial of benefits and restriction of transfers, nationality of management and board of directors, performance requirements and expropriation.

In Asia, Singapore, New Zealand, and Australia's agreements are more encompassing, covering issues related to sectoral coverage, scope—including establishment (greenfield FDI), mergers and acquisitions, post-establishment operations, and resale—as well as addressing denial of benefits. The region's other agreements are very thin on investment. Inter-regional agreements formed by the countries of the Americas are also less encompassing due to the limited coverage of disciplines in the EU–Mexico and EU–Chile agreements, as well as in the Chile–China FTA, P-4, and US–Jordan FTA.

As for liberalization, which is not quantified here, the NAFTA-inspired agreements have a non-discrimination rule in a number of sectors, and create transparency and predictability through one-shot liberalization across all sectors (Houde *et al.* 2007). They also include a ratchet mechanism that locks in future reforms. In the meantime, the EU's FTAs and Asian agreements preserve greater flexibilities and also liberalize more progressively.

Alongside PTAs' investment rules has developed another body of international commitments in investment, bilateral investment treaties (BITs). At the end of 2006, there were no fewer than 2,559 BITs. These treaties address investment issues comprehensively; in fact, PTAs' investment chapters are often very similar to BITs, and some PTAs refer to a pre-existing BIT among the partners as the set of investment rules applicable to the PTA, as well. However, whereas BITs tend to contribute to negative integration—they tend to preclude certain policies that would discriminate against investment, rather than requiring policies that encourage investment—PTAs are seen as more likely to motivate investment by providing a more predictable policy environment for foreign investors and by adding credibility to government policies (Winters 2000).

Besides cross-border investment, services trade is expanding rapidly around the world. Services are seen as providing a new dimension to world

---

[12] In general terms, NAFTA-inspired agreements forged largely by the NAFTA parties with their further partners place investment issues in the investment chapter, with limited interaction with the services chapter (Houde *et al.* 2007). In EU and many Asian agreements, investment disciplines are divided between the services and the investment chapters.

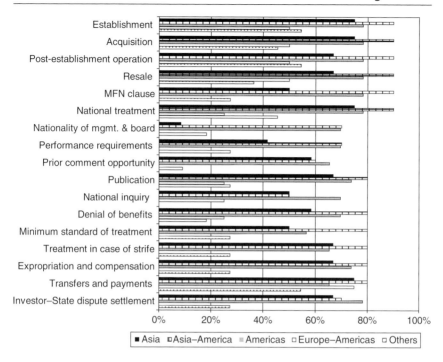

Figure 4.14 Coverage of selected provisions in services in 62 PTAs in selected regions
Source: Authors' calculations.

trade, namely "trade in tasks" that is aided by digitalization and does not require the shipment of physical products.[13] In 2006, commercial services exports alone grew by 11 percent to $2.71 trillion.

Trade negotiators have caught up with these trends. PTAs generally cover a large number of services provisions, particularly most-favored-nation treatment, national treatment, market access, local presence, domestic regulation, recognition of qualifications, transparency, restrictions of transfers, and denial of benefits. Many PTAs also contain (whether in different chapters or in annexes to the services chapters) specific provisions for telecommunications and financial services.

In the Americas, more than 60 percent of PTAs address MFN treatment, national treatment, market access, and unnecessary barriers to trade, and prohibit discriminatory treatment (Fig. 4.14). These areas are generally not addressed in Asian agreements. The exception is the Japan–Singapore

---

[13] See Grossman and Rossi-Hansberg (2006).

135

FTA, which covers national treatment, market access, domestic regulation, recognition of qualifications, transparency, and restriction of transfers, as well as certain provisions on telecommunication and financial services.

EU's agreements with Mexico and Chile differ from each other. The EU–Chile FTA covers national treatment, market access, domestic regulations, recognition of qualifications, transparency and restrictions of transfers, and also contains a thorough regulation of telecommunications and financial services. The EU–Mexico FTA covers only MFN treatment, national treatment, market access, restrictions of transfers, and denial of benefits, while sporting no provisions on telecommunications and covering financial services only rather marginally.

As in investment issues, there is a difference between NAFTA-based agreements and so-called GATS-inspired (per the General Agreement on Trade in Services) EU and Asian models in the form and depth of liberalization. NAFTA is based on a negative-list scheduling modality, whereby everything is liberalized, unless otherwise indicated through lists of reservations. In positive list models, on the other hand, liberalization is effected in sectors that are defined by the agreement.[14] The former approach is viewed as more liberalizing and expeditious for negotiations.

A growing number of PTAs also include competition policy and competition-related provisions. Birdsall and Lawrence (1999) argue that the rationale for including competition policy issues in PTAs is due to domestic incentives to lock in antitrust and other competitive practices, particularly in developing countries. Further explanations might include promotion of stronger competition agencies in developing countries, creating a means for cooperation between the competition agencies of the member countries (especially in "North–South" agreements), as well as to cater to consumer groups—as opposed to only export-oriented producers—when selling a trade agreement domestically (Anderson and Jenny 2005).

The scope of PTAs' competition policy rules tends to be extensive (Anderson and Evenett 2006). The main obligations involve adoption or application of competition laws and closer cooperation among

---

[14] The NAFTA-based agreements are also differently structured. They deal with the different modes of services supply—cross-border supply, consumption abroad, and presence of natural persons (modes 1, 2, and 4, respectively)—in a chapter on cross-border trade in services, while treating disciplines relating to commercial presence, or mode 3, in the chapter on investment. In contrast, the GATS-based model places all modes in the services chapter.

competition authorities of PTA partners. However, competition policy permeates multiple trade disciplines and thus affects policy and business well beyond the core issues of mergers and acquisitions. PTAs carry important competition-related provisions in chapters on services—financial and telecommunication services, in particular—as well as on government procurement, intellectual property rights, and investment.

There is nonetheless notable variation across PTAs in the coverage of services provisions (Fig. 4.15). The EU's FTAs, which draw on the European Communities Treaty of 1958 for competition policy rules, address anti-competitive behaviors ranging from antitrust to abuse of a dominant position, and monopolies, as well as coordination and cooperation issues such as exchange of information. NAFTA, the precursor of the competition policy chapters in NAFTA parties' subsequent agreements, stipulates much more general treatment for the parties to adopt measures to proscribe anti-competitive business practices and take appropriate action with respect to them. NAFTA also exempts competition policy issues from the agreement's dispute settlement provisions. However, it does contain

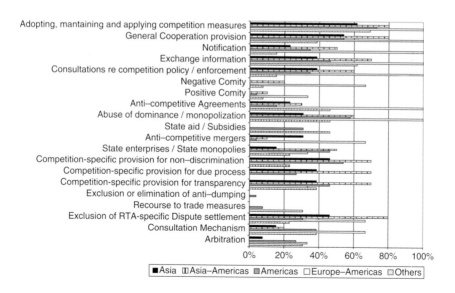

Figure 4.15 Coverage of selected provisions in competition policy in 55 PTAs in selected regions

Source: Authors' calculations.

separate, binding rules for monopolies and state enterprises; Evenett and Anderson (2006) argue that these clauses have facilitated a number of agreements in North America on competition law enforcement.

The Australia–New Zealand Closer Economic Relations Trade Agreement (ANZCERTA) is particularly far-reaching, requiring the parties to amend their national competition laws to ensure their full applicability to anti-competitive conduct or transactions that may affect either country. As a result, courts in both countries are empowered to rule on practices affecting consumers in the other, and there has been stepped-up cooperation between the parties' anti-competition agencies.

Once policy barriers to trade in goods are eradicated, there are a host of issues related to exporting and importing goods that can affect the trade boost from tariff lowering. Tariff liberalization can mean little in the presence of poor customs and high trade costs. This is particularly the case today, as efficiency in processing goods transgressing borders is of increasing importance in light of the expansion of just-in-time production, where the speed of shipping is paramount.[15] According to Hummels (2001), each extra day spent in transit is the equivalent of a 0.5 percent tariff. Inefficient border procedures also are estimated at anywhere between 2 and 15 percent of the total transaction value.[16] The importance of trade facilitation extends beyond procedures to logistics. Moreira (2008) shows that the *ad valorem* tariff faced by Latin American countries in both the intra-regional and US markets pales besides the freight costs of reaching these markets: in Paraguay, for instance, the freight costs are ten times the cost of the tariff barriers faced in foreign markets.[17]

As a reflection of the growing awareness of the importance of transport costs and the complementary relationship between tariff liberalization and trade facilitation, PTA members around the world have adopted comprehensive and specific provisions on customs procedures and trade facilitation. Nearly 60 percent of the PTAs analyzed here include provisions on confidentiality, advance rulings, penalties, review and appeal mechanism, and cooperation in administration, and nearly half provide for technical assistance, transparency, and sharing of information (Fig. 4.16). US agree-

---

[15] Just-in-time is aimed at overcoming market failures in the global economy that stem from disequilibria between the quantity produced and the quantity consumed, and that translate into undue inventory costs on global companies.

[16] Dollar *et al.* (2003) find that firms in countries with a better investment climate, including better logistics, have a higher probability of exporting to international markets and attracting foreign direct investment. Similarly, Subramanian *et al.* (2005) find that long customs clearance times have a significant adverse effect on firms' productivity.

[17] The tariff is here the tariff revenue divided by trade; freight costs as freight charges divided by trade.

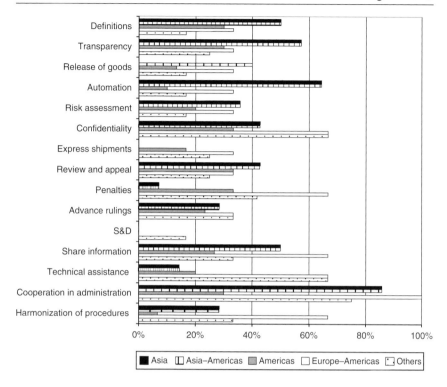

Figure 4.16 Coverage of selected provisions in customs procedures in 48 PTAs in selected regions
Source: Authors' calculations.

ments and the PTA between Brunei, Chile, New Zealand, and Singapore of 2005 (Box 4.2) are particularly comprehensive.

US agreements, as well as EU and many Asian agreements, which are otherwise much thinner on customs procedures, also include clauses on cooperation in the administration of customs, and both EU and US agreements also open up a potential for technical assistance. Indeed, measures going well beyond non-discrimination, such as coordination of policies and enforcement actions, are necessary for the benefits of trade facilitation to be realized (Schiff and Winters 2003). PTAs and other regional cooperation agreements are arguably particularly propitious venues for this. They are, after all, aimed at reducing frictions in members' trade and provide both flexibility and specificity in designing the various rules.[18]

---

[18] Maur (2008) argues that trade facilitation measures in PTAs have not been as effective as hoped.

CAFTA is perhaps a premier example: the agreement contains a specific set of customs procedures in the textile chapter, fashioned in good part to pre-empt transshipment of non-member (such as Asian country) textiles through Central America to the United States.

Box 4.2 CUSTOMS PROCEDURES AND TRADE FACILITATION IN THE TRANS-PACIFIC STRATEGIC ECONOMIC PARTNERSHIP AGREEMENT (SEP)

The Trans-Pacific Strategic Economic Partnership Agreement (SEP) formed by Brunei, Chile, New Zealand, and Singapore has a comprehensive list of provisions regulating customs procedures and trade facilitation between the parties. Some of the key provisions on customs procedures include:

Customs Cooperation (Art. 5.5): The parties' customs administrations are to cooperate on issues pertaining to the implementation of the agreement, movement of goods, investigation and prevention of customs offences, the application of the WTO Customs Valuation Agreement, and the improvement of procedures through such measures as best practices and risk management techniques, technical skills, and technologies.

Advance Rulings (Art. 5.7): The parties are to put forth procedures for advanced rulings on the origin of goods traded between them. The article allows the application for a ruling to be made prior to the importation of a good, and requires the advance ruling to be issued expeditiously (within 60 days of the receipt of the information).

Review and Appeal (Art. 5.8): Importers in each country are to be provided access to independent administrative and judicial reviews.

Paperless Trading/Automation (Art. 5.10): The article strives to increase efficiency of customs procedures through the introduction of modern techniques and new technologies. The parties are also to seek to use electronic procedures that support business transactions.[19]

Express Shipments (Art. 5.11): Parties are to implement procedures aimed at ensuring an efficient clearance of shipments, including pre-arrival processing of information and coverage of all goods in the shipment with a single document (that can be issued electronically).

Risk Management (Art. 5.13): The article refers to customs procedures that facilitate clearance and movement of low-risk goods and focus attention to high-risk goods.

Release of Goods (Art. 5.14): The parties pledged to simplify the release of goods and to release goods at the point of arrival and within a period not exceeding 48 hours. This stands in clear contrast to many other PTAs, which have very few and only general rules governing the release of goods.

---

[19] Notably, the NAFTA countries are developing a concept of trade automation (NATAP) that implies introducing standardized trade data elements, harmonizing customs clearance procedures, and promoting electronic transmission of standard commercial data using UN/EDIFACT MESSAGES and advance processing by governments.

IV. Beyond Rule-Making: Implementing PTAs

Although PTAs are today implemented as a standard operating procedure in many countries, slow and incomplete implementation has long been and still sometimes remains *the* Achilles heel of developing country PTAs in particular. Indeed, analysts and practitioners alike tend to concur that many developing country PTAs have failed to live up to their liberalizing and trade-creating potential, and that one of the key factors behind this performance is slow and incomplete implementation of the common integration commitments.[20] Indeed, while regional integration among developing countries is much more dynamic today than during the era of import substitution industrialization, its actual contribution to members' economic development and global trade remains questionable, in large measure precisely because of concerns about the quality of implementation.[21]

Poor implementation is seen as stemming from various sources, such as domestic political sensitivities and lack of technical capacities in government agencies. Some of the PTAs of the 1960s and 1970s were implemented particularly half-heartedly. While implementation deficits are viewed as being less important today, the fact that modern-day PTAs carry multiple complex issue areas such as rules of origin, sanitary standards, and the environment, implies an expansion in the number of bureaucratic players involved in their implementation process. This, in turn, can render the process hostage to weakest links and multiplies the demands of inter-agency coordination, and broadens the set of actors with an economic and/or political stake in the PTAs' implementation. "Monitoring cascades"—monitoring of multiple bilateral PTAs simultaneously—present challenges that are additional to, and distinct from, those of monitoring intra-regional integration process.

To our knowledge, there are no quantitative, large-sample studies that catalogue the successes and failures of PTA implementation around the world. However, De Lombaerde, Estevadeordal, and Suominen (2008) discuss numerous cases of implementation of developing country integration schemes, such as CACM, ASEAN, and COMESA, as well as in US FTAs and the EU's integration process. They find that the regional and national implementing entities are often viewed as indispensable for the continuity

---

[20] See e.g. World Bank (2005). See Best (2006) for a broader discussion on regional governance.

[21] See e.g. Schiff and Winters (2003).

and deepening of the regional integration process. However, the capacities of these institutions have long been wanting due to poor technical capacities and lack of continuity among implementing staff, especially in national governments. This is something that one-shot capacity building cannot rectify.

However, there are also reasons for optimism. For instance, while the implementation of CACM'c commitments has been sub-optimal over the past four decades, each Central American country has made strides in implementation as a result of the US–Central America–Dominican Republic FTA (DR–CAFTA), which explicitly requires each party to create an implementing unit in their respective ministry of economy. Perhaps paradoxically, then, rather than overburdening the CACM members' implementation processes further, the major extra-regional agreement only facilitated the on-going implementation processes, and created positive externalities for the region's further trade agreements. Good monitoring can also have positive repercussions for trade negotiations. In Mexico, the implementation of prior complex agreements such as NAFTA helped Mexican officials to develop strategies for the negotiation of further agreements.[22]

In general, the learning-by-doing and standardization of implementation processes created by agreements between developed and developing countries may be just the tool for furthering PTA implementation where it is most needed: more may indeed be more. The odds of implementation are improved when the PTA carries a clear, built-in agenda and processes for its administration and implementation, and when it mandates the establishment of implementing entities in each of the member states to interface with each other to see the agreement through. Chapter 7 puts forward policy recommendations for furthering implementation best practices.

V. Conclusion

Today's PTAs are quite strongly liberalizing and comprehensive in the product categories subjected to liberalization. They are also increasingly encompassing in the so-called "behind-the-border" issues from investment to competition policy; from labor issues to dispute settlement; from standards to government procurement and transportation. These provisions can provide for complementarities and synergies, such as those

---

[22] See Suominen (2008a, 2008b).

between tariffs, services, and investment liberalization, that can spur trade well beyond what a simple tariff lowering could. Customs procedures and trade facilitation clauses have proliferated in PTAs, and can facilitate trade not only among the partners, but also with all of their global trading partners. Furthermore, while implementation of agreements is still a challenge, particularly in developing countries, recent evidence seems to indicate that agreements with developed economies may have furthered institutions and processes required for implementation of trade policy commitments—and, subsequently, facilitated the potential for PTAs to live up to their liberalizing potential.

There are marked variations across PTAs in the coverage of trade-related disciplines; yet, the analysis shows that PTAs cluster into distinct "families" by the main world regions—Asia, Europe, and the Americas—and, in particular, by some global trade hubs, such as the United States, EU, and Singapore. It is US agreements formed since NAFTA that are often particularly specific and encompassing, followed by agreements formed by Canada, Mexico, and Chile, respectively, as well as agreements between countries in Asia and the Americas. Thus far, intra-Asian agreements tend to be somewhat less encompassing, precise, and binding than those formed in the Western Hemisphere. However, a closer inspection of the data suggests the exportation of PTA models from one region to the next through trans-continental PTAs, such as exportation of some of the US–Chile FTA's market access provisions in the Chile–Korea FTA; this may suggest some longer-term melding of the Asian agreement models with those of the Americas.

PTAs have furthered liberalization among their members and created a colorful mosaic of trade-related rules around the world. Well implemented, they can have transformative effects on member countries' institutions, policies, and economies. The next chapter surveys some of the potential rewards and risks that PTAs engender both for their members and for the global trading system.

Appendix 4.1 PTAs included in the chapter

Agreements	Product-Level Data					Aggregate Data			
	Tariff Line Lib.	Trade-Weighted Tariff Lib.	Lib. as % of Imports	TRQs	Rules of Origin	Services	Investment	Competition Policy	Customs Proc.
Australia-Singapore	×	×	×	×	×	×	×	×	×
Canada-Costa Rica	×	×	×	×	×	×	×	×	×
Chile-Canada	×	×	×	×	×	×	×	×	×
Chile-China	×	×	×	×	×	×	×	×	×
Chile-Korea	×	×	×	×	×	×	×	×	×
Chile-Peru	×	×	×	×	×	×	×	×	×
EFTA-Mexico	×	×	×	×	×	×	×	×	×
EU-Chile	×	×	×	×	×	×	×	×	×
EU-South Africa	×	×	×	×	×	×	×	×	×
Hong Kong-China	×	×	×	×	×	×	×	×	×
Mexico-Bolivia	×	×	×	×	×	×	×	×	×
Mexico-Costa Rica	×	×	×	×	×	×	×	×	×
Mexico-Nicaragua	×	×	×	×	×	×	×	×	×
Mexico-Uruguay	×	×	×	×	×	×	×	×	×

New Zealand-Singapore	×	×	×	×	×	×	×	×
Panama-Singapore	×	×	×	×	×	×	×	×
USA-Australia	×	×	×	×	×	×	×	×
USA-Chile	×	×	×	×	×	×	×	×
USA-Colombia	×	×	×	×	×	×	×	×
USA-Morocco	×	×	×	×	×	×	×	×
USA-Peru	×	×	×	×	×	×	×	×
USA-Singapore	×	×	×	×	×	×	×	×
Chile-Mexico	×	×	×	×		×	×	×
EU-Morocco	×	×	×	×	×	×	×	×
USA-Jordan	×	×	×	×	×	×	×	×
Australia-Thailand	×	×	×	×	×		×	×
CAFTA-Dominican Republic	×	×	×	×	×		×	×
EU-Lithuania	×	×	×	×	×		×	×
Japan-Mexico	×	×				×	×	×
MERCOSUR -Chile	×	×	×			×	×	×
MERCOSUR –Peru	×	×	×	×		×	×	×

(Continued)

Appendix 4.1 (Continued)

Agreements	Product-Level Data					Aggregate Data			
	Tariff Line Lib.	Trade-Weighted Tariff Lib.	Lib. as % of Imports	TRQs	Rules of Origin	Services	Investment	Competition Policy	Customs Proc.
MERCOSUR-Andean3	×						×	×	×
MERCOSUR-Bolivia	×					×	×	×	×
Mexico-Northern Triangle	×			×		×	×	×	×
NAFTA	×			×		×	×	×	×
P4	×			×		×	×	×	×
Japan-Singapore		×	×	×	×	×	×	×	×
Mexico-Japan			×	×		×	×	×	×
Andean Community									
Argentina-Brazil-Peru									
Argentina-Colombia									
Argentina-Ecuador									
Argentina-Venezuela									
ASEAN						×		×	×

ASEAN-China	×	×	×	×	
ASEAN-Korea		×	×		
Australia-New Zealand	×	×	×	×	
Australia-Papua New Guinea	×	×		×	
BANGKOK					
Brazil-Colombia					
Brazil-Ecuador					
Brazil-Venezuela					
CACM					
CACM-Dominican Republic	×	×	×	×	
CACM-Panama					
Canada-Israel	×	×	×	×	
CARICOM					
Chile-CACM	×	×	×	×	×
Chile-Colombia		×	×		
Chile-Ecuador	×		×	×	
Chile-Japan	×		×	×	

(Continued)

Appendix 4.1 (Continued)

Agreements	Product-Level Data					Aggregate Data			
	Tariff Line Lib.	Trade-Weighted Tariff Lib.	Lib. as % of Imports	TRQs	Rules of Origin	Services	Investment	Competition Policy	Customs Proc.
COMESA						×	×	×	×
ECOWAS									
EFTA-Singapore						×	×	×	×
EU-Egypt								×	×
EU-Mexico						×	×	×	×
EU-Romania						×	×	×	×
G-3						×	×	×	×
GCC									
Japan-Malaysia						×	×	×	×
Japan-Philippines						×	×	×	×
Japan-Thailand						×	×	×	×
Korea-Singapore						×	×	×	×
MERCOSUR									

Mexico-Israel	×	×	×	×
Mexico-Peru	×	×	×	×
New Zealand-Thailand	×	×	×	×
Paneuro				
Paraguay-Colombia				
Paraguay-Ecuador				
Paraguay-Peru				
Paraguay-Venezuela				
Peru-Thailand	×	×	×	×
SADC				
SAFTA				
Thailand-India				
Thailand-New Zealand				
Uruguay-Colombia				
Uruguay-Ecuador				
Uruguay-Peru				
Uruguay-Venezuela				

(Continued)

Appendix 4.1 (Continued)

Agreements	Product-Level Data					Aggregate Data			
	Tariff Line Lib.	Trade-Weighted Tariff Lib.	Lib. as % of Imports	TRQs	Rules of Origin	Services	Investment	Competition Policy	Customs Proc.
USA-Bahrain						×	×	×	×
USA-Israel						×	×	×	×
USA-Korea						×	×	×	×
USA-Oman									
USA-Panama							×		
Total	36	23	27	33	19	62	60	61	61

Methodologies for Measuring Restrictiveness of RoO

Estevadeordal's (2000) observation rule yields a RoO restrictiveness index as follows:

$y = 1$ if $y^* \leq CI$
$y = 2$ if $CI < y^* \leq CS$
$y = 3$ if $CS < y^* \leq CS$ and VC
$y = 4$ if CS and $VC < y^* \leq CH$
$y = 5$ if $CH < y^* \leq CH$ and VC
$y = 6$ if CH and $VC < y^* \leq CC$
$y = 7$ if $CC < y^* \leq CC$ and TECH

where y^* is the potential level of restrictiveness of RoO (rather than the observed level of restrictiveness); CI is the level of restrictiveness imposed by a requirement of a change in tariff classification at the level of tariff item (8–10 HS digits), CS is the level of restrictiveness imposed by a requirement of a change at the level of subheading (6 digits), CH is the level of restrictiveness imposed by a requirement of a change at the level of heading (4 digits), and CC is the level of restrictiveness imposed by a requirement of a change at the level of chapter (2 digits); VC is the level of restrictiveness imposed by a value content criterion; and TECH is the level of restrictiveness imposed by a technical requirement.

Suominen (2004) makes three modifications to the observation rule in the case of RoO for which no CTC is specified in order to allow for coding of such RoO in the Paneuro, SADC, and other regimes in which not all RoO feature a CTC component. First, the level of restrictiveness of RoO based on the import content rule is equated to that imposed by a change in heading requirement (value 4) if the content requirement allows non-originating inputs up to a value of 50 percent of the ex-works price of the product. Value 5 is assigned when the share of permitted non-originating inputs is below 50 percent, as well as when the import content criterion is combined with a technical requirement. Second, RoO featuring an exception alone are assigned a value of 1 if the exception concerns a heading or a number of headings and a value of 2 if the exception concerns a chapter or a number of chapters. Third, RoO based on the wholly obtained criterion are assigned a value of 7.

The restrictiveness index presented in Estevadeordal, Harris, and Suominen (2007) is based on Harris (2004), whereby points are added or subtracted from the restrictiveness score for a particular rule of origin based on different elements used in its definition. The change-in-classification points are based on the magnitude of the required change, as are exception points and addition points (additions are like negative exceptions, in that they permit non-originating inputs that would otherwise be prohibited by the change in classification requirement). Value test points are based on the magnitude of the required value content, with adjustments that depend on the method used for calculating value. The point values were calibrated by observing the relative frequencies of alternative rule combinations in a sample of 13 PTAs in the Americas.

Restrictiveness Points
Change in classification points:

ΔI	+2
ΔS	+4
ΔH	+6
ΔC	+8

where

ΔI represents a required change at the HS item level
ΔS represents a required change at the HS subheading level
ΔH represents a required change at the HS heading level
ΔC represents a required change at the HS item level

Exception points:

exI	+4
> exI and ≤ exS	+5
> exS and ≤ exH	+6
> exH and ≤ exC	+7
> exC	+8

where

exI represents an exception at the HS item level
exS represents an exception at the HS subheading level
exH represents an exception at the HS heading level
exC represents an exception at the HS chapter level

Addition points:

addI	−5
> addI and ≤ addS	−6
> addS and ≤ addH	−7
> addH and < addC	−8
add without CC	+8

where

addI represents an addition at the HS item level
addS represents an addition at the HS subheading level
addH represents an addition at the HS heading level
addC represents an addition at the HS chapter level
add without CC represents an addition without a requirement for a change in classification

Value test points:

> 0% and ≤ 40%	+5
> 40% and ≤ 50%	+6
> 50% and ≤ 60%	+7
> 60%	+8
Net cost	+1

where the percentages represent the value content requirement imposed by the rule

Technical requirement points:	+4
Alternative rule points:	−3
Wholly obtained points:	+16

Part II

What Future for Trade Agreements?

5

Disciplining Trade Agreements: Toward Multilateralization?

I. Introduction

Chapter 4 showed that PTAs often combine tariff liberalization with investment rules, competition policy provisions, services trade liberalization, and rules on customs procedures. As such, not only do they open foreign markets to goods and provide access to cheaper inputs from abroad; they can also improve the quality and lower the costs of services in the partner country markets, facilitate export and import operations throughout the PTA area, and provide enforceable legal protections to traders and investors. In short, PTAs can lower the costs of doing business across borders.

Paradoxically, however, PTAs can also create new risks that contravene globalization. Indeed, there is a wide-ranging, long-standing and contentious debate on whether PTAs are "building blocs" or "stumbling blocs" to multilateral trade liberalization. The "stumbling bloc" camp argues that PTAs are discriminatory instruments that lead to trade diversion, divert attention and sap energy from multilateral trade talks, and potentially even undermine countries' incentives to negotiate and implement multilateral trade rules. Those seeing PTAs as "building blocs" for multilateral liberalization regard them as tools for fueling the liberalizing logic of the multilateral system, as a "WTO+" testing ground for new global trade law, and as preference aggregators at the regional level that can help reduce collective action problems in the mosaic of interests within the multilateral system.

One increasingly important part of this debate concerns the compatibility of PTAs with multilateral trade rules. Chapter 2 showed that today most countries are members of both PTAs and the World Trade Organization

(WTO), and could thus be expected to have a stake in the success of, and compatibilities between, both spheres of integration. However, it is also the case that PTAs carry elements, such as tariff rate quotas and rigid rules of origin, that may create outright new layers of protection in the global trading system, entrench protectionist lobbies, and be in breach of GATT Article XXIV, which sets the conditions for the format of free trade agreements (FTAs) and customs unions (CUs).

And yet, the tools and proposals for dealing with PTAs at the multilateral level have been quite blunt for the greater part of the history of the global trading system. Although the multilateral rules governing PTAs can be seen as too vague and antiquated to managing the proliferating system of PTAs in the interest of global free trade, the WTO membership has been able to make only limited efforts to develop mechanisms to deal, let alone to start dealing, with these arrangements.

One of the reasons for this is political. Many countries have a vested interest in their PTAs and future talks, and in that context, vaguer multilateral rules on PTAs are in many ways seen as better. Changes from the status quo could entail increased scrutiny and stiffer regulations on how countries pursue their trade policy agendas. But another and very important reason is the still rather nascent understanding of the rules and implications of the manifold PTAs criss-crossing the world—and, as such, of what the ideal rules for somehow regulating PTAs might look like.[1]

Encouragingly, however, these questions are receiving growing attention both in the WTO and among trade policy analysts. Recent policy proposals for "multilateralizing" trade agreements have helped move the debate away from the building block–stumbling block seesaw toward ideas on how to enhance compatibilities between PTAs and the multilateral trading system, and on ways in which the system of PTAs could be employed as a pathway to global free trade.

This chapter strives to gauge the extent of compatibilities (divergences) between PTAs and the multilateral trading system, and to develop policy recommendations for furthering (pre-empting) them. The following section looks at the relationship between PTAs and the multilateral trade regime, both in terms of the compatibility of trade rules in these two spheres of integration, and, more broadly, in terms of PTAs' role in altering the incentives of countries to pursue multilateral trade liberalization. Section III discusses policy options for "multilateralizing" PTAs. Section IV concludes.

---

[1] See Schiff and Winters (2003) for a prescient discussion on these issues.

II. Preferential Trade Agreements and the Multilateral Trading System: Friends or Foes?

Are PTAs compatible with the multilateral trading system—multilateral rules established in such agreements as the General Agreement on Tariffs and Trade (GATT) of 1948, the Enabling Clause, General Agreement on Trade in Services (GATS), and other WTO Agreements? This is a hugely important question. After all, incompatibilities between the growing spaghetti bowl of PTAs and the multilateral trading system can create economic distortions and far-reaching negative implications for global trade and production. It is also a huge question, one that has troubled legal experts and economists for decades. And it is a question that is at the heart of the on-going Doha trade round, which has elevated PTAs to a "systemic issue" affecting the entire world trading system.

The multilateral system has started to take steps toward addressing PTAs in a more comprehensive and rigorous fashion. By 1996, the WTO General Council had established the Committee on Regional Trade Agreements, whose main duties are to examine individual PTAs and to consider their systemic, cross-cutting implications for the multilateral trading system. In the Fourth Ministerial of the Doha Round in 2001, WTO members agreed to launch negotiations aimed at clarifying and improving the existing multilateral disciplines and procedures that apply to PTAs. In a further step forward, in December 2006, the members issued a "Transparency Mechanism" that empowers the WTO Secretariat to perform more penetrating and detailed surveys of the contents of PTAs in a way akin to its renowned, country-specific Trade Policy Reviews.[2] While these surveys are to remain "factual" and refrain from value judgments, the increased transparency is particularly hoped to alert the rest of the WTO membership to those rules and practices in a PTA that may have adverse effects on non-members.

Notwithstanding this keen attention to the multilateral–PTA interplay, understanding of the effects of PTAs on the global trading system is still nascent. Five important questions are yet to be conclusively answered:

- Do PTAs comply with GATT Article XXIV?
- Are PTAs WTO+? Do they incorporate a larger number and/or more specific provisions than WTO Agreements do?

[2] See <http://docsonline.wto.org/DDFDocuments/t/WT/L/671.doc>.

159

- Does tariff liberalization in PTAs occur in the context of open regionalism—simultaneous liberalization by PTA partners toward each other and to non-members? Are PTAs ultimately trade-creating or trade-diverting?

- How do PTAs shape countries' incentives for global trade liberalization? Do they encourage countries to pursue multilateral negotiations and liberalize further, or do they divert attention and enthusiasm from multilateralism?

- How should the communication and interplay between multilateral and PTA rules be improved so as to induce compatibilities between them? Should the WTO rules governing PTAs be changed? Should PTA rules be incorporated in multilateral agreements?

The first two questions are legal in nature. The first one centers on GATT Article XXIV (Box 5.1),[3] in particular (1) the extent of product coverage by a PTA; (2) the length of the transition period to the PTA; and (3) PTA instruments that are deemed key arbitrators of market access.

The extent of product coverage and the length of the transition period to the PTA are subject to the Article XXIV stipulation that the elimination of tariffs on "substantially all trade" (SAT) between the PTA parties occur within a "reasonable length of time." Both phrases are ambiguous and a source of numerous interpretations.

Efforts to define "substantially all trade" have followed two main approaches. The first is a quantitative approach geared to a statistical benchmark, such as a percentage of trade between the parties, the most common suggestions being 90, 85, and 80 percent. Whether PTAs meet these thresholds has not been previously submitted to empirical scrutiny. The main problem with this approach is that it would not preclude the exclusion of entire sectors from liberalization. The second approach is more qualitative and stipulates that no sector (or at least no major sector) should be kept from liberalization. This approach is also not without problems. The main disagreement is over the definition of a "sector"; a further question is whether the inclusion of a minor segment of a major sector would satisfy the definition.

Four further approaches have been suggested as possible ways to resolve ambiguities in the calculation of SAT and in defining sectors:

- Defining product coverage in terms of a certain percentage of tariff lines. For instance, Australia has suggested using a threshold of 95 percent of all harmonized system (HS) tariff lines at the six-digit level.

---

[3] See Jackson (1997, 2000), Charnovitz (2002) for background discussion.

Box 5.1 GATT ARTICLE XXIV: TERRITORIAL APPLICATION — FRONTIER
TRAFFIC — CUSTOMS UNIONS AND FREE-TRADE AREAS

---

1. The provisions of this Agreement shall apply to the metropolitan customs territories of the contracting parties and to any other customs territories in respect of
which this Agreement has been accepted under Article XXVI or is being applied
under Article XXXIII or pursuant to the Protocol of Provisional Application. Each
such customs territory shall, exclusively for the purposes of the territorial application of this Agreement, be treated as though it were a contracting party; Provided
that the provisions of this paragraph shall not be construed to create any rights
or obligations as between two or more customs territories in respect of which
this Agreement has been accepted under Article XXVI or is being applied under
Article XXXIII or pursuant to the Protocol of Provisional Application by a single
contracting party.

2. For the purposes of this Agreement a customs territory shall be understood to
mean any territory with respect to which separate tariffs or other regulations of
commerce are maintained for a substantial part of the trade of such territory
with other territories.

3. The provisions of this Agreement shall not be construed to prevent:
   (a) Advantages accorded by any contracting party to adjacent countries in order
   to facilitate frontier traffic;
   (b) Advantages accorded to the trade with the Free Territory of Trieste by countries contiguous to that territory, provided that such advantages are not in
   conflict with the Treaties of Peace arising out of the Second World War.

4. The contracting parties recognize the desirability of increasing freedom of
trade by the development, through voluntary agreements, of closer integration
between the economies of the countries parties to such agreements. They also
recognize that the purpose of a customs union or of a free-trade area should be
to facilitate trade between the constituent territories and not to raise barriers to
the trade of other contracting parties with such territories.

5. Accordingly, the provisions of this Agreement shall not prevent, as between the
territories of contracting parties, the formation of a customs union or of a free-
trade area or the adoption of an interim agreement necessary for the formation
of a customs union or of a free-trade area; Provided that:
   (a) with respect to a customs union, or an interim agreement leading to a formation of a customs union, the duties and other regulations of commerce
   imposed at the institution of any such union or interim agreement in respect
   of trade with contracting parties not parties to such union or agreement shall
   not on the whole be higher or more restrictive than the general incidence
   of the duties and regulations of commerce applicable in the constituent territories prior to the formation of such union or the adoption of such interim
   agreement, as the case may be;
   (b) with respect to a free-trade area, or an interim agreement leading to the formation of a free-trade area, the duties and other regulations of commerce maintained in each of the constituent territories and applicable at the formation of
   such free-trade area or the adoption of such interim agreement to the trade of
   contracting parties not included in such area or not parties to such agreement
   shall not be higher or more restrictive than the corresponding duties and other

regulations of commerce existing in the same constituent territories prior to the formation of the free-trade area, or interim agreement as the case may be; and

(c) any interim agreement referred to in subparagraphs (a) and (b) shall include a plan and schedule for the formation of such a customs union or of such a free-trade area within a reasonable length of time.

6. If, in fulfilling the requirements of subparagraph 5 (a), a contracting party proposes to increase any rate of duty inconsistently with the provisions of Article II, the procedure set forth in Article XXVIII shall apply. In providing for compensatory adjustment, due account shall be taken of the compensation already afforded by the reduction brought about in the corresponding duty of the other constituents of the union.

7. (a) Any contracting party deciding to enter into a customs union or free-trade area, or an interim agreement leading to the formation of such a union or area, shall promptly notify the CONTRACTING PARTIES and shall make available to them such information regarding the proposed union or area as will enable them to make such reports and recommendations to contracting parties as they may deem appropriate.

(b) If, after having studied the plan and schedule included in an interim agreement referred to in paragraph 5 in consultation with the parties to that agreement and taking due account of the information made available in accordance with the provisions of subparagraph (a), the CONTRACTING PARTIES find that such agreement is not likely to result in the formation of a customs union or of a free-trade area within the period contemplated by the parties to the agreement or that such period is not a reasonable one, the CONTRACTING PARTIES shall make recommendations to the parties to the agreement. The parties shall not maintain or put into force, as the case may be, such agreement if they are not prepared to modify it in accordance with these recommendations.

(c) Any substantial change in the plan or schedule referred to in paragraph 5 (c) shall be communicated to the CONTRACTING PARTIES, which may request the contracting parties concerned to consult with them if the change seems likely to jeopardize or delay unduly the formation of the customs union or of the free-trade area.

8. For the purposes of this Agreement:

(a) A customs union shall be understood to mean the substitution of a single customs territory for two or more customs territories, so that

(i) duties and other restrictive regulations of commerce (except, where necessary, those permitted under Articles XI, XII, XIII, XIV, XV and XX) are eliminated with respect to substantially all the trade between the constituent territories of the union or at least with respect to substantially all the trade in products originating in such territories, and,

(ii) subject to the provisions of paragraph 9, substantially the same duties and other regulations of commerce are applied by each of the members of the union to the trade of territories not included in the union;

(b) A free-trade area shall be understood to mean a group of two or more customs territories in which the duties and other restrictive regulations of commerce (except, where necessary, those permitted under Articles XI, XII, XIII, XIV, XV and XX) are eliminated on substantially all the trade between the constituent territories in products originating in such territories.

9. The preferences referred to in paragraph 2 of Article I shall not be affected by the formation of a customs union or of a free-trade area but may be eliminated or adjusted by means of negotiations with contracting parties affected. This procedure of negotiations with affected contracting parties shall, in particular, apply to the elimination of preferences required to conform with the provisions of paragraph 8 (a)(i) and paragraph 8 (b).

10. The CONTRACTING PARTIES may by a two-thirds majority approve proposals which do not fully comply with the requirements of paragraphs 5 to 9 inclusive, provided that such proposals lead to the formation of a customs union or a free-trade area in the sense of this Article.

11. Taking into account the exceptional circumstances arising out of the establishment of India and Pakistan as independent States and recognizing the fact that they have long constituted an economic unit, the contracting parties agree that the provisions of this Agreement shall not prevent the two countries from entering into special arrangements with respect to the trade between them, pending the establishment of their mutual trade relations on a definitive basis.

12. Each contracting party shall take such reasonable measures as may be available to it to ensure observance of the provisions of this Agreement by the regional and local governments and authorities within its territories.

- Defining SAT based on the calculation of the percentage of trade between the PTA parties that is carried out under the PTA's rules of origin.
- A requirement to include all sectors in the agreement.
- Following the approach of footnote 1 of GATS Article V, which precludes an *a priori* exclusion of any sector from an agreement.

The term "reasonable length of time" is also opaque. There are disagreements as to what "reasonable" means, as well as whether the elimination of barriers scheduled for a point beyond reasonable time should be counted toward the fulfillment of the SAT requirement. The multilateral 1994 Understanding on the Interpretation of Article XXIV states that the length of time in question should exceed ten years only in "exceptional cases", yet there is no guidance as to what constitutes an "exceptional case".

How do PTAs measure up to these interpretations? In Chapter 4, we showed that most agreements do attain some of the most common interpretations of SAT and "reasonable length of time"—liberalization of 90 percent of tariff lines and about the same amount of trade by year 10 into an agreement. Moreover, the coverage of products in PTAs tends to become rather homogeneous (uniformly encompassing) by the end of the first decade. However, we also showed that there are also a number of outlier PTA parties (in general developing countries) and product categories (particularly in sensitive sectors—agriculture, textile and apparel, and footwear) that fail to reach the benchmark. In short, when it comes to PTAs' compliance with Article XXIV, the cup seems more full than empty, but not as full as it could be.

Judging PTAs' compliance with the phrase "other restrictive regulations of commerce" on "substantially all trade" is tougher—as is, by implication, determining whether calls to eradicate such regulations are legitimate. A major problem is a lack of agreement as to what constitutes "other restrictive regulations of commerce." There is no clear consensus as to which of the various trade policy instruments should be regarded as such regulations. PTAs carry several disciplines that can impose qualifications on the extent of market access provided by tariff liberalization, such as tariff rate quotas, special safeguards, non-tariff measures, and rules of origin. However, whether these or any other instruments should be subject to the "other restrictive regulations of commerce" phrase is unclear.

To be sure, there may be potential trade-offs between these instruments and the extent of product coverage at the tariff-line level: governments may be more willing to engage in across-the-board liberalization if they know that these instruments are available as defensive measures. However, the distortionary impact can be significant and may grow over time, as many of these potentially protectionist instruments tend to remain in place even after preferential tariffs have been phased out.

Rules of origin is an instrument that some view as particularly fitting the "other restrictive regulation" phrase, as they can effectively insulate entire industries from the PTA's coverage.[4] Justified as tools to avert trade deflection from non-members, RoO can be used for protectionist purposes, and have important implications both for the intra-PTA trade and the trade between the members and the rest of the world (ROW). By tying final goods producers to using intra-PTA sourcing even if it were inefficient, stringent RoO can at the extreme augment intra-PTA final goods producers' production costs to the point where their compliance cost exceeds the benefit of PTA preferences. Indeed, RoO are widely described as a trade policy instrument that can work to offset the benefits of tariff liberaliza-

---

[4] Others argue RoO are not "other regulations", citing clause 8a(i) of Article XXIV as showing that origin is determined *prior* to the operation of the clause. We thank our referee for this observation.

tion.[5] As such, demanding RoO are akin to a tariff on the intermediate product levied by the country importing the final good (Falvey and Reed 2000; Lloyd 2001), and can be used by one PTA member to secure its PTA partners' input markets for the exports of its own intermediate products (Krueger 1993; Krishna and Krueger 1995).[6]

Yet, preferential RoO have thus far escaped multilateral regulation undoubtedly in good part because PTA insiders have few political incentives to subject their RoO to an externally imposed mold, or switch to "looser" rules that could allow free-riding on PTA preferences by third parties. Meanwhile, countries in ROW, against which PTAs are not to raise barriers to trade under paragraph 5 of Article XXIV, have no clear recourse to combat such RoO,[7] and often lack incentives to do so anyway due to themselves being engaged in PTAs with their idiosyncratic rules. The notion of somehow controlling RoO with such negative implications—demanding and complex RoO, in particular—has thus far been largely limited to academic fora.

The definitional issues are part of a bigger problem. Article XXIV has long been criticized as too vague and ambiguous, as allowing countries too much leeway to engage in preferential and discriminatory agreements. To be sure, the designers of the article could not foresee the detail of future PTAs let alone their wildfire-like spread. However, the article's design owes as much to politics. It was the outcome of the 1940s negotiations toward an International Trade Organization (ITO), the GATT's predecessor that never came into being. The article was pushed by the United States, a staunch advocate of multilateralism and non-discrimination, and was in the initial stages to apply to customs unions alone. However, according to Chase (2006), the scope of the article was extended to FTAs to accommodate the imminent US–Canada FTA, which ended up not materializing, either. There may, in other words, be political reasons why the article appears quite inapplicable to the intricacies of today's trade

---

[5] Often negotiated at up to the 8- or 10-digit level of disaggregation, RoO, like the tariff, make a superbly targetable instrument. Demanding RoO can also be employed to favor intra-PTA industry linkages over those between the PTA and the RoW, and, as such, to indirectly protect PTA-based input producers vis-à-vis their extra-PTA rivals (Krueger 1993; Krishna and Krueger 1995). See also Hirsch (2002), Suominen (2004), Estevadeordal and Suominen (2008), Cadot *et al.* (2006).

[6] Furthermore, given that RoO hold the potential for increasing local sourcing, governments can use RoO to encourage investment in sectors that provide high value added and/or jobs (Jensen-Moran 1996; Hirsch 2002).

[7] See Schiff and Winters (2003) for a discussion of the incentives as well as the implications of the vague terminology of GATT Article XXIV.

agreements—and there are reasons why a great many WTO members may prefer it that way.

The second big policy question and one that touches upon virtually all PTA provisions is whether PTAs are WTO+, that is, go beyond multilateral provisions in terms of incorporating a larger number and/or more specific provisions than are implemented at the multilateral level. More generally, the question is whether PTAs are the center of gravity of rulemaking in the global trading system. Is the "real business" of international trade rule-making being done within PTAs, rather than at the multilateral level?

The answer matters. Should PTAs be the engine of trade rulemaking, they could be used as laboratories for the development of new, innovative rules that could be further employed at the multilateral level. Indeed, in such key issue areas as investment and competition policy, further development of multilateral rules has ground to a halt, and the on-going efforts to tackle services and trade facilitation at multilateral level appears more limited than what is being accomplished in the PTA context.

The answer to the question also appears to be largely affirmative. As seen in Chapter 4, PTA rules vary widely across agreements and provisions, but in many instances they do indeed go beyond the multilateral rules. Indeed, the very act of forging a PTA is often motivated by desire to deepen commitments in a bilateral relationship beyond what is already in place globally. The following explores these issues in the areas of investment, services, competition policy, and customs procedures.[8]

INVESTMENT

International investor protection and investment liberalization issues are regulated by a multilayered set of bilateral, regional, sectoral, plurilateral, and multilateral agreements.[9] The main multilateral instruments governing investment issues include the Agreement on Trade-Related Investment

---

[8] In a number of publications, Sally maintains that PTAs are not very WTO+, or even if they go beyond some WTO obligations, the "plus" is not necessarily meaningful. See Sally (2006).

[9] A number of policy proposals have aimed at crafting multilateral principles on investment that would clarify investment rules in the various agreements and instruments, pre-empt the creation of rules that are excessively complex, protectionist, or in other ways sub-optimal, and guarantee the stability of global investment flows. Some of the most prominent attempted coordination devices include the United Nations Code of Conduct on Transnational Corporations created in the late 1970s and 1980s, and a Multilateral Agreement on Investment by the OECD in the late 1990s. Yet, these efforts have not become strongly institutionalized; this is attributed to disagreements over the depth of liberalization, the extent of protection, and, in general, the balance between private and public interests, along with demands by developing countries to address the development dimensions of FDI.

Measures (TRIMs) and the Agreement on Subsidies and Countervailing Measures (ASCM), which limit WTO members' ability to apply certain kinds of measures to attract investment or influence the operations of foreign investors. Also the General Agreement on Trade in Services (GATS), the Agreement on Trade-Related Aspects of Intellectual Property Rights (TRIPs), and the plurilateral Agreement on Government Procurement include provisions pertaining to investments, particularly to the entry and treatment of foreign enterprises and the protection of certain property rights. The Understanding on Rules and Procedures Governing the Settlement of Disputes contains rules for addressing conflicts that arise under these agreements.

TRIMs applies to measures affecting trade in goods. It exhorts the national treatment principles of the GATT, and bars investment measures that lead to quantitative restrictions. TRIMs also requires members to inform each other of any rules that do not conform to it. There are further TRIMs provisions that are viewed as inconsistent with GATT articles, including local content and trade balancing requirements.

As compared to the extensive, in-depth coverage of investment rules in bilateral investment treaties and PTAs, TRIMs is much thinner. The WTO Ministerial Conference in Singapore in 1996 sought to go beyond the current framework and created the Working Group on the Interaction between Trade and Investment to focus on clarifying the scope and definition of transparency, non-discrimination, ways of preparing negotiated commitments, development provisions, exceptions and balance-of-payments safeguards, consultation and dispute settlement pertaining to investment. The plan was to model investment commitments after those in services, particularly by using positive lists rather than negative lists—broad common commitments with selected exceptions.

The subsequent 2001 Doha Declaration aimed at addressing many of the prior grievances that have barred international coordination on investment, such as countries' claims for unilateral rights to regulate investment and development issues affected by investment. However, after a failure at the WTO's Cancun Ministerial in September 2003, the WTO General Council in July 2004 dropped investment along with two other so-called "Singapore Issues", competition policy and transparency in government procurement. The real business and innovation in investment rules continues to be done in the context of BITs and PTAs (Sauvé 2006).

From any one country's perspective, the multilayered approach to investment rules can help signal credibility in the eyes of investors—through commitments to protection, stability, predictability, and transparency.

Yet, at the global level, it has forged a highly complex web of agreements that lacks system-wide coordination. The atomization of international investment rules into different sets of agreements risks the rise of a tangle of non-transparent and divergent rules, which could only be effectively tamed through more comprehensive multilateral provisions.

Further splintering or layering of the global investment rule landscape is not necessarily the trend for the future. PTA and BIT rules could be viewed as potentially conducive to some multilateral consensus for two reasons: there is already a *de facto* harmonization process in place, as most PTAs feature similar main principles, such as non-discrimination; and there are some rather clearly delineated agreements families centered around the US and EU, wherein the differences across agreements are often rather marginal.

SERVICES

GATS has governed multilateral services rules since the Uruguay Round. The agreement contains a number of general obligations applicable to all services, including an MFN rule and a transparency rule; however, in market access, each member defines its own obligations through its own schedule. GATS covers all services except for services provided in the exercise of governmental authority and, in the air transport sector, air traffic rights and all services directly related to the exercise of traffic rights. The commitments of developing countries are in general shallower than those made by the developed countries.

How do PTAs' rules in services interact with GATS? Roy, Marchetti, and Lim (2006) assess 28 PTAs, arguing that PTAs have tended to provide important advances when compared to GATS schedules in three ways:

- PTAs are often very substantive and have helped propel liberalization in sectors that have only thin commitments in GATS, such as financial services, as well as in more traditionally contentious areas such as audiovisual or education services.
- Countries that have used negative-list approaches in PTAs have committed to (i.e. bound) the existing openness for the majority of sectors, a measure that arguably instills predictability in the bilateral relationship and is key to attracting investment and spurring cross-border trade.
- Countries have submitted a high number of sub-sectors to liberalization in the GATS schedules as well as their GATS offers in the Doha Round that they have freed further in PTAs. As such, either the GATS

commitments did not reflect their applied regime or, as is more likely, the improved commitments in PTAs induced actual liberalization and new commercial opportunities.

In particular, NAFTA-inspired agreements feature a much wider schedule of commitments than is made in GATS (Houde *et al.* 2007). Mexico, Morocco, and Singapore make complete commitments with very few reservations in their agreements with the United States in sectors where they have no commitments at the multilateral level. Also the United States, Australia, and Japan have more commitments in their bilateral agreements than in their GATS schedules.

However, there are reservations. The uneven liberalization in services, as in goods, across PTAs as well as at the multilateral level across WTO members can distort services trade. Moreover and paradoxically, a more far-reaching liberalization in PTAs could lower particularly developing countries' incentives to negotiate further at the multilateral level, particularly if the multilateral talks provided for limited reciprocity. Indeed, the way in which developed countries have induced developing countries to open services sectors is by offering, through PTAs, preferential treatment in trade in goods as a *quid pro quo*. The issue-linkage is not as easy to make at the global level.

The Doha Round services negotiations have also proven less far-reaching and ambitious than many developed countries in particular would hope. Industrial countries are looking for developing-country commitments to reform "infrastructure services", such as banking, insurance, telecommunications, and air transport, while developing countries expect new opportunities to provide labor-intensive services, such as health care, construction, and basic information technology services (Schott 2007). However, the concerns that PTAs might divert countries from multilateralism in services issues appears only to accentuate the need to strive for similar depth of commitment at the multilateral level as is awarded in the context of PTAs.

COMPETITION POLICY

The GATT and WTO Agreements do not contain a stand-alone set of competition policy rules. However, there are a number of multilateral provisions that do address competition policy issues (Anderson and Evenett 2006). For instance, GATT Articles VIII and IX on monopolies and exclusive suppliers, and anti-competitive practices restricting trade in services, respectively, as well as the Agreements on Safeguards, bar the signatories from endorsing or encouraging non-governmental measures akin to voluntary export restraints, orderly marketing arrangements, or other governmental arrangements.

The Agreement on Trade-Related Aspects of Intellectual Property Rights (TRIPs) empowers signatories to act against anti-competitive practices in the licensing of intellectual property rights. In the meantime, the United Nations 1980 Set of Multilaterally Agreed Equitable Principles and Rules for the Control of Restrictive Business Practices, while voluntary and of limited practical relevance, iterates the importance of complementing tariff and non-tariff liberalization with non-restrictive business practices.

Attempts to fashion a more comprehensive multilateral framework of competition policy provisions have thus far been unsuccessful. The WTO Ministerial Conference in Singapore in 1996 created the Working Group on the Interaction between Trade and Competition Policy to study the issue; the Doha Ministerial Declaration of 2001 sharpened the Group's focus on clarifying core principles, including transparency, non-discrimination and procedural fairness, provisions on cartels, modalities for voluntary cooperation, and capacity building to support the fostering of competition policy institutions in developing countries. However, in July 2004, the WTO General Council dropped competition policy from the negotiation agenda. Some of the cited reasons included a rejection of the proposed negotiation framework by developing countries as excessively intrusive and a perceived lack of capacity to negotiate this area.[10]

As is the case in investment, the deepest and most comprehensive set of competition policy rules appear to have been forged in the context of PTAs. Perhaps encouragingly for potential future multilateral talks, there are broad similarities between the two most dominant competition policy models in PTAs—those of EU and US PTAs, respectively (Baldwin *et al.* 2007). Moreover, PTA provisions on competition policy have tended to have solid non-discrimination clauses that "multilateralize" the PTA obligations to non-members. For instance, a US firm in Turkey has the same rights before the Turkish competition authorities as an EU firm as a result of the fact that the EU–Turkey agreement gave rise to Turkey's competition policy framework. In other words, in some instances PTAs have helped open up an area where prior national rules, if in place to begin with, may have been too stringent. It is in countries without explicit competition policy rules where nationality concerns, rather than non-discrimination, may arbitrate access.

---

[10] See Anderson and Jenny (2005).

CUSTOMS PROCEDURES

PTAs' customs procedures and trade facilitation provisions are in general compatible with three main international instruments in these areas—the Arusha Declaration and the UN/EDIFACT Initiative that address the use of technology and data processing issues, the World Customs Organization's Revised Kyoto Convention, which addresses such areas as review and appeal, customs clearance, and uses of new technologies, and GATT/WTO trade facilitation provisions, Article V (Freedom of Transit), Article VIII (Fees and Formalities connected with Importation and Exportation), and Article X (Publication and Administration of Trade Regulations). Indeed, trade facilitation and customs procedure measures in PTAs seem to have paralleled the development of international instruments: for instance, PTAs that entered into force after the year 2000 tend to include such provisions as the release of goods, automation, risk assessment, or express shipments—issues also included in the 1999 Revised Kyoto Convention.

The Doha Round negotiations on trade facilitation are relatively narrow in scope, aimed at clarifying and improving GATT Articles V, VIII, and X. The negotiations also contemplate technical assistance and capacity building for developing countries to implement the future commitments. Some private sector observers think that limiting the scope of trade facilitation within the scope of these articles alone can be dangerous, as it might divert attention away from the manifold pressing challenges surrounding the movement of goods.

In contrast, the encompassing scope of the most recent PTAs is in general viewed as positive. As seen in Chapter 4, PTAs' customs procedures and trade facilitation chapters, particularly in US and trans-Pacific agreements, are often highly encompassing and precise. Including customs procedure and trade facilitation disciplines in PTAs can add value in three further ways to dealing with these issues at the multilateral level. First, unlike the World Customs Organization (WCO) provisions, PTA provisions are binding and enforceable via PTAs' dispute settlement mechanisms. Second, given that customs procedure and trade facilitation disciplines are relatively similar across PTAs, PTAs can facilitate and accelerate convergence in these disciplines around the world. Third, to the extent that PTAs streamline customs procedures and facilitate trade, they are inherently good for the multilateral trading system: the resulting lowered trade costs boost trade with *all* of a country's trade partners.

In sum, the relationship between PTAs and GATT/WTO provisions is immensely complex. Overall, most PTAs can be viewed as meeting some of the most common interpretations of Article XXIV. Many of PTAs' key trade-related disciplines, and particularly those of US agreements, often go beyond the multilateral commitments in such areas as services, investment, customs procedures, and competition policy. That PTAs carry deeper commitments than are in effect at the multilateral level in part explains the very appetite for PTAs: they are *the* avenue for greater liberalization, clearer and more elaborate regulations, and stronger protections than can be attained at the multilateral level, at least in the short run. It also reflects the relative ease of finding common ground in the bi- and plurilateral context as opposed to the multilateral talks.

However, some PTA partners offer only limited tariff liberalization in certain sensitive sectors, and/or lower tariffs only very gradually. PTAs also carry various disciplines that open opportunities for protectionist interest to exert themselves, such as rules of origin and tariff rate quotas, both of which can effectively insulate entire sectors from tariff liberalization. And in the longer run, PTAs are suspected of disincentivizing countries from investing resources in multilateral negotiations. Only rigorous economic analyses, which we review next, can help uncover such potential problems.

The Economic Debate: PTAs and Global Trade

Paragraph 5 of Article XXIV was intended to counteract the rise of discriminatory arrangements in global commerce, stipulating that CUs and FTAs do not increase barriers vis-à-vis non-members beyond those in place prior to their formation. Has the article achieved its mission? Are PTAs formed in the spirit of open regionalism—simultaneous freeing of PTA and multilateral tariffs—and are they trade-creating rather than trade-diverting? Are they building or stumbling "blocs" to global trade liberalization?

The 1990s was an era of open regionalism in many countries, with MFN liberalization proceeding in lock-step with PTA liberalization. Latin America exemplified this. During the decade following the late 1980s external *advalorem* tariffs were brought down three-fold to single digits from well above 30 percent in the largest countries in the region (IADB 2002). The simultaneous lowering of PTA and applied MFN tariffs implied that preferential margins remained rather unchanged during the period (IADB 2002).

What is clear is that PTAs do continue to provide a preferential edge, and a substantial one in many of the main emerging markets. Figure 5.1 takes a snapshot of the applied MFN tariff profiles of Argentina, Brazil, Canada, Chile, China, EU, India, Japan, Mexico, and the United States in 2007, as

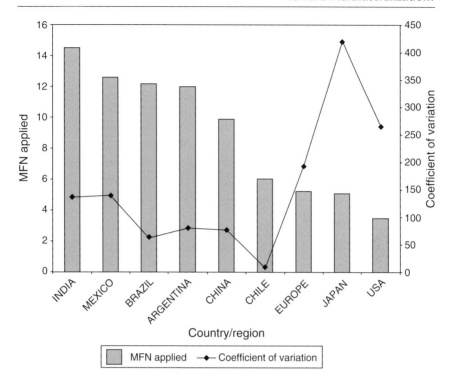

Figure 5.1 Applied MFN tariffs in selected major economies, 2007
Source: World Trade Organization.

well as the coefficient of variation in tariffs, or standard deviation of tariff line duty rates divided by the simple tariff line level average of all duty rates. Simple averages for US and EU tariffs are 3.5 percent and 5.2 percent, respectively, while the figure is 9.9 percent for China, 14.5 percent for India, 12.6 percent for Mexico, 12 percent for Argentina, 12.2 percent for Brazil, and a flat 6 percent for Chile. The coeffient of variation is more marked at up to 421 in Japan and 266 in the United States, although only 8 in Chile. There are extreme outliers, particularly in Mexico (meat, cereals, and tobacco), and India (coffee and tea, animal and vegetable oils, and alcoholic beverages).[11]

Whether PTA signatories feature less or more tariff discrimination than in the late 1990s requires a much more detailed analysis than performed

---

[11] It should be noted that non *advalorem* tariffs are not included in the averages (i.e., calculations do not include *advalorem* equivalents). Since non *advalorem* tariffs are generally more highly protective, the actual level of protection applied by the US and Canada would be slightly higher. Mexico, the EU, and Japan also apply non *advalorem* tariffs to some degree.

here. It is the case that at least in Latin America, the advance of PTA liberalization has been accompanied by a more modest liberalization of external tariffs in the past few years than was the case in the 1990s. However, it is also the case that multilateral tariffs have been lowered around the world following the 1994 conclusion of the Uruguay Round. Moreover, the formation of new PTAs around the world has provided a greater number of countries with preferential access to any one PTA partner's market, thus reducing the preferential edge of the older partners.

Besides PTA members' external tariffs, PTAs contain other, non-tariff instruments that are potentially discriminatory vis-à-vis the rest of the world. One is rules of origin. RoO are used to curb trade deflection—to prevent products from non-PTA members being transshipped through a low-tariff PTA partner to a high-tariff one, and, as such, to preclude outsiders to a PTA from free-riding on the preferential market access granted to the insiders. Sufficiently restrictive RoO can pre-empt such free-riding altogether. This, as discussed earlier, can curb PTA insiders' access to more efficient intermediate goods from the rest of the world, providing incentives for sourcing from within the PTA area. And it can also encourage outsiders to invest in the PTA market so as to meet the RoO's requirements even if the PTA market was not the most efficient venue for production, and export from one PTA member to another under PTA preferences. This happened in the case of NAFTA, where Japanese automakers invested in Mexico in order to use the country for producing and exporting cars to the US market. In general, RoO can provide policy-induced incentives that result in economically sub-optimal outcomes, including discrimination.

Also tariff rate quotas (TRQs) can impart discriminatory effects. TRQs in PTAs are usually additional to TRQ entitlements under the WTO Agreement on Agriculture, and thus do not affect the PTA parties' existing entitlements.[12] The expansion of the quota of one supplying PTA partner will put downward pressure on prices in quota-controlled markets where the Agreement on Agriculture allocates quotas to several supplying countries. This, in turn, can cause some erosion in the quota rents available to all quota-holders, while only the PTA partner is compensated by increased market access. Given the possible negative impact on other quota-holders, it is not clear

---

[12] The Appellate Body in the dispute *Turkey–Restrictions on Imports of Textile and Clothing Products* found that a dispensation could be available in cases where it could be shown that the proposed measure is essential to the formation of the PTA, but did not set the criteria by which this condition could be fulfilled in practice.

that TRQs in PTAs are consistent with the WTO rules on quotas. It is also unclear whether Article XXIV provides a dispensation from those rules—or from GATT Article I, which establishes disciplines on general most-favored-nation treatment and on preferential margins in arrangements that are mentioned in the article.

Academic literature remains divided as to whether PTAs are ultimately trade-creating or trade–diverting, and whether they serve as a stepping stone or a stumbling block to global free trade. There have been a great many approaches to answering this question since Viner's (1950) analysis of the welfare effects of PTAs.[13] Viner went against the existing notion that any form of trade liberalization should be good. Focusing on customs unions, he argued that CUs can be trade-creating or trade-diverting, and the latter can actually undermine both members' and global welfare. A trade-creating CU follows a shift in the location of production from a higher-cost CU member to a lower-cost one; a trade-diverting CU results from a shift from a lower-cost member to a higher-cost one. Analysts such as Meade (1955), Lipsey (1960), Johnson (1965), Mundell (1964), and Corden (1972) built on Viner's theory;[14] Kemp and Wan (1976) break new ground by showing that a CU could always be devised in such a way as to leave non-member countries' welfare unchanged, while boosting the welfare of at least one of the member countries (and leaving all other members unharmed). As such, a CU could always be Pareto-improving as compared to the initial uniform tariff situation of each member country.

---

[13] Richardson (1994) and Panagariya and Findlay (1996) extend the political economy analysis of PTA formation to look at the welfare implications of endogenously determined PTAs. See e.g. Baldwin (2008), World Bank (2000), and Winters (1996) for literature surveys.

[14] Meade puts forth a full-scale general equilibrium analysis of the impact of PTAs on world welfare. The study demonstrates how the welfare effects of trade diversion and trade creation, when jointly present, can lead to either welfare improvement or reduction depending on a number of factors, such as the initial levels of tariffs on the goods subject to trade creation and trade diversion. Lipsey, meanwhile, uses a three-country, two-good general equilibrium model to show that once a CU is formed, the increase in consumption resulting from the reduction in price of the imported good by a union member can more than outweigh the trade diversion effects—the loss from switching imports from a lower-cost third country to a higher-cost CU partner. As such, Lipsey refutes Viner's conclusion that a trade-diverting union is automatically harmful to its members. Johnson, meanwhile, presents a partial-equilibrium analysis, maintaining that both production and consumption effects, as analyzed by Viner and Lipsey, respectively, are to be incorporated in the definition of trade creation and trade diversion. He argues that trade creation implies two types of economic gains: savings on the real costs of goods previously produced domestically and now imported from a partner country, and the gains in consumer surplus resulting from the "substitution of lower-cost for higher-cost means of satisfying wants". According to Johnson, the welfare- and trade-increasing consumption effect arising in Lipsey's model is to be categorized as trade creation, as well.

The Vinerian model is static and thus somewhat limited for examining PTAs' longer-run effects. As a result, analysts have increasingly turned to capturing PTAs' effects through a dynamic time-path analysis. This line of studies was in part triggered by the US inability to launch another multilateral trading round in 1982, and its subsequent move toward PTAs as an alternative mechanism for achieving global trade liberalization. The dynamic path analysis can significantly alter the results and policy implications derived from static analyses. For example, while a CU might be rejected as trade-diverting on static grounds, it could over time lead to multilateral free trade, should it, for example, gradually expand to incorporate new members (Deardorff and Stern 1994), Krugman (1993) argues that the best outcome for world welfare is either few or many PTAs; three blocs divide the global trading system up and represent the worst outcome for world trade and welfare.

A particularly prominent vein of dynamic analyses starts from the political economy incentives in the member states for moving from PTAs to global free trade. Bhagwati (1993) argues that the reduced protection between PTA members will be accompanied by increased protection vis-à-vis outsiders, with PTAs becoming stumbling blocks on the way to multilateral liberalization. Similarly, Krishna (1998) argues that trade-diverting PTAs are in the first place more likely to be supported by member countries, as such PTAs create rents for member countries' producers. As the rents would be lost if the preferences were eliminated, these producers have incentives to oppose multilateral liberalization. Multilateral opening may thus be rendered unfeasible by the establishment of a PTA.

Krueger (1995) develops a similar argument: protectionist lobbies strive to secure captive markets through strict rules of origin, and are subsequently unwilling to relinquish such benefits. She also hypothesizes that PTAs that came to incorporate new members would not become any more disposed toward multilateralism: exporters would likely grow increasingly

---

Besides trade creation and diversion, a PTA's welfare effects also hinge on the changes in the terms of trade between the PTA members and between the PTA and the rest of the world (ROW). Mundell analyzes the terms of trade effects in a systematic manner, showing that when substitutability of consumption is assumed, a discriminatory tariff reduction by a CU member improves the terms of trade of its partner country both vis-à-vis the tariff-reducing country and ROW. However, the terms of trade of the tariff-reducing country vis-à-vis ROW remains ambiguous. Mundell is also among the first to conclude that the higher the initial tariffs of a partner country in an FTA area, the greater the gains to a country from joining the FTA.

For his part, W. Max Corden (1972) explores the effect of the presence of scale economies in a PTA on welfare. He shows that due to trade diversion, the presence of economies of scale does not lead to a greater likelihood that PTAs would be welfare-improving than under constant or increasing costs to scale. Corden also maintains that prospective CU members would be better off liberalizing unilaterally on a non-discriminatory basis than taking the PTA route.

reluctant to invest in lobbying for multilateral liberalization because each new PTA entrant would reduce the marginal benefit of negotiating a multilateral accord (Krueger 1995).[15]

Some authors have gone further, suggesting that PTAs may actually result in higher protection vis-à-vis non-members. Panagariya and Findlay (1996) argue that an FTA makes lobbying against liberalization with third countries cheaper by reducing the incentives to lobby against the partners. Winters (1994) argues that the creation of the EC may have increased world protectionism relative to what it would otherwise have been.[16]

---

[15] There is a substantial body of literature on whether CUs are superior to FTAs as agents of global trade. Sinclair and Vines (1994) see CUs as more likely than FTAs to erode support for global free trade because FTAs offer an incentive for each member country to keep reducing its external tariffs. Similarly, Richardson (1994) also finds FTAs are superior to CUs when the government weighs consumer welfare against the profits of protected industries. The FTA member with a comparative disadvantage in a given good will witness a decline in the political influence of the industry producing the good as a result of the competition within the FTA, which reduces the industry's economic size. The country host to the inefficient industry will thus be able to reduce protection to the industry in a manner that would not be possible were the country bound by the CET of the CU. Also Bagwell and Staiger (1993) see FTAs as more conducive than CUs to global free trade by showing how incentives to liberalize under a CU may wane over time. While plurilateral tariff liberalization is self-enforcing in the early stages of a CU due to members' fear of retaliation by other blocs, the CU's incentives for cutting tariffs decline when the bloc becomes complete and capable of exercising market power. Moreover, if the CU is self-sufficient, it may be less deterred by the prospect of a global trade war, and thus more likely to cheat against third parties. In the case of an FTA, members do not set a CET and are thus unable to exercise such market power as granted by the CU.

The many negative views on CUs notwithstanding, some scholars argue that such arrangements are not inherently disposed against multilateral free trade. For example, Bond, Syropoulos, and Winters (2001) show that the deepening of integration among members of a CU may alter the bargaining relationships in the CU in a manner that could enlarge the possible set of tariff-reducing agreements with non-members. Lawrence (1996) also appears optimistic, arguing that although special interests may effectively capture decision-making processes in a large CU member country, thus thwarting the entire union's prospects for liberalization vis-à-vis ROW, larger CUs can be expected to include countervailing groups that dilute the power of special interests. However, much like Bagwell and Staiger (1993), Bond and Syropoulos (1999) maintain that agreeing on inter-bloc opening grows increasingly difficult with increases in the CU's size and thus its monopoly power.

[16] There are further approaches. Departing from the focus on firms and sectoral lobbies, Levy (1997), drawing on Mayer (1984), uses a model based on the median voter to understand the prospects for global free trade. He finds that in a Heckscher-Ohlin model (of constant returns to scale), voters would never supplant bilateral PTAs for multilateralism, whereas under increased economies of scale they well might. This is because the presence of differentiated product-settings permits trade agreements that would have been politically impossible in the Heckscher-Ohlin scenario and produces gains through greater product variety and price shifts. Thus, "undermining" (multilateral agreements becoming politically unviable) is more likely to occur in bilateral agreements between countries with similar capital/labor ratios and indifferent median voters. McLaren (2002) also explores factors of production, finding that an anticipated trading bloc reduces the members' *ex post* gains from multilateral free trade by inducing its members to specialize toward each other; as a result, regional initiatives may reduce countries' incentives to liberalize multilaterally.

These are rather pessimistic findings. However, the building block camp is equally large if not larger. There are a number of different approaches. Baldwin's (1993) domino theory sees PTAs as ever-expanding and resulting in global free trade. The formation of a PTA or the deepening of integration in an existing PTA is expected to be detrimental to the profits and market shares of firms based in a non-member country. As a result, the non-member country's firms mobilize to compel their government to seek entry to the PTA.

Freund (2000) argues that when any two countries can form a bilateral free trade agreement, any one country is always better off forming a bilateral trade agreement with every other country: without bilateral agreements, countries are better off maintaining a positive tariff, but with bilateral agreements, they are worse off with tariffs than they would be with free trade. This suggests that each new preferential free trade agreement may be a step towards multilateral free trade. Bergsten (1995) arrives at similar results, arguing that PTAs serve to accelerate global opening and enhance world welfare due to producing "competitive liberalization", whereby each member seeks to dismantle trade barriers more rapidly than the others in order to get ahead in the race for international investment.

Kahler (1995) also sees the multilateral and PTA spheres as complementary, arguing that PTAs help streamline the complex global talks by producing larger negotiating units. Once blocs are formed, they may be able to negotiate with a single voice at the global level. Meanwhile, at the regional level, a PTA allows members to focus on issues that are particularly pertinent to their common endeavor, yet possibly more difficult to undertake in the WTO framework, such as macroeconomic coordination and intellectual property rights. Bergsten (2001) and Lamy (2002) take a similar line, arguing that PTAs promote best practices around the world and can thus improve multilateral outcomes.[17] Maggi (1996) takes a different tack, arguing that small countries in particular have an interest in moving from PTAs to multilateralism because the multilateral trading system gives them fairer dispute settlement tools against larger countries.

There can also be purely domestic interests propelling countries from PTAs toward multilateralism. Richardson (1994) shows that PTA member governments may lower external tariffs to lessen the negative impact on tariff revenue caused by the shift of imports from outsiders to PTA part-

---

[17] Bagwell and Staiger (1999) show, in turn, that FTAs are incompatible with the efficiency of GATT's negotiating rules.

ners. Wei and Frankel (1995) engage the median voter, arguing that PTAs may well build political momentum for global opening by mobilizing previously latent support. Under a PTA, more firms will discover their export potential, allowing politicians to build as well as to obtain majority support for previously untenable multilateral opening. Ornelas (2005) shows that whereas political motivations may induce a government to obstruct a welfare-improving multilateral trade agreement, PTA membership can reduce the importance of special interests in shaping trade policy decisions, so that PTA member governments become less inclined to block global free trade.[18]

For many authors such as van der Mensbrugghe *et al.* (2005) and Schott (2004), a large part of PTAs' effects on global trade liberalization depends on the exact characteristics of these agreements. Aghion, Antràs, and Helpman (2006) arrive at two equilibria: one in which global free trade is attained only when preferential trade agreements are permitted to form (a "building bloc" effect), and another in which global free trade is attained only when preferential trade agreements are forbidden (a "stumbling bloc" effect). To be sure, while seeing PTAs as the second-best option to multilateral free trade, most analysts view them as superior to not liberalizing at all. Winters (1997) models PTA's welfare impact on the rest of the world, arguing that it depends on the ROW imports from the PTA and its terms of trade: increasing imports from the PTA are good for the ROW's welfare, while decreasing imports from the PTA are welfare worsening for the ROW. Bond, Syropoulos, and Winters (2001) show that the deepening of integration among the members of a customs union may alter the bargaining relationships between the members in a manner that could enlarge the possible set of tariff-reducing agreements with non-members.

The analysis of PTAs' effects was for long undertaken at a purely theoretical level. The few empirical attempts were generally case studies rather than generalizable analyses with numerous PTAs. However, analysts have made important strides in the past decade toward increasingly sophisticated empirical analyses. Frankel, Stein, and Wei (1997) analyze trade estimates for the EC, MERCOSUR, the Association of Southeast Asian Nations (ASEAN), and East Asia, reaching a tentative conclusion that

---

[18] There are countless further studies. For instance, Bagwell and Staiger (1999) argue that terms of trade changes constitute an extra force toward lower external tariffs. Cadot *et al.* (1999) find that, in the formation of a bilateral PTA, one member will necessarily reduce its external tariffs.

regionalism has over the past decades been "politically consistent with more general liberalization, in the sense that members of trade blocs have tended to increase their trade with nonmembers as they intensify their trade (even more) with each other" (p. 209). Soloaga and Winters (1999) find that except for Latin America, PTAs in the 1990s did not boost intra-bloc trade significantly, but also that there is evidence of trade diversion only for the European Union and the European Free Trade Association. The World Bank (2004) unsurprisingly finds that PTAs that feature high external barriers are trade-diverting, while PTAs where members have reduced external barriers are trade-creating. Adams *et al.* (2003) estimate that 12 of 16 trade agreements, including the EU, ASEAN, and NAFTA have diverted more trade than they have created among members. However, in one of the latest and most rigorous estimates, DeRosa (2007) shows that some of the world's major PTAs, such as EU, NAFTA, ASEAN, MERCOSUR and EFTA, are trade-creating both among members and between members and non-members. However, there is trade diversion against non-members in agriculture, an unsurprising finding in light of the pervasive barriers in the sector around the world.

While most empirical studies still operationalize PTAs as a simple dummy variable, studies engaging tariff concessions are gradually emerging. Limão (2006) finds that the United States and the EU have limited their multilateral tariff liberalization in goods traded with PTA partners. Limão and Olarreaga (2006) make a similar finding in the case of import subsidies afforded to PTA partners by the United States, EU, and Japan. However, Estevadeordal and Robertson (2004) and Estevadeordal, Freund, and Ornelas (2005), operationalizing tariff liberalization in a number of Western Hemisphere PTAs, find that PTAs in the region have not only been conducive to intra-regional trade, but also helped further multilateral liberalization. The greater the tariff preference that a country gives to its PTA partners in a given product, the more the it tends to reduce its MFN tariff in that product. The authors conclude that PTAs can further open regionalism and set in motion a dynamic that attenuates their potential trade-diversionary effects.

A handful of studies have sought to go beyond tariffs. Suominen (2004) and Estevadeordal and Suominen (2008) find that while PTAs help create trade, restrictive rules of origin embedded in them dampen their trade-creating potential. However, various general RoO provisions that can facilitate trade, such as a *de minimis* principle or diagonal cumulation, which expand the pool of inputs available to intra-PTA producers, alleviate the negative effects of restrictive RoO. Meanwhile, restrictive RoO in final goods encourage trade in intermediate goods, and can thus entail trade diversion in inputs. These various different and even countervailing effects of just one PTA discipline illustrate the immense complexities of PTA rules—and highlight the need for a more nuanced analysis of their effects. Mattoo and Fink (2002) analyze PTAs' effects on services trade, finding that if PTAs enable domestic service suppliers to become more efficient and prepare them for global competition, they may create an impetus for global liberalization.[19]

III. Toward Global Free Trade: What Are the Options?

The main insight arising from the above discussion is that asking whether PTAs comply with multilateral rules and whether they are good for global trade is simplistic: the question should be which PTAs are just that, and why. The diversity of PTAs also means that understanding their economic effects requires making finer distinctions than is commonly pursued in empirical literature. Moreover, there is interaction among PTA disciplines. Tariff lowering and restrictive RoO can pull in opposite directions, while tariff lowering and liberalization of services and investment should pull in the same direction, magnifying each other's effects.

Overall, the findings on the compatibilities between PTAs and the multilateral system are rather encouraging: most PTAs do appear to meet the common interpretations of GATT Article XXIV, and particularly PTAs whose members uphold the principle of open regionalism tend to be trade-creating rather than trade-diverting. What is more, PTAs can provide a number of intangibles for propelling global liberalization forward. They can serve as a training ground for trade negotiations, providing a head-start for members in negotiating, absorbing, and implementing multilateral trade disciplines.

However, empirical evidence and policy concerns about trade diversion and about the potential longer-term problems, including the thickening tangle of trade rules criss-crossing the world, cannot be dismissed, either. To be sure, for those skeptical of PTAs, history cannot be reversed: the horse is out of the barn and at least the negotiated and signed PTAs are here to stay. Thus the policy question should go beyond the stumbling

---

[19] Nonetheless, the authors also note that in the longer term, location-specific sunk costs and network externalities inherent in services may generate trade diversion, if preferential liberalization leads to the entry of second-best service providers first.

block–building block seesaw to exploring how to deal with the system of PTAs—and its increasing complexities—in the most constructive fashion.

What are policy options for PTA–WTO interplay going forward? How to ensure that PTAs comply with Article XXIV? More generally, how to minimize potential frictions between PTAs and multilateral trade rules? And more ambitiously, how might the system of PTAs be employed as an avenue to global free trade?

There are a number of broad approaches to tackling these questions, each resting on distinct premises and entailing widely different policy pathways (Schiff and Winters 2003). One premise is that the motivations and actions of any of the big blocs, such as APEC, EU, NAFTA, and ASEAN+6, will have crucial implications for the behavior of the others, set the tone for the evolution of the global system of PTAs, and critically affect the future of the multilateral system. For instance, the creation of a Free Trade Area of the Asia-Pacific could elicit a vigorous response in the EU, a non-member, that might advance the multilateral agenda. NAFTA and the 1993 APEC summit in Seattle were hypothesized to provide just such an impetus for the Europeans to relax their positions in the Uruguay Round agricultural talks so as to conclude the round.[20] In other words, the behavior of any of these bigger blocs would solicit strategic responses from the others as well as from non-member states. Policy proposals to further the complementarities between PTAs and the multilateral system should thus focus on these groupings and their interactions.

Another premise is that PTAs involving any countries—developed or developing countries, large or small countries—will alter the incentives of these countries in the multilateral system. For instance, if a sufficient number of countries are adversely affected by PTAs' discrimination, a large enough group will materialize to support a multilateral solution. Or, more pessimistically, if a large enough set of countries engages in the 1930s-style beggar-thy-neighbor policies, the world trading system could succumb to that logic, as well. Policy recommendations should thus center on propelling large liberalizing groups into existence, and halting tipping points that lead to protectionist cascades.

The third premise is more legalistic in nature, viewing the market access and trade rules embedded in PTAs as crucial shapers of future multilateral negotiations and outcomes. Policy recommendations should thus focus on rulemaking in PTAs. Rules are key not only because they are revealing

---

[20] See e.g. Bergsten (1997).

of members' political economy incentives and, if stacked right, able to pre-empt rent-seeking; they also arbitrate the discriminatory versus liberalizing effects of PTAs, serve as harbingers for WTO members' multilateral negotiations positions, play a role in any potential future exercise to link PTAs together in broader integration areas, and, particularly if they are WTO+ as many PTA rules are, shape the potential for advancing global trade rulemaking.

Multilateralizing PTAs?

An important new concept, "multilateralization of PTAs", is perhaps most closely associated with this third line of thinking, and has become the latest focal point of policy proposals to improve complementarities between PTAs and the global trading system.[21] Multilateralization is an amorphous term; we take it to inherently refer to dealing with the PTA system as a whole, rather than addressing only some of its parts. It is grounded on the assumption that the silver bullet to global trade liberalization, substantial reduction of MFN tariffs and non-tariff barriers, is a long-term possibility at best. And its aim would be to use the PTA system as a back door to global trade, while in the process guaranteeing that PTAs are consistent with the multilateral rules governing them.

Conceptually, multilateralization can be accomplished through two alternative (yet also complementary) measures: (1) deepening tariff liberalization by PTA members vis-à-vis each other while also reducing discrimination toward non-members until it becomes inconsequential; and reducing substantive differences in the various PTA disciplines across PTAs and with multilateral disciplines until one single regime arises; and/or (2) incorporating non-members into a PTA until all countries are members. These measures would help ensure that PTAs meet Article XXIV, and eradicate one of the key potential problems of the PTA spaghetti bowl of overlapping agreements, namely differences in rules between the various PTAs. Since these measures are more theoretical than within our reach, multilateralization can be best conceived as a *process* that drives toward these two outcomes. Simply put, multilateralization is about "flattening" and expanding PTAs; this would also tame the PTA rule tangle.

Multilateralization is a remedy for deep discrimination and is aimed first and foremost at tariffs, where PTAs are the principal point of departure

---

[21] See e.g. Baldwin *et al.* (2007).

from MFN treatment and discrimination is provided via rules of origin. PTAs can spur discrimination in the areas of government procurement and investment measures. In still other instances, however, multilateralization may already be occurring—by default. As Baldwin, Evenett, and Low (2007) argue, PTA provisions on competition policy have tended to be multilateralized through non-discrimination clauses. The multilateralization challenge in these cases is to induce countries to adopt regulations and reforms that are blind to the nationality of producers and suppliers.

Another area where many PTAs are skirting multilateralization is services, as most regimes' services trade rules of origin are quite loose and thus tend to provide only weak discrimination (Fink and Jansen 2007). As such, PTAs automatically multilateralize preferential market access to an extent: third-country service providers can free-ride on the preferences provided by the PTA by establishing a presence in one of the partner's markets.[22]

However, in the many areas where multilateralization is compelling, such as market access of goods and investment rules, it could be achieved through pulling three alternative (yet complementary) levers: multilateral, regional, and a two-way lever.

The multilateral lever can at the most basic level be pulled to ensure PTAs' compliance with Article XXIV. This could entail changing and/or making more precise the multilateral rules governing PTAs, particularly the rather vague requirement of GATT Article XXIV that PTAs liberalize "substantially all trade" among partners and eradicate "restrictive regulations on commerce" within a "reasonable length of time", and not raise new barriers to trade vis-à-vis non-members.

For transparency purposes, the multilateral path could also entail strengthening the notification of PTAs to the WTO and deepening the incipient multilateral examinations of PTAs' compliance with Article XXIV. While the WTO is moving in this direction, including through the December 2006 Transparency Mechanism, multilateral PTA reviews would have to be much more exhaustive. Such PTA surveillance could help developing countries in particular to obtain information on the extent of

---

[22] Baldwin *et al.* (2007) cite the NAFTA-style telecommunications provision as an agent of multilateralization due to the sheer number of countries adhering to it, and because harmonization to a single regulatory regime for telecommunications frees trade in the same way as adoption of an international standard liberalizes technical barriers to trade: a common set of rules that governments apply to private firms in many nations thus tends to foster competition and trade.

the implementation of their PTA commitments—an issue on which many countries have surprising gaps—and rectify implementation deficits.

Comprehensive information on PTAs and their implementation would also enhance the prospects for analyzing their effects. In theory, forceful reviews could also help shame those failing to comply with the multilateral rules on PTAs into adherence, even though it is more likely that political imperatives would outweigh diplomatic considerations unless the reviews were accompanied by a sturdy enforcement mechanism—which, in turn, seems at the present moment as distant as it would be political.

A more ambitious multilateral lever than a review would be to require automatic multilateralization of PTA disciplines and preferences through automatic MFN clauses, as occurred in 19th-century Europe. While several agreements do contain MFN clauses in such areas as competition policy, the MFN clauses are not prevalent enough to effectively eliminate discrimination (Baldwin *et al.* 2007).

Yet another multilateralization tool would be to control rule proliferation and non-transparency in PTAs, for instance through the development of common "caps" or "ranges" for PTA rules in trade disciplines with various types of potentially restrictive rules, such as in the area of product-specific rules of origin. In the area of tariff liberalization, a more specific and easy to monitor definition of substantially all trade, such as at least 90 percent tariff lines *and* 90 percent of trade liberalized by year 10 in the PTA could also be considered. In the area of notifications, the eligibility criteria for the Enabling Clause could be reassessed in light of the rise of many developing countries to the ranks of emerging and developed markets.

The regional lever for multilateralizing PTAs could be applied within each individual PTA or among groups of PTAs. The former would mean driving down intra-PTA barriers and lowering discrimination toward non-members (or incorporating new members). One process that could serve as an example is the liberalization of NAFTA rules of origin. The Working Group in charge of the rules of origin review process has completed two phases of RoO simplification covering such sectors as alcoholic beverages, petroleum/topped crude, esters of glycerol, pearl jewelry, headphones with microphones, chassis fitted with engines, photocopiers, chemicals, pharmaceuticals, plastics and rubber, motor vehicles and their parts, footwear, and copper. The reforms, once complete, are estimated to cover more than US$100 billion of trilateral trade.

In contrast, the regional lever pulled by groups of countries would entail "regional multilateralization" or "convergence" discussed in the following chapter—the creation of ranges, caps, or other ceilings and coordination devices sanctioned at the multilateral level for trade rules within subsets of PTAs. Such a region-by-region convergence process would likely accommodate regional idiosyncrasies better than would a global effort. The European Union pursued such a process with its East European neighbors in the late 1990s. A group of 11 Pacific countries in Latin America are currently considering it, and APEC members are also discussing it as an avenue toward the FTAAP.

The two-way lever would entail using what is "regional" to shape what is "multilateral", and vice versa. For instance, it could mean using empirical measures of liberalization and external discrimination in PTAs as a revealed regional preference and reality check in multilateral rulemaking on PTAs, and as an agreed-upon benchmark for new PTAs to aspire to. It could also mean employing the many tried and tested trade-related disciplines in PTAs that go beyond multilateral rules in coverage and/or precision—such as those on investment, competition policy, or customs procedures—to craft new multilateral trade rules, for instance in services or trade facilitation. This in and of itself could help reduce frictions between the two systems.

Conversely, the two-way lever could be pulled to incorporate new multilateral rules governing PTAs in the texts of new PTAs, and even involve some mechanisms to enforce compliance with multilateral mandates at the regional level. It could also bring some multilateral rules to govern potential regional convergence processes, which we will discuss below, to ensure that expanded PTA zones would not result in discrimination vis-à-vis non-members or systemically problematic, trade-diverting scenarios along the lines of Krugman's (1991) three-bloc world.

There are other, shorter-term, more piecemeal and painless measures that could be taken to blunt the preferential edge of PTAs. One possibility would be to liberalize goods (both in PTAs and vis-à-vis third parties) in product categories that countries in the region have already liberalized for major exporters in or outside the region, so that the marginal pain of liberalization in these sectors is small if not non-existent. For example, in CAFTA, Central American countries freed photographic or cinematographic goods (HS chapter 37) and fruit and nuts (08) to imports from the United States, the key source of their imports in the two sectors, yet they also maintain positive applied MFN rates in these sectors. Another example is wood pulp (47) for Chile in the Chile–US FTA. To be sure, such liberalization would be less consequential for the United States, which might have an interest in retaining its preference margin.[23]

[23] We thank our referee for this point.

Overall, the right tool for multilateralization may differ across policy areas. For instance, on trade in goods, specific tariff liberalization floors may be the way to go, whereas on investment rules, MFN treatment of foreign investors when it comes to performance requirements may be the right approach. Certainly the effects of multilateralization would vary across issues and agreements. However, too little is as yet known about the effectiveness and effects of these various specific remedies for conclusive policy prescriptions.

IV. Conclusion

PTAs incorporate a wide range of rules that can deliver important synergies with each other, and help propel regional and global trade and investment flows. However, as a body of rules and as a trend-setter in global trade, PTAs can also pose challenges to the global trading system. Should their rules contravene GATT Article XXIV, they might undermine the advances of multilateral liberalization in the past six decades. This possibility has inspired a vast body of academic literature and reams of policy debate on whether PTAs are stumbling or building blocks toward global trade. But more recently analysts have turned their attention to means of using PTAs as a gateway to global liberalization, under the broad umbrella concept of multilateralization.

There are various more or less ambitious ways in which PTAs could be multilateralized, such as sturdier multilateral monitoring of PTA commitments, creation of multilateral caps on PTA disciplines, and transposing PTAs' best practices to multilateral trade rules. However, optimism about the effectiveness of multilateralization is not fully warranted, as any progress toward it is bound to be but gradual and rife with political challenges—as well as endogenous to the preferences of existing PTAs.

To be sure, there are a number of challenges to multilateralization, particularly judging by the WTO's history of being a rather ineffectual "innocent bystander" in the face of the PTA proliferation.[24]

First, even if the ambiguities of Article XXIV were resolved, the problem of the article's enforcement would remain on the table. Devising an effective enforcement tool—yet one that would not undermine incentives to notify PTAs to the WTO—might require a critical mass of countries that have pursued highly liberalizing PTAs.

---

[24] See Baldwin (2006).

Second, any definition or rules caps would inherently be endogenous to PTA members' preferences and to existing PTAs. This would mean that while the thorny political economy questions of design of ranges may be resolved *ex ante*, the resulting multilateral framework may be but suboptimal from a purely economic or welfare standpoint.

Third, multilateralization risks perverse incentives. For example, stronger multilateral monitoring of PTAs could turn countries away from regionalism, while doing little to guarantee that they would turn their energies to multilateralism. Or perhaps even more likely, excessively strict multilateral regulations would risk turning countries away from notifying PTAs to the WTO. If rigid, multilateralization also risks straitjacketing regions with unsuitable one-size-fits-all multilateral rules, or, conversely, succumbing to the political economy of PTAs at the multilateral level.

However, positively, the efficiency gains offered by outsourcing and global fragmentation of production may incentivize global companies to call for greater synergies between PTAs and the global trading system, particularly if multilateral trade liberalization proves glacial. In fact, it is quite plausible that globalization is one of the reasons why PTAs continue proliferating and why certain tried and tested PTA rules keep spreading from one agreement to the next—and it is also likely one of the very reasons for the fact that protectionism has abated around the world in the past few decades. It may be that economic drivers will create the political drivers required for advancing toward multilateralization.

6

Managing the Spaghetti Bowl
of Trade Agreements

I. Introduction

International production has fragmented across national jurisdictions over the past two decades. Unlike integrated production activities that were internalized in a company and centered in a few locations, today's production is segmented and spread over an international network of production sites. As a result, a growing share of global trade consists of intermediate goods shipped from one country to another, and many household items, from cars to computers, contain parts hailing from multiple countries (Box 6.1). Trade in parts and accessories has nearly doubled as a share of global trade in 1980–2005, rising to some 20 percent of the total and surpassing the shares of capital goods and consumption goods. The explosion of intermediate trade has been particularly striking in Asia, where parts and accessories constitute some quarter of all trade (Fig. 6.1).

While trade liberalization enables fragmentation of production, it is cross-country differences in factor prices—labor costs, in particular—that drive it. In simple terms, global supply chains can help companies cut production, transaction, and distribution costs because they allow for adjusting to changes in the market—in price and demand.[1] The unbundling of production across several countries can save costs for two main reasons: at given factor costs, the sum of segments of production needed for the

[1] A supply chain is in essence a series of nodes linked by different types of transformations (from raw materials to intermediate manufacturing to the delivery of a finished good to a market). Each successive node involves the acquisition or organization of inputs for the purpose of added value. What makes supply chains complex is that moving from one node to the next involves series of transactions, such as sales and intra-firm transfers, as well as three types of activities—production, trade, and services.

Box 6.1 MAKING A COMPUTER IN THE FLAT WORLD

In his 2005 book *The World is Flat,* Thomas Friedman uses the example of the Dell Inspiron 600m computer as an illustration of the fragmentation of production. After his order for such a laptop arrived at the firm's headquarters, it went to a Dell plant in Malaysia for assembly—one of Dell's six factories in the United States, Ireland, China, Brazil, and Malaysia. The Malaysian factory constructed the computer from parts made by contractors and stocked in supply centers in Asia. Friedman tracked down the origins of the parts going into the 5.6 pound machine, ending up with no fewer than 20 countries:

- the hard disk drive was made by Seagate's (American) Singapore factory, Toshiba's plant in the Philippines, or Thailand-based Hitachi and Fujitsu plants;
- motherboards and memory chips came from Taiwanese original design manufacturers (ODMs) Quanta and Compal, with factories around Shanghai and Suzhou in mainland China;
- Intel microprocessors came from plants in the Philippines, Malaysia, China, or Costa Rica;
- graphics cards were from Taiwan;
- the cooling fan and keyboard were made in mainland China;
- the liquid crystal display (LCD) came from Japan, Taiwan, or Korea;
- the battery was Malaysian, Korean, or Taiwanese;
- the power adapter came from Thailand;
- the removable memory stick came from Israel, or else from Malaysia itself;
- the power cord was made in China, India, or Malaysia.

And where do Dell 1505 and 1100 "Made in China" notebooks originate? Licenses, manufacturers' mark and other stamps hail from Latvia, Argentina, Singapore, the United States, Romania, Chile, and the Philippines.

final good is less than under integrated production; and factor price differentials between countries allow at least one fragment to be produced more cheaply in another country (Deardorff 2001).

Globalization of production has boosted company profits the world over, and helped bring consumers a greater variety of products at lower prices. Trade liberalization and PTAs have been part of the story. Paradoxically, however, PTAs can also create new risks that contravene globalization. One is the risk of their potential incompatibilities with multilateral trade rules discussed in the previous chapter; another, distinct risk is posed by the growing "spaghetti bowl" of PTAs. While the prospect of exclusive regional preferential megablocs appears to have been eclipsed by the rise of prolific bilateral transcontinentalism, the rise of multiple, overlapping agreements risks a movement to the other extreme—"balkanization" of global trade into bilateral miniblocs.

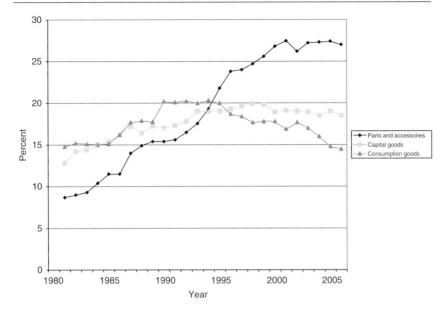

Figure 6.1 Trade in parts and accessories, capital goods, and consumption goods as a percentage share of total trade in East Asia, 1980–2005

Note: Parts and accessories are broad economic classification (BEC) categories 42 (parts and accessories except for transport equipment) and 53 (parts and accessories for transport equipment).

Source: IDB calculations based on COMTRADE.

In such a world, differences across PTAs can produce transactions costs for firms operating on two or more PTA fronts, above and beyond the costs of operating under one single set of trade rules. A splintering of the global trading system can also provide firms with strong incentives to create supply chains and pool production within the PTA area, rather than unbundling production in the globally most efficient fashion. And yet, the contours of an optimal PTA architecture for facilitating global production have eluded both analysts and practitioners.

Encouragingly, to the extent that these potential frictions generated by PTAs are real and matter to countries, companies, and global trade, there are a number of strategic alternatives for ameliorating them. Indeed, countries around the world are at a crossroads: they can choose to continue trading amid the trade agreement tangle, or they can pursue proactive policies that may overcome its potential problems and expand their market access and production possibilities. One alternative is multilateralization, as discussed in the previous chapter; another and complementary one is converging the existing PTAs into broader common integration schemes.

This chapter explores the potential internal frictions in the PTA spaghetti bowl, and discusses existing efforts to reduce them through such "convergence". The following section examines the conceptual underpinnings of convergence. Section III looks at the feasibility of convergence across PTAs in the area of market access. Section IVconcludes.

II. Conceptualizing Convergence

The PTA system carries an internal paradox. PTAs can, and are designed to, lower the costs of cross-border business, and they can indeed pave the way for efficient supply and distribution networks and sequential production. And yet, the spaghetti bowl of multiple overlapping PTAs can also contain internal frictions that create transactions costs for companies operating across various PTA theaters simultaneously, above and beyond what such costs would be if operating under one single set of trade rules.

Conceptually, the potential "systemic frictions" in the PTA universe can be broken down into (1) differences in disciplines *across* PTAs; (2) PTA hub-and-spoke formations; and (3) the strategic implications of PTAs for outsiders.

First, differences across PTAs can produce transactions costs for firms operating on two or more PTA fronts simultaneously, and, as such, can potentially limit firms' prospects for locating in different markets and/or for diversifying export markets. Each discipline in each new PTA potentially represents a new policy for firms to consider in their export, outsourcing, and investment decisions.

Figure 6.2a is a simple illustration of the PTA divergence problem. When PTA 1 and PTA 2 differ from each other, firms in country A may need to apply different sets of tariff schedules, rules of origin protocols, and other rules when seeking access to B's market than when seeking access to C's market. Similarly, customs in A will need to refer to different agreements when dealing with the respective imports of the two spokes. To the extent that the divergence across the two PTAs accentuates transactions costs and uncertainties to firms in A, this could be solved by making the two agreements more compatible with each other.

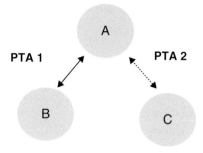

Figure 6.2a PTA divergence and hub-and-spoke problems

Box 6.2 DOES THE PTA SPAGHETTI BOWL MATTER? CONSIDER RULES OF ORIGIN

The effects of cross-regime diversity in market access disciplines are only starting to be subjected to theoretical and empirical assessments. What is clear, however, is that such effects are bound to befall the PTA spokes—countries that are party to several relatively different RoO models, such as Chile and Costa Rica. Such countries (1) must have customs that are well equipped to verify the different RoO governing all of the RoO regimes; (2) must be prepared to implement a number of different certification methods; and (3) may have to tailor their production structures differently for each PTA market.

Consider a Chilean producer of typewriters (heading 8469): he/she will have to comply with RoO that stipulate a ceiling of 50 percent import content to enter the EU; a change of subheading except from subheading 8469.12 to enter the United States, and a change of heading except from heading 84.13 (or, alternatively, a change from heading 84.13, provided there is a regional value content of not less than 45 percent when the build-down method is used, or of not less than 30 percent when the build-up method is used) to enter Korea; and a 60 percent regional value content (i.e. a ceiling of 40 percent import content) to enter MERCOSUR. Meanwhile, an EU producer in the same heading can, by virtue of the EU's application of a uniform list of product-specific RoO across its PTAs, use the same RoO (in this case, 50 percent import content) to enter the EU's PTA partners such as Mexico, Chile, and South Africa, as well as the entire, European-wide "Paneuro" system market.

The example illustrates also the comparative complexities faced by customs: Chilean customs would basically have to verify the RoO for all the products *times* the number of PTAs that Chile has, while customs in the EU would need to verify one single list of RoO for goods coming in under the EU's PTAs.

The potential problems of the spaghetti bowl can be particularly pronounced for small producers who lack the capacity to tailor their production patterns to meet the different sets of trade disciplines across the various FTA markets. However, they are a crucial consideration also for multinational companies that decentralize and stage their production in multiple countries.

Besides complicating life at the firm level, the spaghetti bowl problems can affect customs and governments. Customs authorities administering trade with numerous different PTA partners may have to refer to multiple, divergent sets of rules rather than a single list. The complexities at customs can have repercussions on firms. For example, they can result in delays in customs clearance, which, in turn, increases time to market for finished goods and can increase inventory costs when the delayed shipments are intermediates. Administrative complexities can also increase the odds on errors in the application of rules of origin and thus the potential denial of preference for originating products. In general, all the spaghetti bowl problems can increase uncertainties for traders, depressing trade. Traders in developing countries can be disproportionately affected given the frequent gaps of institutional capacities in these countries' customs.

More generally, the spaghetti bowl of agreements can create administrative costs for integrating governments beyond those that they would incur in the presence of a single trade agreement. Engaging in agreements with multiple trade partners poses a challenge for the coordination of negotiations and implementation of the different agreements, and accentuates the importance of ensuring compatibilities between agreements. This is a particular consideration in such regions as the Americas and Asia, where each country belongs to multiple different kinds of PTAs and is negotiating many more—while also negotiating and implementing multilateral trade agreements. Compounding the complexity is the expansion in the scope of PTA into such areas as services, investment, standards, and intellectual property rights.

The second policy question posed by the PTA tangle is whether it has yielded hub-and-spoke systems where the potential cost savings from connecting the spokes (B and C in Fig. 6.2b) remain untapped. Hub-and-spoke patterns would augur especially poorly for the capacity of firms in the spoke countries to obtain inputs from each other for goods destined for the hub market. As such, they could give incentives to firms from the spokes to migrate to the hub market. At the regional level, a hub-and-spoke system could also undermine the propensity for firms, whether located in the hub or in the spokes, to build efficient region-wide supply chains, pool production, and take advantage of region-wide scale economies.

Note that hub-and spoke patterns could materialize even if all PTA nodes A, B, and C were connected to each other. Stringent disciplines in

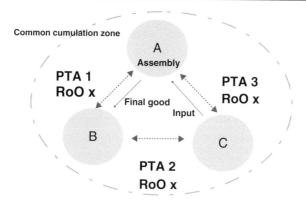

Figure 6.2b Three-PTA cumulation zone

one PTA, such as standards and rules of origin, can lock area ABC manu-facturers into sourcing from one PTA market over another, even if the latter were a more efficient producer. Similarly, foreign investors can "go PTA shopping"—opt to locate in PTA partners where compliance with the trade rules is easiest, rather than in partners with the most efficient production, *ceteris paribus*. At the aggregate level, such hub-and-spoke patterns can result in trade- and investment diversion and policy-driven agglomeration effects, leaving everyone worse off.

The third systemic policy problem of the PTA tangle is the treatment of outsiders. Being left outside PTA zones may place small outsider firms in par-ticular at a competitive disadvantage vis-à-vis PTA insider firms. Some out-sider firms that are exporting into a PTA may decide to invest in the PTA area in order to access the PTA market. The issue is particularly acute for firms that are outsiders in relation to *multiple* PTAs. In such cases, firms may locate in a PTA hub market so as to maximize trading and sourcing possibilities with the spokes. They may also strive to structure their supply chains so as to take advantage of the interlinked PTA nodes. To be sure, in sectors where the cost differential for using the MFN and the PTA channels is marginal, an outsider firm may opt to "do business as usual", discarding PTA preferences.

These problems are potentially hugely important for international trade. One mechanism for pre-empting balkanization and hub-and-spoke problems is "convergence" among the affected PTAs. Convergence goes beyond multilateralization, discussed in Chapter 5, by entailing a process whereby the member countries establish a common rules of origin regime that covers their common PTAs, and subsequently permits cumulation among these PTAs. "Cumulation" means a situation where countries applying the same origin regime can use inputs that originate in any part of the common area as if they originated in the country exporting the final good.

How would cumulation work in practice? In a simple illustration, should the "PTAless" corridor between B and C be connected (Figure 6.2b), *and* the rules of origin regimes in PTAs 1, 2, and 3 be the same, the three countries A, B, and C would have in place preconditions for cumulating production in the ABC region. Once cumulation is agreed on, it would enable producers of, say, A to use materials from C without losing the preferential status of the final product when exporting it to B under an A–B PTA (Box 6.3). In essence, the aim of cumulation would be to transform the PTA spaghetti bowl into a lasagna plate.[2]

Box 6.3 WHAT IS CUMULATION?[3]

Cumulation allows producers of one PTA member to use materials from another PTA member (or other members) without losing the preferential status of the final product. As such, cumulation can counteract restrictive product-specific RoO.

Bilateral cumulation refers to provisions that permit goods that qualify as originating in any one signatory country to be considered as such when incorporated into a subsequent product in another signatory country. For our purposes, bilateral cumulation can be based either on products or processes (full cumulation).[4] Virtually all PTAs have bilateral cumulation in place.

Diagonal cumulation allows countries that are all linked to each other via separate bi- or plurilateral PTAs and whose PTAs have the same set of preferential origin rules to use products that originate in any part of the common RoO zone as if they originated in the exporting country.

Full cumulation extends diagonal cumulation. It provides that countries tied by the same RoO regime can use goods produced in any part of the common RoO zone even if these were not originating products: any and all processing done in the zone is calculated as if it had taken place in the final country of manufacture. As such, full cumulation is mostly concerned with processes. It can notably expand the scope of diagonal cumulation.

---

[2] Bhagwati (2008) crafts a lively discussion on the potential problems that would ensue after such lasagna plates were in place and covered the globe, including on his argued impossibility of translating them into a global pizza of full-fledged global free trade.

[3] This box draws on Estevadeordal, Harris, and Suominen (2007).

[4] The distinction between cumulation based on products or processes is significant but not essential to our policy analysis.

Importantly, for cumulation to work well in practice, RoO convergence is not enough. Rather, each PTA in the triangle ABC should also drive bilateral preferential tariffs to very low levels or zero. Indeed, preferential tariff elimination is very important: even if PTAs A–B, A–C, and B–C had common RoO and cumulation in place, positive preferential tariffs on any side of the triangle could distort trade and production patterns, with trade likely flowing through the lowest-tariff channels and production agglomerating in the hub country that faces the lowest preferential tariffs in the other two countries.

It is also important to note that restrictive rules of origin accentuate the urgency for cumulation. Rules of origin effectively set up walls around PTA members that prevent the use of some inputs in each product. Multiple overlapping PTAs with divergent origin regimes thus entail many such barriers to free and efficient sourcing of inputs. When the rules are more restrictive, the walls are higher, and efficient allocation of resources is even more difficult (Fig. 6.3a). In this sense, then, more restrictive rules of origin will accentuate the RoO divergence problem for countries that have entered into multiple PTAs, as both the number and height of the walls will be higher. When rules of origin are less restrictive, the RoO barriers to trade are lower, both across PTAs and between PTA members and ROW, and inputs can be sourced efficiently raising the global gains from trade (Fig. 6.3b).

In simple terms, in the presence of persistent tariff barriers in the two-way trade between any of the three parties, the tripartite zone would feature a

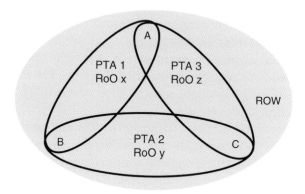

Figure 6.3a Siloing trade within PTAs: RoO divergence with high restrictiveness of rules of origin

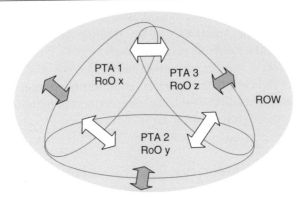

Figure 6.3b Enabling trade across PTAs and with rest of the world: RoO divergence with low restrictiveness of rules of origin

problem of poor "connectivity" (i.e. lack of liberalization), whereas in the presence of restrictive, differing, and disconnected RoO regimes, it would contain a problem of lack of "convergence". It is the absence of connectivity and convergence that creates the spaghetti bowl problem; it is high tariffs around each PTA that amplify the problem. Particularly problematic are situations where RoO are highly restrictive, as restrictive RoO compound the effects of high external tariffs and reduce the benefits of liberalized tariffs.

To the extent that market access obstacles to efficient region-wide supply chains and pooling regional production exist, the zone ABC could be converted into "cumulation triangle" in three stages: first, by eliminating tariffs within each PTA—something that will automatically result from tariff phase-outs—second, by adopting a common rules of origin regime for the three PTAs; and third, enabling cumulation among the parties applying the common regime. The point here is that *both* connectivity (tariff elimination) and convergence (compatible RoO) are key to cumulation. For the purposes of cumulation, without good connectivity, convergence has little practical value.

Convergence would "flatten" the regional PTAs and tame the PTA rule tangle. It would facilitate trade and production across the connected region, and, as such, harness regional scale economies and opportunities for cost savings. It might also undermine protectionist interests and prospects for trade diversion, and serve as a base for further region-wide and global negotiations. In short, the idea of convergence is to make the PTA spaghetti greater than the sum of its parts.

Existing Convergence Efforts

Convergence would surely be a challenging endeavor, both technically and politically. Yet, it is no new idea, nor is it unprecedented in practice. There have been a number of notable efforts around the world to create broad-based cumulation zones among PTAs.[5]

The foremost example of pure diagonal cumulation is the creation of the EU's Pan-European system of cumulation in the 1990s.[6] The process entailed harmonizing EU's RoO protocols with the European Free Trade Association (EFTA) countries that dated from 1972 and 1973, as well as among EU's PTAs forged in the early 1990s in the context of the European Agreements with Bulgaria, Czech Republic, Estonia, Hungary, Latvia, Lithuania, Poland, Slovakia, and Romania.[7] The Paneuro system finalized in 1997 established identical RoO protocols across the EU's existing PTAs as well as for the PTAs among the EU's partners, providing for cumulation among the participating countries. The Commission's Regulation 46 of January 1999 reiterates the harmonized protocols, outlining the so-called Single List RoO. These RoO are highly complex, combining change of tariff classification mainly at the heading level with exceptions, value content

---

[5] Besides the regional efforts at RoO harmonization and/or some form of cumulation, there is an on-going global drive to harmonize non-preferential RoO. These RoO are inherently national rather than bi- or plurilateral, and are used for purposes distinct from those of preferential rules. Unlike preferential RoO that have thus far escaped multilateral regulation, non-preferential RoO have been under a process of harmonization since 1995 as mandated by the Uruguay Round's Agreement on Rules of Origin (ARO). Indeed, the rapid evolution of the preferential RoO panorama stands in contrast to the glacial progress of harmonizing non-preferential RoO. The harmonization work, propelled precisely by growing concerns about divergent national RoO's effects on trade flows, has been carried out under the auspices of the Committee on Rules of Origin (CRO) of the World Trade Organization (WTO) and the Technical Committee on Rules of Origin (TCRO) of the Brussels-based World Customs Organization. The latter has been responsible for the technical part of the work, including discussions on the RoO options for each product.

The harmonization drive was initially scheduled for completion by July 1998. However, the deadline has been extended several times since then. As of now, the pending product-specific issues involve some 30 products. There are also two major issues that have yet to be resolved—use of the value added vs. change in tariff classification principle in assembly in Harmonized System chapters 84–90, and implementation issues, particularly the use of the harmonized non-preferential RoO in anti-dumping cases.

While ARO is centered on non-preferential RoO, its Common Declaration with Regard to Preferential Rules of Origin spells out a requirement for the members to keep the WTO Secretariat informed about their preferential RoO. In their current structure, the non-preferential RoO approximate the Paneuro and NAFTA models in sectoral specificity, yet are less demanding than either of the two main RoO regimes. However, since the final agreement has yet to be reached, the ultimate degree of complexity and restrictiveness of the non-preferential RoO remains to be gauged.

[6] The Paneuro rules are also known as the Pan-European Cumulation System (PECS) or the Paneuro-Med rules.

[7] See Driessen and Graafsma (1999) for a review.

rules, and technological requirements, and varying markedly across products. However, the harmonized RoO do not represent a dramatic break with those of the pre-1997 era.[8]

The Single List became incorporated in the Euro-Mediterranean Association Agreements between the EU and various southern Mediterranean countries, and the system of cumulation operates among the regional countries that have signed bilateral agreements with each other. The so-called Paneuro-Med cumulation zone covers the 27 EU members and is gradually incorporating 17 other countries or territories.[9] While the object of this "cumulation system" is to enable goods that fulfill the RoO of one agreement to automatically qualify in other agreements within the system, this also requires that all the countries within the system have PTAs in force with all other countries in the system, which is not yet the case for some bilateral relationships.

The Paneuro RoO model is incorporated also in the EU's PTAs outside the cumulation zone, including the EU's Stabilization and Association Agreements with Albania, Bosnia and Herzegovina, Croatia, the former Yugoslav Republic of Macedonia, and Serbia and Montenegro, and the EU's extra-regional PTAs with South Africa, Mexico, and Chile.[10] Also the RoO of the EU's Generalized System of Preferences (GSP) and the 2000 Cotonou Agreement with the African Caribbean, and Pacific (ACP) developing countries are nearly identical to the Paneuro rules. The European Free Trade Association's recently concluded PTAs with Mexico and Singapore also follow the model, albeit providing an additional alternative rule in selected sectors, such as plastics, rubber, textiles, iron and steel products, and some machinery products.

---

[8] For example, the RoO in nearly 75 percent of the products (in terms of tariff subheadings) in Paneuro and the original EU–Poland RoO protocol published in 1993 are identical. Both the new and the old versions combine CTC with VC and/or TECH. Indeed, EU RoO feature remarkable continuity: the RoO of the European Community–Cyprus PTA formed in 1973 are strikingly similar to those used today. One notable difference between the older and the newer protocols is that the latter allow for an optional way of meeting the RoO for about 25 percent of the products, whereas the former specify mostly only one way of meeting the RoO. The second option, alternative RoO, much like the first option RoO, combine different RoO criteria; however, the most frequently used alternative RoO is a stand-alone import content criterion.

[9] The Paneuro-Med system of cumulation operates between the EU and the member states of the European Free Trade Association (Iceland, Liechtenstein, Norway, and Switzerland) and Turkey, and countries which signed the Barcelona Declaration, namely Algeria, Egypt, Israel, Jordan, Lebanon, Morocco, Syria, Tunisia, and the Palestinian Authority of the West Bank and the Gaza Strip. The Faeroe Islands have been added to the system as well.

[10] See Estevadeordal and Suominen (2003).

There are various examples of cumulation that do not fully attain the Paneuro-type diagonal cumulation. In SPARTECA, Australia and New Zealand allow members of the South Pacific Forum Islands to cumulate among themselves and still receive preferential treatment. The Forum Islands may not, however, cumulate inputs from New Zealand to export to Australia, or vice versa, as trade between Australia and New Zealand is governed by the ANZCERTA agreement (which does not provide for cumulation of Forum country-originating inputs).[11]

The Canada–Israel PTA permits cumulation with the two countries' common PTA partners as of the agreement's entry into force, a set of countries which includes the United States and no other. This extension of cumulation most likely accommodates existing integration of Canadian industry with US suppliers.

US agreements with Israel and Jordan also have some cumulation. The US–Israel PTA permits cumulation of inputs from the West Bank and the Gaza Strip, but not Jordan. Prior to the negotiation of a PTA with Jordan, the United States established a classification of qualifying industrial zones (QIZ) with Jordan and also with Egypt. This program allowed for cumulation of inputs from Israel, the West Bank, and Gaza, but not between Jordan and Egypt. The subsequent PTA between Jordan and the United States includes rules that permit cumulation only bilaterally, but the QIZ program remains in effect, allowing continuation of the cumulation of inputs from Israel and the Palestinian territories. The QIZ, however, are still a unilateral concession of the United States, not a bilateral treaty obligation like the PTA.

Singapore has pursued innovative mechanisms in its PTAs that, while not extending cumulation in the conventional sense of the term, do allow for greater participation of non-members in the production of originating goods. The main mechanism is outward processing (OP), which is recognized in all of Singapore's PTAs. OP enables Singapore to outsource part of the manufacturing process, usually lower value-added or labor-intensive activities, to neighboring countries, yet to count the value of Singaporean production done prior to the outsourcing activity toward local, Singaporean content when meeting the RoO required by the export market.

As yet, there have been only limited efforts to carve out cumulation areas within the Americas. The DR–CAFTA agreement between the United

---

[11] The ANZCERTA rules were completely renegotiated in 2006 with the new rules going into force in 2007.

States, Central America, and the Dominican Republic contains provisions for cumulation of inputs from Canada and Mexico in the production of garments of woven fabric (HS chapter 62). These provisions are subject to negotiation of origin verification protocols different from those in NAFTA as well as adjustments to the rules in the agreements of the Central American countries with Mexico. Thus far, Mexico has participated actively in the negotiation and implementation of these changes. This provision is available to the Dominican Republic for a transition period, by the end of which it must negotiate a PTA with Mexico in order for it to remain in effect.[12]

The agreements between members of MERCOSUR and the Andean Community share a common origin text, including a provision for cumulation that includes all nine countries (including Bolivia). However, the product-level rules were negotiated bilaterally, resulting in 16 sets of rules of origin that in principle permit cumulation throughout the common bi-regional space. That these rules are not uniform across bilateral relationships complicates the attainment of genuine regional cumulation.

However, there are moves toward convergence in the Americas. In January 2007, the Pacific Basin Forum of 11 countries in Latin America, including Chile, Colombia, Costa Rica, Ecuador, El Salvador, Guatemala, Honduras, Mexico, Nicaragua, Panama, Peru, formed a work agenda to study, among other things, trade convergence and integration. The group has held a number of regular meetings, furthering analysis of tangible ways of advancing toward convergence. Some US trade lobby groups focused on manufacturing industries have also expressed interest in a convergence among US agreements.

There is furthermore growing discussion on convergence among the nearly three dozen PTAs criss-crossing the Asia-Pacific space among APEC members. Indeed, many see a convergence process among these existing intra-regional PTAs—rather than a full-blown megaregional negotiation from scratch—as the key means in the search for a Free Trade Area of the Asia-Pacific (FTAAP).

These efforts are not made without a reason. The effects of belonging to larger trade zones can ensure major economic gains particularly for small countries with limited production possibilities. Figure 6.4 illustrates this

---

[12] The beginning of these negotiations has already been announced.

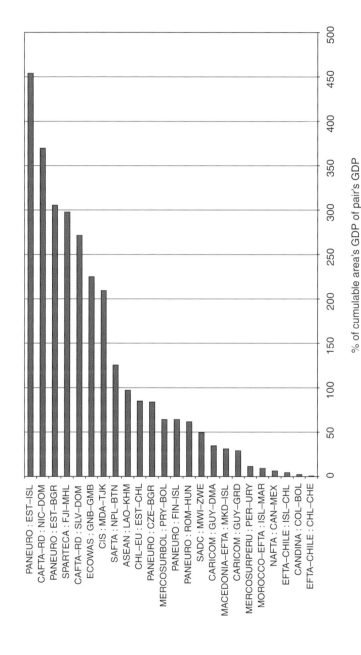

Figure 6.4 Size of additional cumulation area as a multiple of a PTA pair's GDP, selected PTA pairs

Source: IDB calculations.

by showing the size of the additional "cumulable" zones of pairs of countries that have a common PTA with each other. The measure is a multiple of the pair's combined GDPs. For instance, by virtue of both Estonia and Iceland belonging to the Paneuro cumulation zone (which here is the only pure diagonal cumulation system), the total size of their cumulable area (i.e. the size of the Paneuro zone) from which they can source inputs for their bilateral trade is more than 450 times their combined GDP. Similarly, the fact that El Salvador and the Dominican Republic can use inputs for the United States and other Central American countries in their bilateral trade under DR–CAFTA means that their "real" or effective cumulation area is 250 times larger than is their combined size. The figure for Canada–Mexico trade under NAFTA is about six due to the US economy being six times as large as the combined economies of Canada and Mexico.

The results are illustrative: cumulation can vastly expand the zone from which PTA partners can source inputs and/or in which they can perform operations. For small countries with small partners, the size of the beyond-PTA cumulable zone in many cases dwarfs the size of the combined economies, expanding production possibilities well beyond what could ever be accomplished within national borders.

Besides potentially vastly expanding the regional production pool and streamlining trade, convergence in areas where it has yet to be employed could potentially have substantial effects also on world trade. For instance, just connecting US agreements into a one large "lasagna plate" would impact nearly 11 percent of world trade. Connecting PTAs criss-crossing the Americas would cover nearly 10 percent of global trade, and those of Mexico alone some 9 percent. The effects of connecting the entire Asia-Pacific region into a huge cumulation bowl could be remarkable, as a large share of global trade takes place within this region.

Trade Effects of Convergence

What are the economic effects of convergence? This question is hugely important yet completely under-researched. There are only a few studies. Augier *et al.* (2007) is the foremost empirical assessment. The authors make a distinction between changes in spoke–spoke trade and changes in hub–spoke trade. Spoke–spoke trade would see a combination of trade creation and trade reorientation. Going back to the above figures, the former occurs as spoke B would now be able to source more intermediates from spoke C instead of supplying the good itself domestically. This reverses the trade suppression caused by the original RoO. The latter occurs as, say, country B switches its supply of inputs away from A and towards country C. This reverses some of the trade diversion arising from the original RoO in A–B. Given the original impact of the constraining RoO, this is likely to be the most significant direct effect.

Hub–spoke trade would also experience changes. As for flows from the hub to the spoke, to the extent that country B reorients its sourcing of intermediates away from A to country C, there would be a negative impact on hub–spoke trade. With regard to flows from the spoke to the hub, it is possible that the hub A could be reorienting its sourcing of intermediates toward country B for final goods made in and exported from country A. Hence there could be some increase in spoke–hub trade flows.

Augier *et al.* (2005) perform a natural experiment on the effects of cumulation in the Paneuro system, finding that the introduction of the continental cumulation served to increase trade between the Eastern European spokes by between 7 percent and 22 percent. They also find that trade was lower between the countries that were not part of the Paneuro system by up to 70 percent.

Gasiorek *et al.* (2007) examine the effects of the Paneuro system in 28 industries in Europe. The industries where the effects of cumulation are consistently positive are food manufacturing, textiles, apparel, leather and products of leather, furniture, other chemical products, rubber products, plastic products, non-ferrous metal basic industries, fabricated metal products, electrical machinery, and transport equipment; cumulation served to increase trade between 14 and 72 percent in these sectors. The largest impact of cumulation is in apparel, leather products, fabricated metal products, and electrical machinery. Unsurprisingly, these are also the industries where the EU tariff is highest and RoO most restrictive. As such, it appears that cumulation has liberalizing effects and helps reduce the tariff and RoO constraints.

Harris and Suominen (2008) strive to globalize these studies. They argue that the trade effects should vary by country size. Assuming that countries with a larger GDP (productivity) produce more goods than countries with a low GDP, the probability that imported intermediates from a third country C (that A and B can use for final goods trade in their bilateral PTA) will substitute for A and B intermediates will likely be increasing in the third country's GDP. This, in turn, should yield efficiency gains in A and B production, boosting final goods trade between them. But if the third country is very small, it will at best complement the intermediates of A and B, if it has much intermediate production at all. However, when A and B are also very small, adding any third country could augment their intermediate products pool and again likely help boost bilateral trade in final goods.

The effect of allowing cumulation from C to final goods trade between A and B should thus be increasing in the size of C, as well as decreasing in the size of the original PTA members, A and B. Trade diversion in intermediates between A and B should be decreasing with C's size.[13] Harris and Suominen perform a global analysis covering most PTAs and attempts at cumulation over the past 40 years, preliminarily finding that having access to a large cumulation zone (a country or spoke C, or something like the European Union) can significantly expand preferential bilateral trade between small countries (countries A and B, say Estonia and Iceland). Adding partners representing 10 percent of world output to a cumulation zone is associated on balance with a 3 percent increase in small countries' bilateral aggregate trade.[14] Importantly, this ought to be the net effect of increased final goods trade between A and B, and a reduction in intermediate trade (and reduced trade diversion in intermediates) between them. Some bilateral trade in final goods may also be substituted by cumulation if cumulation is taken also to mean a reduction in tariffs between the PTA members and their cumulation partner C.

The larger the "extra" cumulable zone is, the greater the trade effects of cumulation become. Harris and Suominen also find that the impact of cumulation has accentuated over time and particularly since the 1990s, an expected result considering that the EU's Paneuro regime encompassing most of Europe, and various other smaller-scale cumulation zones, went into effect during those years. This result is in line with Suominen (2004) and Estevadeordal and Suominen (2008), who find cumulation clauses in PTAs to have a significant effect on trade in the period of 1981–2001.

What, then, are the effects on the trade between the new "convergent" cumulation zone ABC and the rest of the world? Gasiorek et al. (2007) argue that the potential for cumulation could result in trade diversion between A and B on the one hand, and C, on the other: both A and B may now choose to import more from country C than from the ROW. The reason for so doing is that country C intermediate inputs can be cumulated

---

[13] Empirically, Suominen (2004) and Estevadeordal and Suominen (2008) find that restrictive rules of origin in final goods divert trade in intermediates to the PTA zone.

[14] Without operationalizing rules of origin, Hufbauer and Schott (2007) estimate that a Free Trade Area of the Asia-Pacific (FTAAP) covering 21 countries would provide gains of more than 50 percent for the United States, China, and Korea over their existing trade with their 20 other APEC partners. The gains would be more than 65 percent for Association of Southeast Asian Nations (ASEAN), and nearly 90 percent for Japan.

in A–B trade while ROW inputs cannot. If those imports replace, say, A's more expensive imports from the ROW, trade reorientation occurs. If they replace domestic production, trade creation results. The changes in hub–ROW trade would be analogous to spoke–ROW trade. There could be some trade diversion away from B's imports from the ROW if B switches to A or C suppliers. However, there could also be some trade creation or trade reorientation.

Aside from the more abstract trade effects, what would be the immediate value of cumulation to the end-users, the private sector players? How much do the RoO divergence and hub-and-spoke issues matter to firms in practise?

In a forthcoming survey of PTAs' effects on 360 firms' costs in four Latin American countries, Estevadeordal *et al.* (forthcoming) preliminarily finds that companies in the region foresee important gains from convergence. In the case of Colombia, 54 percent of small and medium-sized enterprises (SMEs, or firms that in the study are smaller than 200 employees) report that cost-savings from connecting and cumulating across Colombia's various PTAs would be "high" or "very high"; the figure is 34 percent for larger firms (Fig. 6.5a). The estimated savings are particularly high in food

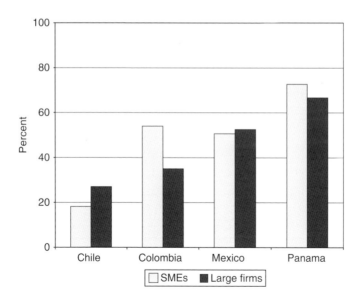

Figure 6.5a Percent of firms stating cost savings from cumulation across their country's PTAs would be "high" or "very high", by country and size of firm
Source: IDB (2008).

product and textile sectors, both of which feature particularly restrictive RoO. Illustrative of the importance of cumulation is that if cumulation was *not* allowed yet the various PTAs were harmonized, the estimated cost savings would be "high" or "very high" for 42 percent of Colombian SMEs and 17 percent of larger firms (Fig. 6.5b).

Mexico exhibits similar patterns, with 50 percent of small and medium-sized firms and 52 percent of larger firms arguing that cost-savings from convergence among the country's various PTAs would be "high" or "very high". Without cumulation, the figures drop to 28 and 29 percent, respectively. In the case of Chile, a country with a larger number of PTAs but a longer trajectory of learning to use RoO, the corresponding figures are 18 and 27 percent, respectively; that the benefits are viewed as greater by larger firms may be due to their exporting to a larger number of different markets. Harmonization without cumulation would pull these figures down to 9 and 18 percent, respectively. Meanwhile, in Panama, a country that entered the PTA spaghetti bowl only recently, the cost-savings from connecting the country's various PTAs would be "high" or "very high" for as many as 73 percent of SMEs and 67 percent of larger firms. Without

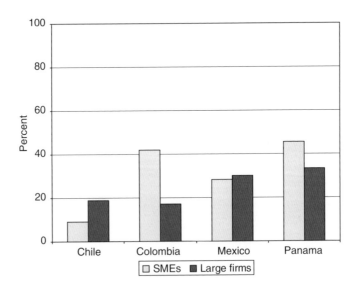

Figure 6.5b Percent of firms stating cost savings from harmonizing rules across their country's PTAs (but not allowing cumulation) would be "high" or "very high", by country and size of firm

Source: IDB (2008).

cumulation, the figures drop to 28 and 29 percent, respectively. The bulk of all these savings would come from reductions in administrative costs, such as paperwork.

III. Feasibility of Convergence across PTAs around the World

High-yield cumulation requires all members of a cumulation zone to share common rules of origin and to have zero or low tariffs in their respective bilateral PTAs. Attaining convergence should be easiest where compatibilities among RoO regimes pre-exist. Are there such preconditions for cumulation across PTAs around the world?

Figure 6.6 provides a staring point, mapping the degree of similarities among RoO across PTAs within some of the main RoO families: US agreements (13 agreements), and Mexican (9) and Chilean (8) families;

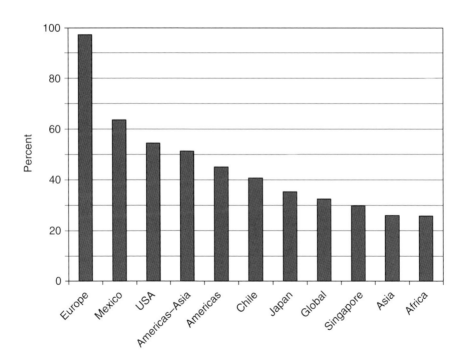

Figure 6.6 Index of similarity in product-specific RoO within selected RoO families
Source: Estevadeordal, Harris, and Suominen (2007) based on "Regímenes de Origen de las Americas" database.

Japanese and Singaporean families (4 agreements each); the family of EU agreements (4) and of African agreements (4); Americas–Asia agreements (8); as well as an Americas-wide sample (41) and a global sample (73) (Appendix 6.1). The height of the bar measures the average share of agreements within the family that have common RoO (average of product-level RoO as proxied by Harris's RoO restrictiveness index value discussed in Chapter 4). Agreements within a family may have exactly the same RoO in some sectors and fully divergent RoO in others; the bars thus measure the average coincidence.

In the Paneuro family of agreements, on average nearly all of the agreements apply the same rule[15] for a given product, as measured at harmonized system (HS) sub-heading level. Also the Mexican and US family regimes show significant internal similarities. On average, nearly two-thirds of Mexican agreements have coinciding product-specific RoO; the figure is well above 50 percent for US and Americas–Asia agreements. Also the Americas–Asia family, driven by US, Mexican, and Chilean PTAs, is quite internally coherent. Chile's PTAs diverge from each other more than those of the United States and Mexico, reflecting the diversity in Chile's partners and perhaps also bargaining power differentials. For the full global set of agreements, on average about one-third of agreements' rules will coincide on any given product. In the African agreements, in fact, the 25 percent outcome actually implies complete divergence, as there are only four agreements included in the analysis, and their rules never coincide.

Figure 6.7 examines similarities in RoO within the main regional families at the sectoral level. The first finding is the notable correlation *between* the families: sectors with most similar RoO in one family tend to be so also in another. There are, however, more nuanced findings. The only divergence in the homogeneous European family arises from RoO in plastics (section 7), textiles and footwear (sections 11 and 12), and machinery and equipment and transport equipment (sections 16–18). In the Americas, there are only a few PTAs, with a common, most frequently occurring RoO in agricultural products (sections 1–4), textiles (10), and machinery and equipment (17). The "New Generation (NG)" US agreements (i.e. excluding those with Middle Eastern countries) are rather diverse. Only eight

---

[15] By "the same rule" we here mean "rules with the same level of restrictiveness". We thus employ a simplified set of 28 different measures of RoO for the similarity analysis, rather than a typology of RoO types, of which there is a total of 211 in our analyzed set of agreements. However, while it abstracts away from the RoO types, it provides a solid and in our view sufficiently nuanced basis for capturing cross-regime divergences.

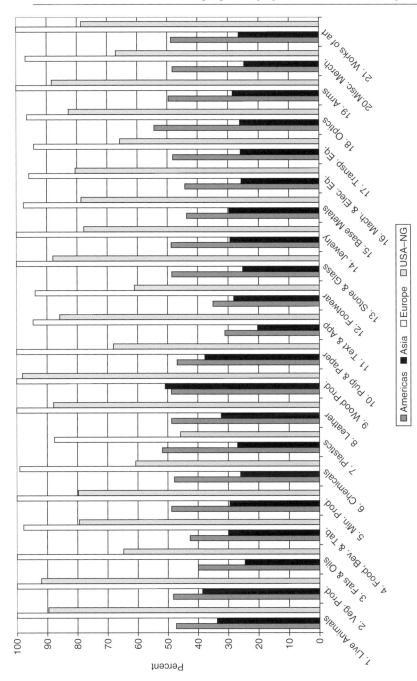

Figure 6.7 Similarity of RoO within PTA families of the Americas, Asia, Europe, and United States (percent of agreements by family with the same RoO)

Source: Estevadeordal, Harris, and Suominen (2007) based on "Regímenes de Origen de las Americas" database.

of the 21 sectors in US agreements have RoO that coincide 80 percent or more of the time across these agreements. Regimes in the Americas and Asia are even less homogeneous, rarely exceeding 50 percent agreements coinciding on average.

At the global level, there are no sub-headings out of a total of 4,100 in which *all* PTAs analyzed here would have the exact same RoO. In the Americas, among 30 PTAs considered here, there are only 59 such sub-headings. These span such sectors as chemical and industrial products (12 sub-headings with common rules), wood and wood articles (2), footwear (5), base metals (19), motor vehicles (2), and precision instruments (19). This number is quite significant in light of the widely distinct production structures and interests of the countries party to the various PTAs analyzed here.[16]

Does the second precondition to effective cumulation, tariff elimination among each pair within a "cumulation triangle", exist in the different world regions? Exploring this question at the global level is near-impossible due to the countless PTA triangle permutations. We thus choose to focus on the Americas, a region with particularly intense PTA activity and numerous potential cumulation zones.[17]

A set of 20 regional countries yields a total of 1,140 possible triangular relationships. However, since some countries do not have PTAs with each other and because there are other cases where all three countries are parties to a single plurilateral PTA (such as NAFTA, the Mexico–Northern Triangle FTA, or MERCOSUR), there are a total of 74 potential cumulation triangles in the region. One example of such a triangle is that among Chile, Mexico, and Uruguay: each country has a PTA with each of the other two, yet the three PTAs do not provide for cumulation among them.

Figure 6.8 maps out liberalization in the 74 potential cumulation triangles. The bars depict the share of the common six-digit sub-headings of the harmonized system (HS) that are duty-free in the six liberalization

---

[16] Zooming into the smaller families raises the specter of common RoO. In the NAFTA members' family, there are 477 products in which all PTAs share the exact same rule; particularly alike are RoO in agricultural goods and paper goods (with all PTAs in the family sharing the exact same RoO in live animals, plants, vegetables, vegetable products, fruit, and books and newspapers). In MERCOSUR's family, there are 407 such products, with RoO on pharmaceuticals, fertilizers, tannins, and furskins being universally shared within the group.

[17] Many of the findings are based on Estevadeordal *et al.* (forthcoming).

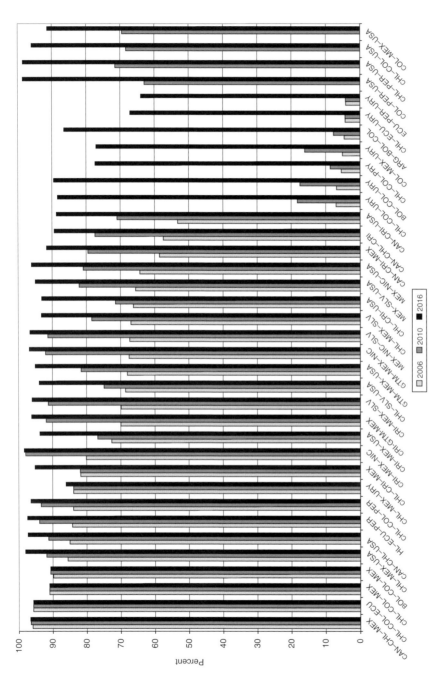

Figure 6.8 Share of common liberalized tariff universe in selected potential cumulation triangles in the Americas, 2006, 2010, and 2016

Source: IDB calculations.

schedules (one for each of the two parties in all three PTAs) within the triangle in 2006, 2010, and 2016, respectively.[18]

Although there is a wide divergence in the share of sub-headings liberalized by parties vis-à-vis one another that persists through 2010, most triangles will feature free bilateral trade in more than 80 percent of sub-headings by 2016. Overall, connectivity among the NAFTA countries and their subsequent FTA partners, Chile and Central American countries, is high and will become particularly significant starting in 2010.

Particularly "ripe" are the triangles among Mexico and the various Central American countries, as well as the triangles among Mexico, Chile, Costa Rica, and El Salvador; Chile, Colombia, Ecuador, and Peru; and Chile, Colombia, and Mexico. The entry into effect of the US–Colombia and US–Peru FTAs would lead to a rapid liberalization between 2010 and 2016, which entails that the triangle Colombia–Peru–United States would free nearly all lines by 2016, while liberalization in the triangle Colombia–Mexico–United States would soar above 90 percent. Triangles among most Andean and MERCOSUR countries reach an average liberalization of slightly over 70 percent by 2016.

To be sure, while a survey of cumulation triangles provides useful information on the extent to which liberalization schedules match in terms of product composition and temporal sequencing, it is less useful for immediate policy prescriptions. Countries aiming at cumulation would be much better served by a broader, multi-country cumulation zone—one where *all* countries are currently linked to each other via bi- or plurilateral PTAs. One example of such a zone is one encompassing Canada, Chile, Costa Rica, Mexico, and the United States, all of which are linked to one another and have relatively advanced liberalization in their respective common FTAs. An analysis of the five-member pentagon shows that no fewer than 65 percent of all products in the ten bilateral trade channels will be liberalized in 2010, while 85 percent will be free of duty by 2016. In other words, connectivity in these products will be at its maximum, facilitating the prospects of meaningful cumulation.

These findings are quite notable given that the figure focuses only on common products with *zero* tariffs and is thus based on a highly conservative estimate. There are various other products in the bilateral

---

[18] The analysis here is restricted to only the 4,201 HS subheadings that do not change between the 1992, 1996, and 2002 versions of the HS. This is so that triangles can be formed among agreements that were negotiated at different points in time.

relationships that feature very low yet not zero tariffs, which implies that the extent of liberalization across the region is even greater than the figure suggests.[19]

In sum, the analysis of the potential for convergence around the world has yielded two results.

First, the extent of compatibilities in rules of origin regimes—a factor that can augur well for negotiation of one precondition for cumulation, a common origin regime—varies across subsets of PTAs and across economic sectors. There are marked differences across RoO regimes around the world: on average about one-third of all agreements' rules will coincide on any given product. Nonetheless, there are clear RoO families centered around the United States, the EU, and Mexico, in particular, which suggests potential for some form of regional RoO convergence. Similarly, although PTAs differ quite notably in their definition of product-specific rules for agricultural products, textiles, and machinery, there are also a number of sectors, such as arms, wood products, and precision instruments, where the differences in rules of origin across agreements are marginal and, in some cases, non-existent.

Second, today, tariff elimination—the first precondition for effective cumulation—in a case study on the Americas is advanced: not only do many PTA members belong to many PTAs in the region, serving as key nodes between agreements, but most PTA members examined here have already liberalized at least some four-fifths of their tariff lines to each other, and nearly all of them will have freed trade on more than 90 percent of the products by 2016.

These are encouraging results, particularly for some sub-regional groupings. In practice, initial interest in expanded cumulation is implicit in recent US agreements (chapter 62 provisions in CAFTA, for example), and the interest by the Pacific Basin Forum of 11 countries in Latin America and by APEC members in examining the prospects for intra-regional

---

[19] The figure begs the question whether the various countries' preferential liberalization applies also on their external tariff regimes—that is, whether the most-favored-nation (MFN) tariffs of the PTA member countries are also zero. The question is of policy relevance: both preferential tariffs and rules of origin lose meaning, as does the rationale for pursuing cumulation, when MFN tariffs among all parties to a potential cumulation zone reach zero. However, calculations based on the latest available MFN tariff data show that the share of common products that are duty free for all countries in any of the cumulation triangles in Figure 6.7 is below 20 percent, and in all but one is below 10 percent: introducing meaningful cumulation in the triangles would thus inherently require addressing the differences in rules across the various PTAs.

convergence. The EU's new PTAs will likely carry the Paneuro rules, expanding the uniformity conducive to expanded cumulation. The growing discussion on the Free Trade Area of the Asia-Pacific (FTAAP) might also center increasingly around some form of convergence rather than a full-blown megaregional negotiation.

However, convergence in any region merits careful consideration in light of the vast range of PTA provisions beyond market access that would potentially have to be reconciled for full-blown convergence. There are three main alternatives (or alternatively, stages) for proceeding further. The first option is an "all countries–all disciplines" approach; the second and one that has been our primary focus here, a "selected countries–selected disciplines" approach; and the third the most *laissez-faire* "case-by-case" approach, whereby countries agree to implement some common reforms in their PTAs, but do not negotiate across PTAs. A fourth possibility might be a variable geometry process, whereby a sub-group of countries pursues convergence across all disciplines, while the other group members settle for a less expansive set of trade rules. But even if the approach was defined, there are at least half a dozen questions that should be answered prior to proceeding. They are complicated as in the case of rules of origin:

- What should the sectoral coverage of a negotiation aimed at a common regime be? The answer to this question can be aided by a diagnosis of the degree of tariff liberalization in the various PTAs and of the extent to which their RoO regimes are compatible. However, for any one country, the decision to join a convergence effort is ultimately a political one, and the choice of sectors can play a major role in that decision.

- What format should the common RoO regime take so as to be agreeable to all countries, *and* not to jeopardize the existing degree of liberalization in the converging region? In the case of RoO, a common regime would preferably not be more stringent than any of the RoO regimes in the region, but, rather, be based on a simple and flexible model.

- How would a common regime relate to the existing bi- and plurilateral regimes it is going to overlap with? Would it replace the existing PTAs altogether, would it coexist with them? Under the former model, traders would be able to use the common regime only; under the latter, they could choose between the common regime (and reap the benefits of cumulation) or the existing bi- or plurilateral RoO (and forgo cumulation). It would behoove on the origin certificate to specify the RoO regime (common or PTA-specific) under which the good is being shipped. Some flexibilities (such as partial exclusions of products) could be adopted for the application of a general regime to address sensitive sectors.

- What would be the implications for the multilateral trade regime? Would convergence be compatible with GATT Article XXIV, and would it require to be notified to the WTO as a "new" agreement? This is relevant in light of the concerns that diagonal cumulation may be inconsistent with the principle of most-favored-nation treatment and the Article XXIV requirement that PTAs not raise barriers vis-à-vis third parties.[20] And what should the multilateral responses to convergence be, particularly if pursued in major regions around the world? Should there be multilateral rules to govern regional convergence processes to ensure that expanded PTA zones would not result in discrimination against non-members?

- How would a common regime interface with extra-regional PTAs and other rising cumulation zones? For instance, in the Americas, a rapidly growing share of the PTAs formed by the regional countries is with extra-regional partners. Most countries should thus have an interest in a common regime that is both compatible with the extra-regional PTAs, and amenable to trading with extra-regional partners, rather than sealing them off from the hemisphere. And surely all extra-regional players have an interest in continuing to see their market access expanded rather than curtailed in the Americas.

- Who would do the talking? While governments are necessary for forming and redefining international agreements, considerations of cumulation should incorporate actors in the private sector, not least given that they are the end-users of PTAs and thus hold the best information about the operation of PTAs and the relevance of the hypothetical problems posed by the PTA spaghetti bowl. As such, any process aimed at building bridges across PTAs should inherently involve public–private sector partnerships. Such a consultative process could yield positive externalities, such as to generate fresh ideas on how best to educate private sector actors to take advantage of PTAs.

---

[20] In the late 1990s, the United States and Japan raised several objections to the EU's Paneuro system of cumulation as a potentially discriminatory entity.

IV. Conclusion

The proliferation of PTAs has been accompanied by globalization of production, a trend that has transformed ways of doing business around the world. Providing new market access channels, the spaghetti bowl of PTAs can help companies split production across the most efficient locations.

And yet, the PTA spaghetti can also pose a number of challenges for the global trading system, countries, and companies. Should its rules contravene GATT Article XXIV, it could undermine the advances of multilateral liberalization in the past six decades; should it contain agreements with widely distinct rules, it could increase the complexities facing customs authorities and augment the costs of doing business for traders and investors dealing across multiple markets; should it result in hub-and-spoke patterns, it could impede the cost savings that would result from connecting the spokes and creating broader production regions. The transactions costs of the system of PTAs can be particularly acute for small- and medium-sized companies seeking to enter international trade and expand production and exports to multiple different PTA markets, as they often lack in-house expertise in navigating global trade rules.

The potential drawbacks of the PTA web have engendered a growing debate on ways to reconcile the various agreements through such mechanisms as "multilateralization" and "convergence". While these terms are ill-defined and amorphous, they are starting to attract the attention of policymakers around the world.

There are various more or less ambitious ways in which PTAs could be multilateralized, such as sturdier multilateral monitoring of PTA commitments, creation of multilateral caps on PTA disciplines, and transposing PTAs' best practices into multilateral trade rules. However, optimism about the effectiveness of multilateralization is not fully warranted, as any processes toward it are bound to be but gradual and rife with political challenges—as well as endogenous to the preferences of existing PTAs.

Convergence, meanwhile, would entail harmonizing a subset of PTA partners. and allowing cumulation of production among them. The starting point and initial focus of such an effort would be market access provisions in the intra-regional PTAs, particularly rules of origin. Successful convergence would facilitate trade and production across the member PTAs, and, as such, help harness regional scale economies and opportunities for cost savings. Potentially thus attractive to export lobbies, convergence could also be politically more palatable and faster to attain than multilateralization.

However, convergence is neither simple nor risk-proof. For one thing, the process toward convergence must be carefully planned. There are a number of ways to create a common origin regime—carve one from and for the many. All approaches have their trade-offs and benefits that will have to be weighed carefully prior to negotiations, and also among all the stakeholders in bridge-building across PTAs. Moreover, the potential implications of convergence must be considered with care before convergence can be advocated as a remedy to the PTA spaghetti bowl. Convergent subsets of PTAs must be firmly nested in a liberal global trading system, lest the benefits of convergence be defeated by the rise of exclusive megablocs.

To be sure, there are various alternatives to multilateralization and convergence. The one magic bullet for reducing complexities of the PTA system is global trade liberalization and multilateral harmonization of trade rules. This would resolve the spaghetti bowl problems around the world at a single blow. However, the odds of this option are relatively low, especially in the near-term, and something over which any one grouping of liberalizing countries has only limited control. Perhaps a more likely scenario would entail gradual advances at the multilateral sphere.[21] Indeed, the road to multilateral liberalization may have to travel through multilateralization of PTAs.

The second main option, and a more important one in light of the likely gradualism at the multilateral level, would be to pursue a broader intra-regional integration scheme among a group of countries, such as regional partners. Essentially superseding criss-crossing PTAs in a region— say, Asia or the Americas—a megaregional agreement would have effects similar to those of convergence: it would streamline the regional PTA architecture, and help circumvent the rise of hub-and-spoke systems and produce a level playing field, eliminating the increasing discrimination stemming from the proliferation of PTAs. However, since multiple bi- and pluriliteral PTAs are already in place and proliferating further, and since region-wide all sectors–all countries talks can be prolonged, attaining a full-fledged region-wide deal anywhere is unlikely in the viable short-term. Future megaregionalism may have to travel through convergence.

---

[21] See, for instance, Hufbauer and Schott (2007).

Appendix 6.1 Rules of Origin Regimes Included in Calculations

Agreement	Europe	Americas	USA	Asia	Africa	Americas–Asia	Chile	Mexico	Singapore	Japan
PANEURO	✓									
EU–Chile (EUCHL)	✓						✓			
EU–Mexico (EUMEX)	✓							✓		
EU–South Africa (EUZAF)	✓									
Chile–USA (CHLUSA)		✓	✓				✓			
NAFTA		✓	✓					✓		
USA–Colombia (USACOL)		✓	✓							
USA–Panama (USAPAN)		✓	✓							
USA–Peru (USAPER)		✓	✓							
Argentina–Brazil–Peru (ARGBRAPER)		✓								
Paraguay–Peru (PRYPER)		✓								
Uruguay–Peru (URYPER)		✓								
Argentina–Colombia (ARGCOL)		✓								

Argentina–Ecuador (ARGECU)	✓	
Argentina–Venezuela (ARGVEN)	✓	
Brazil–Colombia (BRACOL)	✓	
Brazil–Ecuador (BRAECU)	✓	
Brazil–Venezuela (BRAVEN)	✓	
Paraguay–Colombia (PRYCOL)	✓	
Paraguay–Ecuador (PRYECU)	✓	
Paraguay–Venezuela (PRYVEN)	✓	
Uruguay–Colombia (URYCOL)	✓	
Uruguay–Ecuador (URYECU)	✓	
Uruguay–Venezuela (URYVEN)	✓	
CACM	✓	
CACM–Dominican Republic (CACM–DR)	✓	
CAFTA–Dominican Republic (CAFTA–RD)	✓	
Canada–Costa Rica (CANCRI)	✓	
Andean Community (CANDINA)	✓	
CARICOM	✓	
Chile–Canada (CHLCAN)		✓
Chile–CACM (CHLCACM)		✓
Chile–Mexico (CHLMEX)		✓ ✓
Chile–Peru (CHLPER)		✓

(Continued)

221

Appendix 6.1 (Continued)

Agreement	Europe	Americas	USA	Asia	Africa	Americas–Asia	Chile	Mexico	Singapore	Japan
G3		✓								
MERCOSUR		✓								
MERCOSUR–Bolivia (MERCOSURBOL)		✓								
MERCOSUR–Chile (MERCOSURCHL)		✓								
Mexico–Bolivia (MEXBOL)		✓						✓		
Mexico–Costa Rica (MEXCRI)		✓						✓		
Mexico–Nicaragua (MEXNIC)		✓						✓		
Mexico–Northern Triangle (MEXNT)		✓						✓		
Mexico–Uruguay (MEXURY)		✓						✓		
Chile–Colombia (CHLCOL)		✓								
Chile–Ecuador (CHLECU)		✓								
USA–Australia (USAAUS)			✓			✓				
USA–Bahrain (USABAH)			✓							
USA–Israel (USAISR)			✓							
USA–Jordan (USAJOR)			✓							
USA–Korea (USAKOR)			✓			✓				
USA–Morocco (USAMOR)			✓							

- USA–Singapore (USASING)
- USA–Oman (USAOMN)
- ASEAN
- ASEAN–China (ASEANCHN)
- ASEAN–Korea (ASEANKOR)
- Australia–New Zealand (AUSNZ)
- Australia–Singapore (AUSSING)
- Australia–Thailand (AUSTHA)
- BANGKOK
- Chile–China (CHLCHN)
- Chile–Korea (CHLKOR)
- COMESA
- ECOWAS
- Japan–Malaysia (JPNMYS)
- Japan–Singapore (JPNSING)
- Japan–Thailand (JPNTHA)
- Mexico–Japan (MEXJAP)
- P4
- SADC
- SAFTA
- Thailand–New Zealand (THANZ)
- Peru–Thailand (PERTHA)

7

Conclusion: Making More of Trade Agreements

I. Introduction

PTAs have blanketed the world over the past two decades. Never before have so many countries been connected to each other through PTAs, and never has the network of trade agreements been as dense. Also quite unprecedented is the depth of liberalization and comprehensiveness of today's PTAs, as is their backdrop of a liberal multilateral trading order and expansion of world trade.

The chapters of this book have sought to provide a deeper empirical understanding of PTAs, their implications for the global economy and politics, and measures by which the proliferating system of trade agreements could be shaped further so as to foster and facilitate global trade for the benefit of all countries.

The key underlying theme running through this volume is that trade agreements are no longer of consequence only for their members or certain world regions, but exert *systemic* effects in the international economy and politics. These system effects are inherently beyond the control of any one country, yet no country escapes them. The PTA system is in many ways synergistic, or greater than the sum of its parts; the whole can have both positive and negative implications beyond those that could ever be spawned by any one agreement or smaller group of agreements.

From the perspective of any one country, the "whole" of the system of trade agreements has three implications. First, while any one country is likely to be an insider in several agreements, it is also bound to be an outsider in relation to a larger and more rapidly growing set of agreements than ever before. This carries various implications. It accentuates the salience of the provisions of the other trade agreements—the depth of discrimination they confer, the range of product they cover, and their treatment of external trade partners—to any one country. It can also provide countries with incentives to negotiate (and incur negotiations costs) further agreements simply in order to hedge against the prospect of becoming placed at a competitive disadvantage in the new agreements. And the proliferation of trade agreements can also mean that the value of preferential edge gained in prior or new trade agreements is eroding: not only are other countries forging agreements with the country's PTA partners, but they are also forming agreements elsewhere in relation to which the country is an outsider.

It follows from these considerations not only that strategic acumen and capacity to grasp opportunities to negotiate new agreements are required, but there is also a possibility that, at the system level, the PTA panorama could splinter further, driving up the transactions costs stemming from a system of multiple overlapping agreements.

Second, overlapping agreements can introduce policy frictions that increase the costs of doing business for countries and their companies dealing on two or more trade agreement fronts simultaneously, particularly if and when the obligations of the agreements differ. Firms may need to alter their production patterns to meet each agreement's idiosyncratic rules of origin and other requirements; customs may have to refer to multiple, divergent sets of rules instead of a single document. The usefulness of some form of compatibilities, let alone cumulation, between agreements can thus be viewed as accentuating for a growing number of countries.

Third, each sequential trade agreement does not necessarily entail diminishing returns to a country; much depends on the types of partners that are being courted and, importantly, on possibilities for the country to link up with the partner country's trade agreements. Each new agreement may well be additive, and the whole of a country's PTAs may be made larger than the sum of the parts through such measures as MFN tariff liberalization, non-discrimination clauses, flexible rules of origin, and cumulation of production across agreements.

In other words, the upside of the web of agreements is that accepting an invitation from a new partner can enable a country to link with its partner's partners—much as accepting an invitation to the social networking sites MySpace or Facebook does. The logic of the MFN system is somewhat different: to serve as a club where members are treated equally.[1] With the

---

[1] We thank our referee for stressing this point.

right policies such as open regionalism, non-discrimination, and convergence, these can be logical also for the PTA system.

The system of PTAs certainly also has implications for the multilateral trading system. For instance, it is one thing for an agreement to breach the GATT Article XXIV stipulation that the elimination of tariffs on "substantially all trade" between the parties must occur within a "reasonable length of time" and that an agreement is not to raise barriers vis-à-vis third parties; it is quite another for all agreements to do so. This would surely undermine the credibility of multilateral rules. It is also somewhat different for the major economy and the majority of global economies to favor trade agreements on multilateralism than it is for a handful of small countries to do so. Perhaps most apocalyptically, the PTA system is feared to create protection cascades: even though agreements are liberalizing, the sectoral exceptions and "hidden protection" embedded in such instruments as rules of origin can help entrench protectionist lobbies opposed to multilateral liberalization. There are some specific issues to watch out for:

- The first pertains to the liberalization within PTAs. We have found that while most PTAs are deeply liberalizing and free tariffs quite rapidly, there are a number of outlier parties and sensitive sectors that lag behind in liberalization, or preclude it altogether. We have also found that many a PTA sports instruments that are non-conducive to trade opening, such as tariff rate quotas, special safeguards, and demanding rules of origin. While these instruments may be the price that liberalizers will have to pay to move the trade agenda forward, their downsides have made many analysts think twice about the benefits of preferential agreements.

- As for the discrimination imparted by trade agreements, the record is mixed. PTA preferences in some disciplines, such as services and competition policy, have to an extent been multilateralized. But in other areas, such as in investment and certainly in market access of goods, PTAs can be highly discriminatory. Furthermore, although PTAs often aggregate in families, each applying a blueprint of types of trade rules, the proliferation of distinct rules can cause the global trade system to degenerate into a rule tangle, with the attendant heightened transactions costs to the end-users of such rules.

- The spread of PTAs is creating new and perhaps unexpected constellations. To the extent that discrimination matters, a balkanization of the global trading system into hundreds of bilateral PTAs could accentuate the transactions costs of dealing on multiple PTA fronts beyond those of a single megabloc or a global agreement. In turn, hub-and-spoke formations centered around a few countries could augur poorly for the spokes' incentives to trade with each other and to pool resources for exports destined to the hub market.

• Just as the liberalization that is occurring through PTAs can assist multilateral trade further, so the rise of protectionism in the PTA system can both signal and propel the spread of protectionism in the multilateral trading system. The rapid and often sequential clip at which PTAs are brought to domestic constituents can aggravate and mobilize protectionist interests, which, if awakening in the main trading powers, may spread around the world, decelerating the multilateral trade bicycle. The PTA system can magnify the benefits of global trade liberalization, but problems therein can also shut the system down. As we hypothesized in Chapter 3, gaps in trade cooperation would not only have hugely damaging economic consequences; they can lead to the appetite for international cooperation grinding to a halt. Conversely, isolationism in international relations can undercut the incentives for trade cooperation.

And yet, while PTAs raise some question marks, there is an important body of literature that quite credibly speaks to the value-added of PTAs for the global trading system. At their best, trade agreements can serve as engines of liberalization, focal points of inter-state cooperation, incubators of new global trade rules, and as testing grounds for mechanisms to adjust to an open trading environment. They can also help aggregate national and global pro-trade forces to lobby for further liberalization.

It may also be the case that a critical mass of trade agreements can create dynamics conducive to global trade liberalization, perhaps well beyond what could be accomplished through multilateral negotiations alone. An MFN principle that extends any one PTA's preferences to further PTA partners, a non-discrimination principle that is oblivious to the nationality of the producer or service provider, and flexible rules of origin that allow for global production linkages can be forceful yet simple starting points for spreading liberalization and legal guarantees from PTAs to the global economy. The rise of a critical mass of agreements could also incentivize countries to develop mechanisms to multilateralize PTAs, and/or to pursue multilateral negotiations so is pre-empt any discrimination provoked by PTAs.

Furthermore, the lure of trade facilitation and costs savings that businesses could realize from connecting trade agreements at regional levels could propel countries to search for convergence among their agreements, along the lines of efforts on the Pacific side of the Americas. Convergent zones would automatically simplify the global rule tangle and potentially aggregate their member countries' disparate preferences for multilateral bargaining. Finally, a cascade of similar trade disciplines across multiple agreements, something that is brewing within many PTA families and sometimes across them, can result in a tipping point whereby rules tested and tried in multiple PTAs or perhaps similarly modified across multiple PTAs, become accepted enough to be incorporated into the multilateral framework.

II. Managing Trade Challenges: Global and National Measures

How are countries to face up to the opportunities and challenges these patterns present—take and sustain the good and get rid of the bad? How can the potential positive synergies of PTAs be stoked, while attenuating their potential negative consequences?

There are three broad policy areas for making more of PTAs that inherently require some form of international coordination—designing, connecting, and building on PTAs.

First, PTAs can be better designed. Most PTAs today are much more encompassing in product and issue coverage than PTAs in the past, boost trade between the members, are trade-creating rather than trade-diverting, and attain the most commonly used multilateral benchmarks for assessing their compliance with GATT Article XXIV. However, there are a number of outlier PTA parties and product categories that fall short due to prolonged tariff phase-outs, various non-tariff barriers, and restrictive rules of origin.

What, then, are the best designs? Prescribing specific rules for all idiosyncratic circumstances and sectors is difficult, but four general keys are simplicity, rapid liberalization, precision, and transparency. Yes, political economy studies and politicians alike have found that sectoral protectionism may be the price to pay for liberalizing agreements—and may be the prerequisite for an agreement to begin with. It is also the case that precision and simplicity may conflict: getting the language right may require complexity. And it is also the case that one size is unlikely to fit all partners or all sectors; a certain rule of origin in one sector may have completely different implications in another. But overall, an agreement should do more to elucidate than to obscure, much more to open than to protect, as well as to aim at compatibilities with other agreements and WTO rules.

Second, PTAs can be connected through innovative policies, such as those under the larger umbrellas of multilateralization and convergence. In light of the political economy constraints and resource gaps for the WTO to oversee much less regulate all PTAs, multilateralizing may have to occur organically and partly by default. However, with enough countries with an interest in taming the PTA tangle, some form of multilateralization can be feasible, for example, the development of common rule ranges in disciplines where distinct types and potentially restrictive rules have proliferated, such as in the area of product-specific rules of origin.

Convergence may be a more feasible process: the target and the end-result are clearer (region-wide cumulation of production), pro-trade lobbies may be easier to mobilize, foreign policy spillovers may be particularly tangible, and a single large regional hegemonic actor may be able to propel the process in a way quite unlike that which could be accomplished at the global level. There are several major considerations that would have to be addressed in such a process, including the coexistence between the new set of converged rules and the rules of the other PTAs, and the actual contents of the resulting rules—which would ideally be more liberalizing than those of any of the component agreements. Prior examples show that the task can be done and can result in important synergies. If multilateralization is a backhanded way of arriving at global liberalization, perhaps convergence presents a backhanded way of getting at multilateralization.

Third, PTAs can be built upon to achieve greater cross-border gains and public goods. This is particularly noteworthy in light of the fact that the degree of integration and policy coordination between states—even those sharing a border—continues to pale in comparison with the degree of integration within states. In the meantime, the on-going expansion of regional and global cross-border externalities, such as migration, financial shocks, and environmental hazards, places an added premium on international coordination and pooling of resources for common policy responses. Trade agreements can serve as a powerful focal point with real economic incentives to pursue further cross-border integration—but can only do so if their members consciously use them for such purposes. PTA partners can do much more to stoke the apparent complementary relationship between trade and cooperation, and build on their past collaboration.

The National Dimension of Trade Integration

Each country has a set of unilateral policies at its disposal for managing and making more of the hard-earned PTAs. These are needed: while the growing spaghetti bowl of trade agreements presents thorny strategic considerations for any one country, so does any one PTA create a sizable set of challenges to its members. First, trade agreements carry numerous trade disciplines, requiring capacities to design, negotiate, and implement them. Second, trade agreements, like trade liberalization itself, are political, and thus require investment in lobbying for them. Third, trade agreements have economic effects, requiring capacities to adjust to free trade and cushion the effects on those affected negatively by trade liberalization. And fourth, PTAs generate new opportunities, yet are no silver bullet for trade, much less for translating trade into growth and development: they require an enabling environment to take advantage of the opportunities of international markets.

This list of challenges means that trade liberalization in general, and trade agreements in particular, will have to be accompanied by complementary policies—national policies amenable to implementing agreements, trading across borders, fostering the supply side of trade, and pre-empting a backlash against trade by cushioning those hurt by liberalization.

IMPLEMENTING PTAs

As noted in Chapter 4, implementation of trade agreements is crucial for their effects to start taking hold—yet many an integrating economy still struggles with this crucial stage of PTA formation. Implementation, and, more broadly, monitoring—the processes carried out by national and regional public and private sector institutions (rules, roles, and actual physical organizations) to ensure that the contractual obligations assumed in PTAs will be implemented—can be improved in manifold ways so as to make more of PTAs.[2] Monitoring takes place in the "monitoring system", the framework of public and private sector institutions that are involved and/or employed in agreement implementation. Monitors—generally located in ministries of the economy or trade—are the grand coordinators of PTA implementation. They quarterback institutions and individuals charged with implementing the various parts PTAs, such as customs and ministries of health, agriculture, finance, and labor.

A solid national monitoring system is also not a luxury, but a necessity: it lends credibility to a country in the global trading arena, makes a country more attractive as a PTA partner, and plays a crucial role in

---

[2] This section draws on Estevadeordal, de Lombaerde and Suominen (2008) and Suominen (2008) therein.

facilitating trade and investment flows with the partners. At the bilateral level, the foremost benefit of monitoring is its provision of an institutionalized channel of regular communications between the trading partners. Problems and disputes can arise in any trade relationship; however, routinized institutional channels allow the partner countries to quickly put out any fires, avoid politicization of the agreement, and bring predictability to the economic exchange.

In a study of two seasoned monitors,[3] Mexico and the United States, Suominen (2008) finds lessons for meeting some of these challenges:

- Comprehensive PTAs. The better the various trade disciplines governing commerce between the FTA partners can be "bunched" together under the FTA umbrella, rather than negotiated separately or *ex post*, the clearer the monitoring mandate and the better the monitoring process can be centralized and coordinated.

- Clear monitoring agenda embedded in the PTA. A clear pre-defined agenda for implementation sets the agenda for work and, as such, serves as a commitment device for the member state monitors in their interactions with the partner country, and helps them to break bureaucratic inertia and logjams at the domestic level. The most powerful guarantee of compliance with such an agenda is by building it into the very FTA.

- High-quality, motivated monitors. High-quality monitoring staff—staff that is well-trained, seasoned, and flexible—is a key prerequisite for an effective monitoring system. While funding for monitoring work is important both for improving staff quality and retaining experienced staff, the right institutional designs and agility—staff able to rapidly "switch gears" and work across trade disciplines, across agreements, and across functions—can help do more with less.

---

[3] The two countries opened their respective FTA sprees in North America—the United States with Canada in 1989, and Mexico with the North American Free Trade Agreement (NAFTA) with the United States and Canada in 1994. Each has since reached some dozen further agreements with Western Hemisphere and extra-regional partners alike, which makes them the most prolific integrators in the world. Both cases can provide insights for countries that are only starting to set up monitoring systems and/or are entering manifold trade agreements. Furthermore, currently deepening and widening their bilateral integration in the context of NAFTA, Mexico and the United States also offer lessons to monitors of maturing and evolving trade agreements. Indeed, while trade in the NAFTA zone will be fully liberalized by 2008, in March 2005 the three partner countries launched the Security and Prosperity Partnership of North America (SPP), an extensive undertaking aimed at a wide range of areas of trilateral cooperation from energy to migration, port security, and trade facilitation—all of which require negotiation, technical work, and, indeed, monitoring.

- Inter-agency coordination. Inter-agency work has proven crucial to agreement implementation in light of the expansion of the agencies involved in PTA implementation. A prerequisite for coordination is that the national monitoring units have a clear mandate to be the sole coordination center of the implementation of trade agreements, and should reinforce the mandate through periodic inter-agency coordination meetings that keep all the players up to date and synchronized. Decentralization adds speed and agility to the monitoring process, but also requires the monitors to step up the coordination work.

- Political tie-breaker. A strong decision-making nucleus within the executive branch—such as a designated official in the executive office—is key to breaking political logjams over the implementation of agreements between government agencies. Even if decisions are not always favorable to the monitors, backlogs will be avoided and inter-agency coordination becomes more fluid.

- Flexibility of the monitoring system. High-quality monitoring does not necessarily require an elaborate institutional apparatus, particularly at the technical level. Rather than creating numerous committees with a heavy meeting agenda *ex ante*, the partner governments are often better off opting for ad-hoc working groups that can be convened when the need arises. A lighter institutional structure can be particularly useful for governments with limited staff resources for monitoring.

COMPLEMENTING PTAs

A large body of research, albeit some of it quite contested, has shown that countries with better institutions and countries that trade more grow faster, and that countries with better institutions also tend to trade more.[4] Conversely, trade can fail to stimulate growth in economies with poor institutions, such as excessive regulation.

There are a host of institutions and policies that must be honed lest PTAs fail to deliver on their full potential. One immediate area is trade costs. Trade costs are increasingly important in light of the expansion of just-in-time delivery and globalization of production. The importance that firms attach to fast transit is evinced by shippers' willingness to pay a premium for faster delivery. It is also reflected in the simultaneous rise

---

[4] See e.g. Dollar and Kraay (2002) and Bolaky and Freund (2006).

in the share of transportation costs and decline in the share of inventory costs in international logistics expenditures.[5]

In today's global trade, time is literally and increasingly money. Yet, as we briefly discussed in Chapter 4, delays in international trade are still hugely consequential for the competitiveness of many developing economies in particular. According to the World Bank's *Doing Business Report* data, in OECD countries, importing a shipment takes on average less than two weeks, while in developing regions such as South Asia or South Africa, the average number of days to import a shipment is nearly two months. The far-reaching implications of delays in and costs of shipping are particularly vexing for landlocked countries, such as Bolivia or Uzbekhistan, that depend on their neighbors for moving goods in and out of ports, and also for countries distant from the main global markets, such as Chile. Investments in infrastructure and streamlining customs procedures are crucial for countries to take advantage of the market access provided by trade agreements.

Besides trade costs, entering foreign markets requires a reduction of informational costs. There are two main types of imperfect information in trade. The first concerns information gaps overseas about a country's products and their quality. This is a severe entry barrier, particularly for developing country firms, as they tend to have a weaker country brand and lower national reputation than do developed countries. The informational asymmetries are even more acute when a country's firms enjoy only a small share of the overseas market, as consumers tend to attach informational value to quantity—they interpret low market shares as a sign of low quality. The second main informational gap resides at home: domestic firms lack information about foreign markets and means to penetrate foreign markets.

One way of overcoming the informational hurdles is export promotion—sustained campaigns to inform consumers in the export markets through efforts to polish and promote national image and brand, and to keep exporters at home aware of opportunities overseas, be it through efforts by the government, a trade association, or a chamber of commerce. Bridging informational gulfs in essence is to increase the odds that a given product becomes exported.

Export promotion has various benefits. It can most immediately increase export volumes and product variety. Export promotion offices abroad are found to be particularly useful instruments: they increase both the volume

---

[5] See Hummels (2001) and UNCTAD (2006).

and the number of new products, while export promotion by embassies and consulates helps increase the volume of goods that are already exported. Also lowered transportation and market entry costs help diversify exports, which a number of studies link to sustained economic growth.[6]

There are further policy areas that are key for any country or region to take advantage of trade agreements. One is the uneven participation in (and exposure to) of regions within countries to the stream of global trade. The case of Mexico is emblematic: only four northern states accounted for 60 percent of the country's trade boom in the decade following NAFTA; with five additional states, the figure rises up to 90 percent. In the meantime, 16 central and southern states remained by and large disconnected from integration, contributing less than 1 percent to Mexican export growth during the period. These patterns are related to inequality: states with greatest participation in global trade saw a decrease in inequality, while inequality deepened in states that remained disconnected from global trade.[7] Not surprisingly, the high-trade growth states have vastly superior infrastructures, educational attainment, access to credit, and other fundamentals crucial to competitiveness.

One final and increasingly crucial domestic policy area for making more of PTAs is assuaging those concerned about trade liberalization for their jobs and livelihoods. While technological chance is empirically the main driver of economic dislocations and job losses, import competition and outsourcing have received the bulk of the blame, leading many observers to fear a backlash against globalization. Pressures in the US Congress today against trade agreements and for tariffs on imports from China, along with intense scrutiny of foreign investment inflows, suggest that such concerns are not unfounded—as well as that those hurting from dislocations are able to aggregate their preferences effectively in the national policymaking process. And as Chapter 2 of this volume illustrated, countries have tended to turn away from trade cooperation and to protectionism when economic times turn sour, particularly for influential constituents.

Attention to economic dislocations, whatever their source, is increasingly recognized as crucial for nurturing the trade liberalization attained the world over in past decades.[8] However, the effectiveness of the proposed

---

[6] For studies on export promotion and diversification, see e.g. Volpe (2007), Dennis and Shepherd (2007), and Herzer and Novak-Lehnmann (2006).

[7] See López-Córdova (2006).

[8] See Blinder (2008), Aldonas *et al.* (2007a), and Rosen (2008) for discussion and specific proposals.

and implemented shorter-term remedies, such as training and unemployment insurance for those adversely affected, is not always clear. While there are numerous institutional and political insurances against protectionism, such as entrenched export and producers' lobbies around the world and strong intellectual backing for free trade, the domestic protectionist pressures can prove politically overwhelming. This may just be the most important overarching trade policy challenge of our times for sustaining the liberal order painstakingly carved out in the past half a century.

III. Conclusion

The rise of the system of trade agreements has become increasingly consequential in the global economy. One of the main notions of this book is that while trade agreements can be a "sovereign remedy", delivering important benefits for member states and the global trading system, their full potential for fostering multilateral trade, global production, international cooperation, and national welfare is yet to be fully harnessed. Such outcomes require better agreement designs, new, innovative ways to connect agreements, and an intense focus on complementary policies conducive to trade at both regional and national levels.

To be sure, the evolution of trade agreements and the benefits they can deliver depend on several external forces that are beyond the control of any one region or country, such as the state of the world economy, exchange rates, the price of energy, and the outcome of the Doha Round. Yet, steering trade agreements in the right direction might give their members greater leverage over the unexpected storms ahead.

Bibliography

Adams, R., P. Dee, J. Gali, and G. McGuire (2003), "Trade and Investment Effects of Preferential Trading Arrangements—Old and New Evidence", Productivity Commission Staff Working Paper, Canberra.

Aghion, P., P. Antràs, and E. Helpman (2006), "Negotiating Free Trade", mimeo, Harvard University.

Aldonas, Grant D., Robert Z. Lawrence, and Matthew J. Slaughter (2007a), "Succeeding in the Global Economy: A New Policy Agenda for the American Worker", Financial Services Forum Policy Research Paper.

—————(2007b), "New Policy Agenda for the American Worker", Financial Services Forum Policy Research Paper.

Anderson, J. E., and J. P. Neary (2005), *Measuring the Restrictiveness of International Trade Policy* (Cambridge, Mass.: MIT Press).

——and Eric van Wincoop (2001), "Gravity with Gravitas: A Solution to the Border Puzzle", NBER Working Paper No. 8079.

Anderson, Kym, Will Martin, and Dominique van der Mensbrugghe (2006), "Market and Welfare Implications of the Doha Reform Scenarios", in Kym Anderson and Will Martin (eds.), *Agricultural Trade Reform and the Doha Development Agenda* (London and Washington: Palgrave Macmillan and World Bank).

Anderson, Robert D., and Simon Evenett (2006), "Incorporating Competition Elements into Regional Trade Agreements: Characterization and Empirical Analysis", Working Paper, available at <http://www.evenett.com/working/CompPrincInRTAs.pdf >.

——and F. Jenny (2005), "Competition Policy, Economic Development and the Role of a Possible Multilateral Framework on Competition Policy: Insights from the WTO Working Group on Trade and Competition Policy", in E. Medalla (ed.), *Competition Policy in East Asia* (London: Routledge).

Arashiro, Z., C. Marin, and A. Chacoff (2005), *Challenges to Multilateralism: The Explosion of PTA's* (Sao Paulo: Institute for International Trade Negotiations).

Augier, Patricia, Michael Gasiorek, and Charles Lai-Tong (2005), "The Impact of Rules of Origin on Trade Flows", *Economic Policy*, 20/43 (July): 567–624.

—————(2007), "Multilateralising Regionalism: Relaxing the Rules of Origin or Can those Pecs be Flexed?" CARIS Working Paper No. 3, from Centre for the Analysis of Regional Integration, University of Sussex.

Axelrod, R. (1984), *The Evolution of Cooperation* (New York: Basic Books).

Bagwell, Kyle, and Robert W. Staiger (1997), "Multilateral Tariff Cooperation during the Formation of Free Trade Areas", *International Economic Review*, 38/2 (May): 291–319.

——— (1999), "An Economic Theory of GATT", *American Economic Review*, 89/1 (Mar.): 215–48.

Baier, Scott L., and Jeffrey H. Bergstrand (2004), "Economic Determinants of Free Trade Agreements", *Journal of International Economics*, 64/1 (Sept.): 29–63.

Bairoch, Paul (1989), "European Trade Policy 1815–1914", in Peter Mathias and Sidney Pollard (eds.), *Cambridge Economic History of Europe, Vol. XIII* (New York: Cambridge University Press).

Balassa, B. (1961), "Towards a Theory of Economic Integration", *Kyklos*, 16: 1–17.

Baldwin, R. (1993), "A Domino Theory of Regionalism", NBER Working Paper No. W4465.

—— (2006), "Multilateralising Regionalism: Spaghetti Bowls as Building Blocs on the Path to Global Free Trade", CEPR Discussion Paper No. 5775.

—— (2008), "Big-Think Regionalism: A Critical Survey", NBER Working Paper No. 14056.

—— Simon Evenett and Patrick Low (2007), "Beyond Tariffs: Multilaterising Deeper PTA Commitments", Conference on Multilateralising Regionalism, Geneva, Switzerland, 10–12 September 2007.

Barrett, Scott (2007), *Why Cooperate? The Incentive to Supply Global Public Goods* (Oxford: Oxford University Press).

Bergsten, C. Fred (1995), "APEC: The Bogor Declaration and the Path Ahead", APEC Working Paper No. 95-1, Institute for International Economics, Washington.

—— (1996), "Competitive Liberalization and Global Free Trade: A Vision for the Early 21st Century", IIE Working Paper No. 96-15.

—— (1997), "Open Regionalism", in C. Fred Bergsten (ed.), *Whither APEC: The Progress to Date and Agenda for the Future* (Washington: Institute of International Economics).

—— (2007), "Toward a Free Trade Area of the Asia Pacific", *Policy Briefs in International Economics* (Washington: Peterson Institute).

Best, E. (2006), "Regional Integration and (Good) Regional Governance: Are Common Standards and Indicators Possible?" in P. De Lombaerde (ed.), *Assessment and Measurement of Regional Integration* (London: Routledge), 183–214.

Bhagwati, J. (1993), "Regionalism and Multilateralism: An Overview", in J. de Melo and A. Panagariya (eds.), *New Dimensions in Regional Integration* (New York: Cambridge University Press).

—— (2008), *Termites in the Trading System: How Preferential Agreements Undermine Free Trade* (New York: Oxford University Press).

—— and Arvind Panagariya (1996), "The Theory of Preferential Trade Agreements: Historical Evolution and Current Trends", *American Economic Review*, 86/2: 83–7.

237

Birdsall, N. and R. Lawrence (1999), "Deep Integration and Trade Agreements: Good for Developing Countries?" in I. Kaul, I. Grunberg and M. Stern (eds.), *Global Public Goods: International Cooperation in the 21st Century* (Oxford: Oxford University Press).

Blattman, Christopher, Michael A. Clemens, and Williamson, Jeffrey G. (2002), 'Who Protected and Why? Tariffs the World around 1870–1938', Conference on the Political Economy of Globalization, Trinity College, Dublin.

Blinder, Alan (2008), "Stop the World (and Avoid Reality)", *New York Times*, 6 Jan.

Blomström, M., and Ari Kokko (1997), "Regional Integration and Foreign Direct Investment: A Conceptual Framework and Three Cases", Policy Research Working Paper No. 1750. International Trade Division, International Economics Department, the World Bank, Washington. Apr.

Bolaky, Bineswaree, and Caroline Freund (2004), "Trade, Regulations, and Growth", Policy Research Working Paper No. WPS3255, Washington: The World Bank.

Bond, Eric W., and Constantinos A. Syropoulos (1999), "The Size of Trading Blocs: Market Power and World Welfare Effects", in Carsten Kowalczyk (ed.), *Economic Integration and International Trade* (Northampton, Mass.: Edward Elgar).

——C. Syropoulos, and L. A. Winters (2001), "Deepening of Regional Integration and Multilateral Trade Agreements", *Journal of International Economics*, 53/2: 335–61.

Brunthaver, Carroll G. (1965), "U.K. Grain Agreement: Format for an International Grain Agreement?" *Journal of Farm Economics*, 47/1 (Feb.): 51–9.

Cadot, Olivier, Jaime de Melo, and Marcelo Olarreaga (1999), "Regional Integration and Lobbying for Tariffs against Non-members", *International Economic Review*, 40: 635–58.

————(2001), "Can Regionalism Ease the Pain of Multilateral Trade Liberalization?", *European Economic Review*, 45: 27–44.

——A. Estevadeordal, and A. Suwa-Eisenmann (2004), "Rules of Origin as Export Subsidies", Working Paper, IADB.

————J. de Melo, A. Suwa-Eisenmann, and B. Tumurchudur (2002), "Assessing the Effect of NAFTA's Rules of Origin", mimeo, University of Lausanne.

Charnovitz, Steve (2002), *Trade Law and Global Governance* (London: Cameron May).

Chase, Kerry A. (2006), "Multilateralism Compromised: The Mysterious Origins of GATT Article XXIV", *World Trade Review*, 5/1: 1–30.

Clemens, Michael A., and Jeffrey G. Williamson (2004), "Why did the Tariff-Growth Correlation Change after 1950?" *Journal of Economic Growth*, 9/1: 5–46.

Coatsworth, J. H., and Williamson, J. G. (2004a), "The Roots of Latin American Protectionism: Looking before the Great Depression", in A. Estevadeordal, D. Rodrik, A. Taylor, and A. Velasco (eds.), *FTAA and Beyond: Prospects for Integration in the Americas* (Cambridge, Mass.: Harvard University Press).

————(2004b), "Always Protectionist? Latin American Tariffs from Independence to Great Depression", *Journal of Latin American Studies*, 36 (May): 205–32.

Corden, W. M. (1972), "Economies of Scale and Customs Union Theory", *Journal of Political Economy*, 80/3: 465–75.

Crawford, Jo-Ann, and Roberto V. Fiorentino (2005), "The Changing Landscape of Regional Trade Agreements", WTO Discussion Paper No. 8, World Trade Organization, Geneva.

Crawford, V., and Joel Sobel (1982), "Strategic Information Transmission", *Econometrica*, 50: 1431–51.

De Lombaerde, Philippe, Antoni Estevadeordal, and Kati Suominen (eds.) (2008), *Governing Regional Integration for Development: Monitoring Experiences, Methods and Prospects* (Aldershot: Ashgate).

Deardorff, Alan V. (2001), "International Provision of Trade Services, Trade, and Fragmentation", *Review of International Economics*, 9/2: 233–48.

——and Stern, Robert (1994), "Multilateral Trade Negotiations and Preferential Trading Arrangements", in Alan Deardorff and Robert Stern (eds.), *Analytical and Negotiating Issues in the Global Trading System* (Ann Arbor: University of Michigan Press).

Dennis, Allen, and Ben Shepherd (2007), "Trade Costs, Barriers to Entry, and Export Diversification in Developing Countries", World Bank Policy Research Working Paper No. 4368 (Sept.).

DeRosa, Dean A. (2007), "International Trade and Investment Data Set by 1-Digit SITC, 1976–2005: Gravity Model Data Set on DVD Developed for the Peterson Institute and the World Trade Institute", Washington, DC: Peterson Institute for International Economics.

Destler, I. M. (2005), *American Trade Politics* (Washington: Institute of International Economics).

Devlin, R., and A. Estevadeordal (2004), "Trade and Cooperation: A Regional Public Goods Approach", in A. Estevadeordal, B. Frantz, and T. R. Nguyen (eds.), *Regional Public Goods: From Theory to Practice* (Washington, DC: Inter-American Development Bank).

Dollar, D., M. Hallward-Driemeier, and T. Mengistae (2003). "Investment Climate and Firm Performance in Developing Economies", World Bank, Development Research Group, Washington.

————(2004), "Investment Climate and International Integration", World Bank Policy Research Working Paper No. 3323, World Bank.

——and Aart Kraay (2002), *Institutions, Trade, and Growth* (Washington: The World Bank).

Drezner, Daniel W. (2006), *U.S. Trade Strategy: Free versus Fair* (New York: Council on Foreign Relations).

Driessen, Bart, and Folkert Graafsma (1999), "The EC's Wonderland: An Overview of the Pan-European Harmonised Origin Protocols", *Journal of World Trade*, 33/4: 19–45.

Eichengreen, B., and Frankel, J. A. (1995), "Economic Regionalism: Evidence from Two 20th Century Episodes", *North American Journal of Economics and Finance*, 6/29 (Fall): 89–106.

Eichengreen, B., and D. Irwin (1995), "Trade Blocks, Currency Blocs and the Reorientation of Trade in the 1930s", *Journal of International Economics*, 38/1–2: 1–24.

Estevadeordal, Antoni (2000), "Negotiating Preferential Market Access: The Case of the North American Free Trade Agreement", *Journal of World Trade*, 34/1 (Feb.): 141–66.

——B. Frantz, and T. R. Nguyen (2004), *Regional Public Goods: From Theory to Practice* (Washington: Inter-American Development Bank).

——Caroline Freund, and Emanuel Ornelas (2005), "Does Regionalism Help or Hinder Multilateralism? An Empirical Evaluation", paper presented at the Conference on The Sequencing of Regional Economic Integration: Issues in the Breadth and Depth of Economic Integration in the Americas, Kellogg Institute for International Studies, University of Notre Dame, Notre Dame, Ind., 9–10 Sept. 2005.

——J. Harris, and K. Suominen (2007), "Multilateralizing Preferential Rules of Origin around the World" (Washington: Inter-American Development Bank).

——José Ernesto, López-Córdova and Kati Suominen (2006), "How do Rules of Origin Affect Investment Flows? Some Hypotheses and the Case of Mexico", INTAL-ITD Working Paper No. 22.

——and R. Robertson (2004), "From Distant Neighbors to Close Partners: FTAA and the Pattern of Trade", in A. Estevadeordal, D. Rodrik, A. M. Taylor, and A. Velasco (eds.), *Integrating the Americas: FTAA and Beyond* (Cambridge, Mass.: Harvard University Press).

——and Kati Suominen (2003), "Rules of Origin in FTAs in Europe and in the Americas: Issues and Implications for the EU-Mercosur Inter-Regional Association Agreement", in Alfredo G. A. Valladão and Roberto Bouzas (eds.), *Market Access for Goods & Services in the EU-Mercosur Negotiations* (Paris: Chaire Mercosur de Sciences Po).

——————(2006), "Mapping and Measuring Rules of Origin Around the World", in Olivier Cadot, Antoni Estevadeordal, Akiko Suwa-Eisenmann, and Thierry Verdier (eds.), *The Origin of Goods: Rules of Origin in Regional Trade Agreements* (New York: Oxford University Press), 69–114.

——————(2008), *Gatekeepers of Global Commerce: Rules of Origin and International Economic Integration* (Washington: IADB).

——————with Jeremy Harris and Matthew Shearer (forthcoming), *Bridging Trade Agreements in the Americas*, IADB report.

——————and Robert Teh (2008). *Handbook on Regional Trade Agreements* (Cambridge: Cambridge University Press).

Ethier, W. J. (1998), "Regionalism in a Multilateral World", *Journal of Political Economy,* 106/6: 1214–45.

Evenett, Simon (2007), "EU Commercial Policy in a Multipolar Trading System", University of St Gallen Law and Economics Working Paper No. 15.

——and Robert Anderson (2006), "Incorporating Competition Elements into Regional Trade Agreements: Characterization and Empirical Analysis", Working Paper (July).

Falvey, R., and G. Reed (2000), "Rules of Origin as Commercial Policy Instruments", Research Paper No. 2000/18, Centre for Research on Globalization and Labor Markets, University of Nottingham.

Fearon, J. D. (1997), "Signaling Foreign Policy Interests: Tying Hands Versus Sinking Costs", *Journal of Conflict Resolution*, 41/1: 68–90.

Fernández, Raquel (1997), "Returns to Regionalism: An Evaluation of Non-traditional Gains from RTAs", CEPR Discussion Paper 1634.

Ferrantino, Michael (2006), "Policy Anchors: Do Free Trade Agreements and WTO Accessions Serve as Vehicles for Developing-Country Policy Reform?" Paper No. 2006-04-A, Office of Economics Working Paper, US International Trade Commission.

Findlay, Ronald, and O'Rourke, Kevin H. (2007), *Power and Plenty: Trade, War, and the World Economy in the Second Millennium*, Princeton: Princeton University Press.

——and Stanislaw Wellisz (1982), "Endogenous Tariffs, the Political Economy of Trade Restrictions and Welfare", in Jagdish Bhagwati (ed.), *Import Competition and Response* (Chicago: University of Chicago Press), 158–87.

Fink, Carsten, and Marion Jansen (2007), "Services Provisions in Regional Trade Agreements: Stumbling or Building Blocks for Multilateral Liberalization?" Paper presented at the Conference on Multilateralizing Regionalism, sponsored and organized by WTO–HEI, co-organized by the CEPR, Geneva, Switzerland, 10–12 Sept.

Frankel, J. A., E. Stein, and S. Wei (1995) "Trading Blocs and the Americas: the Natural, the Unnatural, and the Super-Natural," *Journal of Development Economics*, 47: 61–95.

————(1997), *Regional Trading Blocs in the World Economic System* (Washington: Institute for International Economics).

Freund, Caroline (2000), "Multilateralism and the Endogenous Formation of Preferential Trade Agreements", *Journal of International Economics*, 52: 359–76.

Frieden, J. (1996), "The Impact of Goods and Capital Market Integration on European Monetary Politics", *Comparative Political Studies*, 29/2.

Friedman, Thomas L. (2005), *The World is Flat* (New York: Farrar, Straus and Giroux).

Goldstein, J. L., M. Kahler, R. O. Keohane, and A. Slaughter (2000), 'Introduction: Legalization and World Politics', *International Organization*, 54/3: 385–99.

Gourevitch, Peter A. (1977), "International Trade, Domestic Coalitions, and Liberty: Comparative Responses to the Crisis of 1873–1896", *Journal of Interdisciplinary History*, 8/2: 281–313.

Gowa, J. (1994), *Allies, Adversaries, and International Trade* (Princeton: Princeton University Press).

Gowa, J., and E. D. Mansfield (1993), "Power Politics and International Trade", *American Political Science Review*, 87/2: 408–20.

Grossman, Gene M., and Elhanan Helpman (1994), "Protection for Sale", *American Economic Review*, 84/4 (Sept.): 833–50.

241

Grossman, Gene M. and E. Rossi-Hansberg (2006), "The Rise of Offshoring: It's Not Wine for Cloth Anymore", paper prepared for the Symposium sponsored by the Federal Reserve Bank of Kansas City on The New Economic Geography: Effects and Policy Implications, Princeton University.

Haas, E. B. (1958), *The Uniting of Europe: Political, Social, and Economic Forces, 1950–57* (Stanford, Calif.: Stanford University Press).

Haftel, Y. Z. (2004), "Variation in Regional Integration Arrangements and Intramural Violent Conflict", paper prepared for the 100th Annual Meeting of the American Political Science Association, Chicago, 2–5 Sept.

Haggard, Stephen (1997), "Regionalism in Asia and the Americas", in Edward Mansfield and Helen Milner (eds.), *The Political Economy of Regionalism* (New York: Columbia University Press).

Harris, Jeremy (2007), "Measurement and Determination of Rules of Origin in Preferential Trade Agreements", PhD dissertation, University of Maryland.

——and Kati Suominen (2008), "Expanding Production Possibilities in Global Commerce: Effects of Cumulation on Bilateral Trade Flows, 1965–2005", draft, Inter-American Development Bank, Washington.

Haveman, J. D. (1992), "On the Consequences of Recent Changes in the Global Trading Environment", PhD dissertation, University of Michigan.

——(1996), "Some Welfare Effects of Sequential Customs Union Formation", *Canadian Journal of Economics*, 29/4: 941–58.

Helpman, Elhanan, and Paul R. Krugman (1985), *Market Structure and Foreign Trade: Increasing Returns, Imperfect Competition, and the International Economy* (Cambridge, Mass.: MIT Press).

Herzer, Dierk, and Felicitas D. Nowak-Lehnmann (2006), "What does Export Diversification do for Growth? An Econometric Analysis", *Applied Economics*, 38/15: 1825–38.

Hirsch, Moshe (2002), "International Trade Law, Political Economy and Rules of Origin: A Plea for a Reform of the WTO Regime on Rules of Origin", *Journal of World Trade*, 36/2: 171–89.

Hiscox, Michael (1999), "The Magic Bullet? The RTAA, Institutional Reform, and Trade Liberalization", *International Organization*, 53/4 (autumn): 669–98.

Houde, Marie-France, Akshay Kolse-Patil, and Sébastien Miroudot (2007), "The Interaction between Investment and Services Chapters in Selected Regional Trade Agreements", OECD Trade Policy Working Paper No. 55.

Hufbauer Gary, and Jeffrey Schott (2005), *NAFTA Revisited: Achievements and Challenges* (Washington: Institute of International Economics).

————(2007), "Multilateralizing Regionalism Fitting Asia-Pacific Agreements into the WTO System", Working Paper, Peterson Institute for International Economics, Washington.

Hummels D. (2001), "Time as a Trade Barrier", Purdue University, West Lafayette, Ind.

Inter-American Development Bank (IADB) (2002), "Beyond Borders: The New Regionalism in Latin America", *Economic and Social Progress in Latin America, 2002 Report* (Washington: IADB).

Irwin, D. A. (1993), "Multilateral and Bilateral Trade Policies in the World Trading System: An Historical Perspective", in J. de Melo and A. Panagariya (eds.), *New Dimensions in Regional Integration* (New York: Cambridge University Press).

——(1995), "The GATT in Historical Perspective", *American Economic Review*, 85/2: 323–8.

——(1997), *Against the Tide: An Intellectual History of Free Trade* (Princeton: Princeton University Press).

Ivanic, Maros (2006), "The Effects of a Prospective Multilateral Trade Reform on Poverty in Developing Countries", in Thomas W. Hertel and Alan Winters (eds.), *Poverty and the WTO: Impacts of the Doha Development Agenda* (New York: Palgrave).

Jackson, J. H. (1997), *The World Trading System: Law and Policy of International Economic Relations*, 2nd edn. (Cambridge, Mass.: MIT Press).

——(2000), *The Jurisprudence of the GATT and the WTO: Insights on Treaty Law and Economic Relations* (New York: Cambridge University Press).

——J.-V. Louis, and M. Matsushita (1984), *Implementing the Tokyo Round: National Constitutions and International Economic Rules* (Ann Arbor: University of Michigan Press).

Jensen-Moran, J. (1996), "Trade Battles as Investment Wars: The Coming Rules of Origin Debate", *Washington Quarterly,* 19/1: 239–53.

Johnson, H. (1965), "An Economic Theory of Protectionism, Tariff Bargaining, and the Formation of Customs Unions", *Journal of Political Economy*, 73: 256–83.

Kahler, Miles (1995), *International Institutions and the Political Economy of Integration* (Washington: Brookings Institution).

——(2000), "Conclusion: The Causes and Consequences of Legalization", *International Organization,* 54/3: 549–71.

Kee, H. L., A. Nicita, and M. Olarreaga (2006), "Estimating Trade Restrictiveness Indices", Policy Research Working Paper No. 3840, World Bank (Feb.).

Kemp, M. C., and H. Y. Wan Jr. (1976), "An Elementary Proposition Concerning the Formation of Customs Unions", *Journal of International Economics*, 6: 95–8.

Keohane, R. O. (1984), *After Hegemony: Cooperation and Discord in the World Political Economy* (Princeton: Princeton University Press).

Kindleberger, Charles P. (1975), "Germany's Overtaking of England, 1806–1914 Part I", *Review of World Economics*, 111/2 (June).

——(1989), *Manias, Panics and Crashes: A History of Financial Crises* (New York: Basic Books).

Koremenos, Barbara (2001), "Loosening the Ties that Bind: A Learning Model of Agreement Flexibility", *International Organization*, 55: 289–325.

——(2003), "International Law for an Uncertain Environment", paper presented at UCSD Project on International Affairs Seminar, 3 Dec.

Koremenos, Barbara, C. Lipson, and D. Snidal (2001), "The Rational Design of International Institutions", *International Organization,* 55/4: 761–99.

Krishna, Kala, and Anne O. Krueger (1995), "Implementing Free Trade Areas: Rules of Origin and Hidden Protection", in Alan Deardorff, James Levinsohn, and Robert Stern (eds.), *New Directions in Trade Theory* (Ann Arbor: University of Michigan Press).

Krishna, P. (1998), "Regionalism and Multilateralism: A Political Economy Approach", *Quarterly Journal of Economics,* 113/1: 227–51.

——and Jagdish Bhagwati (1997), "Necessarily Welfare-Enhancing Customs Unions with Industrialization Constraints", *Japan and the World Economy,* 9/4: 441–6.

Krueger, A. O. (1993), "Free Trade Agreements as Protectionist Devices: Rules of Origin", NBER Working Paper No. 4352.

——(1995), "Free Trade Agreements versus Customs Unions", NBER Working Paper No. W5084.

——(1999), "Are Preferential Trading Agreements Trade-Liberalizing or Protectionist?" *Journal of Economic Perspectives,* 13: 105–24.

Krugman, Paul (1991), "The Move toward Free Trade Zones", paper presented at a symposium on Policy Implications of Trade and Currency Zones, sponsored by the Federal Reserve Bank of Kansas City, Jackson Hole, Wyoming.

——(1993), "Regionalism versus Multilateralism: Analytical Notes", in J. de Melo and A. Panagariya (eds.), *New Dimensions in Regional Integration* (Cambridge: Cambridge University Press).

Laird, S. (1999), "Regional Trade Agreements: Dangerous Liaisons?" *World Economy,* 22/9: 1179–200.

Lake, D. A. (1988), *Power, Protection, and Free Trade: International Sources of U.S. Commercial Strategy, 1887–1939* (Ithaca, NY: Cornell University Press).

——(1999), *Entangling Relations: American Foreign Policy in its Century* (Princeton: Princeton University Press).

——and Angela O'Mahony (2004), "The Incredible Shrinking State: Explaining Change in the Territorial Size of Countries", *Journal of Conflict Resolution,* 48/5 (Oct.): 699–722.

Lamy P. (2002), "Stepping Stones or Stumbling Blocks? The EU's Approach Towards the Problem of Multilateralism vs Regionalism in Trade Policy", *The World Economy,* 25/10: 1399–413.

Lawrence, Robert Z. (1996), *Regionalism, Multilateralism and Deeper Integration* (Washington: Brookings Institution).

——(2008), *Blue-Collar Blues: Is Trade to Blame for Rising U.S. Income Inequality?* (Washington: Peterson Institute for International Economics).

Levy, Philip I. (1997), "A Political-Economic Analysis of Free-Trade Agreements", *American Economic Review,* 87/4: 506–19.

Limão, N. (2006), "Preferential Trade Agreements as Stumbling Blocks for Multilateral Trade Liberalization: Evidence for the US", *American Economic Review,* 96/3: 896–914.

——and M. Olarreaga (2006), "Trade Preferences to Small Developing Countries and the Welfare Costs of Lost Multilateral Liberalization", *World Bank Economic Review*, 20/2: 217–40.

Lipsey, R. G. (1960), "The Theory of Customs Unions: A General Survey", *Economic Journal*, 70: 498–513.

Lloyd, P. J. (1997), "Towards a Framework of Trade and Competition Policy", *Asia-Pacific Economic Review*, 3/2.

——(2001), "Rules of Origin and Fragmentation of Trade", in Leonard Cheng and Henryk Kierzkowski (eds.), *Globalization of Trade and Production in South-East Asia* (New York: Kluwer Academic Press).

López-Córdova, Jose Ernesto (2006), "México: Nota Sectorial Sobre Comercio e Integración", Inter-American Development Bank.

——and Meissner, Christopher M. (2005), "The Globalization of Trade and Democracy, 1870–2000", NBER Working Paper No. W11117.

McLaren, J. (1997), "Size, Sunk Costs, and Judge Bowker's Objection to Free Trade", *American Economic Review*, 87/3: 400–20.

——(2002), "A Theory of Insidious Regionalism", *Quarterly Journal of Economics*, 117(2).

Magee, Stephen P. (1989), "Three Simple Tests of the Stolper-Samuelson Theorem", in Stephen P. Magee, William A. Brock, and Leslie Young (eds.), *Black Hole Tariffs and Endogenous Policy Theory* (New York: Cambridge University Press), 101–10.

Maggi, G. (1996), "Strategic Trade Policies with Endogenous Mode of Competition", *American Economic Review*, 86: 237–58.

——and Andres Rodriguez-Clare (2007), "A Political-Economy Theory of Trade Agreements", *American Economic Review*, 97/4: 1374–1406.

Mansfield, Edward D. (1998), "The Proliferation of Preferential Trading Arrangements", *Journal of Conflict Resolution*, 42/5: 523–43.

——and H. V. Milner (1999), "The New Wave of Regionalism", *International Organization*, 53/3: 589–627.

——and J. C. Pevehouse (2000), "Trade Blocs, Trade Flows, and International Conflict", *International Organization*, 54/4: 775–808.

——and B. P. Rosendorff (2000), "Free to Trade: Democracies, Autocracies, and International Trade", *American Political Science Review*, 94/2: 305–21.

Mattli, W. (1999), *The Logic of Regional Integration: Europe and Beyond* (Cambridge: Cambridge University Press).

Mattoo, A., and F. Carsten (2002), "Regional Agreements and Trade in Services: Policy Issues", World Bank Policy Research Working Paper No. 2852, World Bank, Washington.

Maur, Jean-Christophe (2008), "Regionalism and Trade Facilitation: A Primer", Policy Research Working Paper No. 4464, World Bank (Feb.).

Maxfield, S. (1990), *Governing Capital: International Finance and Mexican Politics* (Ithaca, NY: Cornell University Press).

Mayer, Wolfgang (1984), "Endogenous Tariff Formation", *American Economic Review*, 74/5: 970–85.

Meade, J. (1955), *The Theory of Customs Unions* (Amsterdam: North-Holland).

Melatos, Mark, and Alan D. Woodland (2007), "Pareto-Optimal Delegation in Customs Unions", *Review of International Economics*, 15/3: 441–61.

Milner, Helen V. (1988). *Resisting Protectionism: Global Industries and the Politics of International Trade*. Princeton: Princeton University Press.

——(1997a), "Industries, Governments, and the Creation of Regional Trade Blocs", in E. D. Mansfield and H. V. Milner (eds.), *The Political Economy of Regionalism* (New York: Columbia University Press).

——(1997b), *Interests, Institutions, and Information: Domestic Politics and International Relations* (Princeton: Princeton University Press).

Milward, A. S. (1984), *The Reconstruction of Western Europe, 1945–51* (London: Methuen).

Moravcsik, Andrew (1998), *The Choice for Europe: Social Purpose and State Power from Messina to Maastricht* (Ithaca, NY: Cornell University Press and (European edn.) London: Routledge/UCL Press, 1998).

Moreira, Mauricio (2008), "Trade Costs in Latin America", mimeo, IDB.

Morrow, J. D. (1992), "Signaling Difficulties with Linkage in Crisis Bargaining", *International Studies Quarterly*, 36/2: 153–72.

——(1994), "Modeling the Forms of International-Cooperation-Distribution versus Information", *International Organization*, 48/3: 387–423.

——(1999), "How Could Trade Affect Conflict?" *Journal of Peace Research*, 36/4: 481–9.

Mundell, R. A. (1964), "Tariff Preferences and the Terms of Trade", *Manchester School of Economic and Social Studies*, 32: 1–13.

Nye, Joseph (1992), "What New World Order?" *Foreign Affairs* (spring).

O'Rourke, K., and J. G. Williamson (1994), "Late Nineteenth-Century Anglo-American Factor-Price Convergence: Were Heckscher and Ohlin Right?" *Journal of Economic History*, 54: 892–916.

Oatley, Thomas H. (2001), "Multilateralizing Trade and Payments in Postwar Europe", *International Organization*, 55/4: 949–69.

Olarreaga, Marcelo, and Isidro Soloaga (1998), "Endogenous Tariff Formation: The Case of MERCOSUR", *World Bank Economic Review*, 12/2: 297–320.

Ornelas, E. (2005), "Trade Creating Free Trade Areas and the Undermining of Multilateralism", *European Economic Review*, 49/7: 1717–35.

Oye, Kenneth (1986), 'Explaining Cooperation under Anarchy: Hypotheses and Strategies', in K. Oye (ed.), *Cooperation under Anarchy* (Princeton: Princeton University Press).

——(1992), *Economic Discrimination and Political Exchange: World Political Economy in the 1930s and 1980s* (Princeton: Princeton University Press).

Pahre, Robert (2001), "Most-Favored-Nation Clauses and Clustered Negotiations", *International Organization*, 55/4: 859–90.

Panagariya, A., and R. Findlay (1996), "A Political-Economy Analysis of Free-Trade Areas and Customs Unions", *The Political Economy of Trade Reform: Essays in Honor of Jagdish Bhagwati* (Cambridge, Mass.: MIT Press).

Parry, Clive (1969–81), *Consolidated Treaty Series* (Dobbs Ferry, NY: Oceana).

Pastor, R. (2001), *Toward a North American Community: Lessons from the Old World for the New* (Washington: Institute for International Economics).

Polaski, Sandra (2006), *Winners and Losers: The Impact of the Doha Round on Developing Countries* (Washington: Carnegie Endowment for International Peace).

Pollard, S. (1974), *European Economic Integration 1815–1970* (London: Thames and Hudson).

Putnam, Robert. D. (1988), "Diplomacy and Domestic Politics: The Logic of Two-Level Games", *International Organization*, 42: 426–60.

Ray, Edward, J. (1987) "The Impact of Special Interests on Preferential Tariff Concessions by the United States", *Review of Economics and Statistics*, 69/2: 187–93.

Richardson, M. (1994), "Why a Free Trade Area? The Tariff Also Rises", *Economics and Politics*, 6/1: 79–96.

Rosen, Howard (2008), "Strengthening Trade Adjustment Assistance", Policy Brief 08-2, Peterson Institute for International Economics.

Roy, M., J. Marchetti, and H. Lim (2006), "Services Liberalization in the New Generation of Preferential Trade Agreements (PTAs): How Much Further than the GATS?" WTO Staff Working Papers No. ERSD-2006–07.

Russett, Bruce, and John O'Neal (2001), *Triangulating Peace: Democracy, Interdependence, and International Organizations* (New York: W. W. Norton).

Sally, Razeen (2006), "Asian Trade Needs Coalitions of the Willing", *The Times of India*, Mumbai, 22 Nov.

Sauvé, Pierre (2006), "Multilateral Rules on Investment: Is Forward Movement Possible?" *Journal of International Economic Law*, 9/2: 325–55.

Schelling, Thomas (1960), *The Strategy of Conflict* (Cambridge, Mass.: Harvard University Press).

Scheve, Kenneth F., and Matthew J. Slaughter (2007), "A New Deal for Globalization", *Foreign Affairs*, July/Aug.

Schiff, Maurice, and L. Alan Winters (2002), "Regional Cooperation, and the Role of International Organizations and Regional Integration", Policy Research Working Paper No. 2872, World Bank.

————(2003), *Regional Integration and Development*, London and New York: Oxford University Press for the World Bank.

Schott, Jeffrey (2004), *Free Trade Agreements: US Strategies and Priorities* (Washington: Institute for International Economics).

——(2007), "Completing the Doha Round", Policy Brief 06/7, Peterson Institute for International Economics.

Scollay, Robert (2005), "Substantially All Trade: Which Definitions are Fulfilled in Practice? An Empirical Investigation", Report prepared for the Commonwealth Secretariat, APEC Study Center, University of Auckland (15 Aug.).

Sinclair, Peter, and David Vines (1994), "Do Fewer, Larger Trade Blocs Imply Greater Protection? The Good News and the Bad News about Regional Trading Blocs", University of Birmingham and Oxford University, June.

Smith, Peter H. (1996), *Talons of the Eagle: Dynamics of US–Latin American Relations* (New York: Oxford University Press).

Soloaga, I., and L.W. Winters (1999), "Regionalism in the Nineties: What Effect on Trade?" World Bank Working Paper No. 2156.

Spruyt, Hendrik (1994), *The Sovereign State and its Competitors: An Analysis of Systems Change* (Princeton: Princeton University Press).

Stein, Emesto (1994), "Essays on the Welfare Implications of Trading Blocs with Transport Costs and on Political Cycles of Inflation", PhD dissertation, University of California, Berkeley.

Subramanian, Uma (2006), "Being Competitive: Value Chain Analysis and Solution Design", FTAs, World Bank Group, April 2006.

——William Anderson, and Kihoon Lee (2005), "Measuring the Impact of the Investment Climate on Total Factor Productivity: Cases of China and Brazil", Working Paper, World Bank, Washington.

Summers, L. (1991), "Regionalism and the World Trading System", in Policy Implications of Trade and Currency Zones, a Symposium sponsored by the Federal Reserve Bank of Kansas City, Jackson Hole, Wyoming.

Suominen, Kati (2004), "Rules of Origin in Global Commerce", PhD dissertation, University of California, San Diego.

——(2008a), 'Monitoring Regional Integration: The Case of Central America', in De Lombaerde *et al.* (2008).

——(2008b), "Seasoned Monitoring of Trade Agreements: The Case of North America", in De Lombaerde *et al.* (2008).

Syropoulos, C. (1999), "Customs Unions and Comparative Advantage", *Oxford Economic Papers*, 51/2: 239–66.

United Nations (1947), *Customs Unions* (New York: UN).

Van Biesebroeck, Johannes (2005), "Exporting Raises Productivity in Sub-Saharan African Manufacturing Firms", *Journal of International Economics*, 67/2 (Dec.): 373–91.

van der Mensbrugghe, Dominique Richard Newfarmer, and Denisse Pierola (2005), "Regionalism vs. Multilateralism", in Richard Newfarmer (ed.), *Trade, Doha and Development: A Window into the Issues* (Washington: World Bank).

Viner, J. (1950), *The Customs Union Issue* (New York: Carnegie Endowment for International Peace).

Volpe, Christian (2007), "Export Promotion Institutions and Export Diversification", mimeo, IDB.

Waltz, Kenneth (1972), *Theory of International Politics* (New York: McGraw-Hill).

Wei, S., and J. A. Frankel (1995), *European Integration and the Regionalization of World Trade and Currencies: The Economics and the Politics* (Berkeley: University of California at Berkeley).

Wendt, A. (1992), "Anarchy is What States Make out of it: The Social Construction of Power Politics", *International Organization,* 46/2: 391–425.

Whalley, John (1996), "Why do Countries Seek Regional Trade Agreements?" in J. Frankel (ed.), *The Regionalization of the World Economy* (Chicago: Chicago University Press).

Williamson, Jeffrey G. (2004), "The Tariff Response to World Market Integration in the Periphery before the Modern Era", paper presented at the Market Integration Workshop, European University Institute, Fiesole, Italy, 1–4 July 2004.

Winters, L. Alan (1994), "The EC and Protectionism: The Political Economy", *European Economic Review,* 38: 596–603.

——(1996), "Regionalism versus Multilateralism", Policy Research Working Paper No. 1687, The World Bank, Washington.

——(1997), "Regionalism and the Rest of World: The Irrelevance of the Kemp-Wan Theorem", *Oxford Economic Papers,* 49/2: 228–34.

——(2000), "Regionalism and Multilateralism in the Twenty-First Century", paper prepared for the High-Level Regional Policy Dialogue, IDB, 20–21 November 2000.

Wonnacott, Paul, and Mark Lutz (1989), "Is there a Case for Free Trade Areas?" in Jeffrey Schott (ed.), *Free Trade Areas and U.S. Trade Policy* (Washington: Institute for International Economics), 59–84.

World Bank (2000), *Trade Blocs* (Oxford: Oxford University Press).

——(2004), *Global Economic Prospects 2005: Trade, Regionalism and Development 2005* (Washington: World Bank).

——(2005), *Global Economic Prospects* (Washington: World Bank).

World Trade Organization (WTO) (2002), "Coverage, Liberalization Process and Transitional Provisions in Regional Trade Agreements", Committee on Regional Trade Agreements (5 Apr.).

Yarbrough, B. V., and R. M. Yarbrough (1992), *Cooperation and Governance in International Trade: The Strategic Organizational Approach* (Princeton: Princeton University Press).

————(1997), "Dispute Settlement in International Trade: Regionalism and Procedural Coordination", in E. D. Mansfield and H. V. Milner (eds.), *The Political Economy of Regionalism: New Directions in World Politics* (New York: Columbia University Press).

Yi, S.-S. (1996), "Open Regionalism and World Welfare", *Eastern Economic Journal,* 22/4: 467–75.

Index